9x13

THE PERFECT-FIT DISH

MORE THAN 180 FAMILY FAVORITES
TO FIT AMERICA'S MOST POPULAR PAN

MEREDITH PRINT ADVANTAGE
DES MOINES, IOWA

9x13: THE PERFECT-FIT DiSH

Meredith Corporation Print Advantage
Vice President, Production: Bruce Heston
National Sales Director: Linda Hyden
Associate Director, Production: Doug Johnston

Waterbury Publications, Inc.
Editorial Director: Lisa Kingsley
Associate Editor: Tricia Laning
Creative Director: Ken Carlson
Associate Design Director: Doug Samuelson
Production Coordinator: Mindy Samuelson
Contributing Project Editor: Spectrum Communication Services, Inc.
Contributing Copy Editor: Terri Fredrickson
Contributing Proofreaders: Gretchen Kauffman, Peg Smith
Contributing Indexer: Elizabeth T. Parson

Meredith Publishing Group
President: Jack Griffin
Executive Vice President: Andy Sareyan
Vice President, Manufacturing: Bruce Heston

Meredith Corporation
Chairman of the Board and Chief Executive Officer: Stephen M. Lacy
In Memoriam: E. T. Meredith III (1933–2003)

All of us at Meredith Print Advantage are dedicated to providing
you information and ideas to enhance your home. We welcome your
comments and suggestions. Write to us at: Meredith Print Advantage,
1716 Locust St., Des Moines, IA 50309-3023.

TABLE OF CONTENTS

HOW TO CHOOSE THE RIGHT PAN AND MAKE IT WORK

4

It goes by many names: that rectangular pan, your lasagna dish, the 3-quart casserole, Mom's favorite cake pan, and the one you always make the layered salad in for the neighborhood potluck. With endless uses, the 9×13 is the No. 1 pan or dish working in kitchens across America.

Many cooks received their first pan or dish as a bridal shower gift. Others bought theirs when they spotted a great cake or casserole and continue to use the pan on a regular basis.

Whether you're choosing bakeware for a new kitchen or you've been relying on your trusty old pans for years, check out the current selection of 9×13s and discover more exciting uses for them.

WHICH 9×13 IS FOR YOU?

Having the right pan or dish opens a world of possibilities for foods you can make—everything from savory roasts and lasagnas to gelatin salads and casseroles to cakes, cobblers, and bars. Today the variety of materials

the pans are made of is endless: glass, aluminum, plastic, silicone; with nonstick finishes and without; with racks or with ridges. When choosing the perfect pan or dish, consider these helpful suggestions based on recipes you'll find in this book.

Tomato-based recipes: If you're fond of making lasagna or red-sauced casseroles, glass bakeware is best. Baking pans made of aluminum, iron, or tin can react with acidic ingredients such as tomatoes or lemons, causing the foods to discolor. Nonstick pans may work if you use serving utensils that won't scratch the surface.

No-bake bars, gelatin salads, and freezer desserts: Sturdy plastic containers will give you the best storage results. Choose a container that has an airtight seal that can store food at room temperature, in the fridge, or in the freezer.

Avoid choosing light-weight plastic containers because they have a tendency to bend or fold when full.

Bars, brownies, and cakes: Dark- or dull-finish pans (metal, nonstick, or glass) absorb heat, which produce nice even browning. Shiny finishes, such as steel or stainless reflect heat, causing cakes to have thin golden crusts.

Numerous 9×13 pans available with removable roasting racks can do double duty. With the rack it's a roasting pan; without it's great for baking. You can also fashion your own roasting pan by inserting a roasting rack into a 9×13 pan or dish. Or if you are roasting meat and vegetables together, line the pan or dish with foil, add the vegetables, and roast the meat on top, letting the juices run down into the vegetables. Just be sure the meat or poultry sits at least ¾ inch above the bottom of the pan to prevent the roast from stewing in the pan juices.

PAN COMPARISON

	+	−
Glass or Stoneware	<ul><li>Nonreactive surface</li><li>Retains heat well</li><li>Good for tomato-based casseroles such as lasagna, and citrus-sauced poultry or fish</li><li>Rims/handles make it easy to grab with oven mitts for oven-to-table serving</li><li>Clear glass makes it easy to monitor browning</li><li>Shows off beauty of gelatin or layered salads</li><li>Some pans come with lids</li><li>Dishwasher-safe</li></ul>	<ul><li>Breakable</li><li>Cannot withstand sudden temperature change</li><li>Unsafe for stovetop or broiler</li><li>Some stoneware dishes require initial seasoning and cannot go in the dishwasher</li></ul>
Metal	<ul><li>Good for roasting meats and poultry; cleans up easily</li><li>Helps promote even cooking</li><li>Can be used on stovetop</li><li>Many pans come with lids</li><li>Pans travel well and won't break</li><li>Pans with handles are easy to remove from oven</li></ul>	<ul><li>Less-sturdy pans show wear over time and may need to be replaced more frequently</li><li>Can't use knives or forks, and other pointed items may damage the surface</li><li>Some pans are not dishwasher-safe</li></ul>
Plastic	<ul><li>Good for no-bake recipes, refrigerator salads, and freezer desserts</li><li>Good for storing cakes and cookies</li><li>Good for toting</li><li>Most are dishwasher-safe</li></ul>	<ul><li>May not be used for baking</li><li>Sharp utensils damage surface</li></ul>

5

MORE PAN POINTERS

SAFE TOTING

Choose a pan or dish with a tight-fitting lid. Pack cold foods in an insulated cooler with ice packs. Insulated casserole carriers are great for transporting hot dishes. You can also wrap a tightly covered dish of hot food in layers of newspaper or towels and transport it in an insulated carrier. Fill gaps around the food container with crumpled newspaper or towels to prevent shifting or spills.

SERVING SAVVY

Nonmetal spoons or spatulas are great serving utensils when using nonstick pans because they won't scratch or damage the surface. If you're looking for a quick way to get bars out of a pan without using a knife or spatula, line the pan with foil. After baking grab the foil ends and lift the bars out of the pan before cutting. This way your pans won't become damaged by knife cuts and cleanup will be easier.

LEFTOVERS AND FREEZING

Whether you have one serving of a hot dish left or are dividing a casserole for another meal, keep these pointers in mind:

- It is best to refrigerate leftovers immediately after you have finished eating. Never let perishable foods cool at room temperature.
- Divide cooked foods into small portions in shallow containers. Place in refrigerator to chill. Then, if freezing, move food to the freezer.
- If you are freezing an entire dish before or after baking, always use freezer-to-oven dishes lined with foil. Cover them with plastic freezer wrap or with foil. When frozen, lift out the foil-lined food and place it in a storage container or freezer bag or wrap it in additional foil and return to the freezer. Be sure to label and date the food.

SLICK WAY TO GREASE A 9×13

When a recipe calls for greasing a pan or dish, dip a ball of waxed paper into shortening and wipe the pan with a light coating. Or use a light coating of nonstick cooking spray.

BAKING BARS AND BROWNIES

Lining the 9×13 pan with foil makes removing bars from the pan easier. Foil also helps keep pans from being damaged from knife cuts and makes cleanup easier. Just shape the foil over the outside of the pan, extending it over the edges about 1 inch, then place the shaped foil inside the pan. If your recipe calls for a greased pan, grease the foil inside the pan (or choose no-stick foil). Bake and cool the bars as usual, then grasp the extra foil at the edges to pull the uncut bars out of the pan.

WHEN TO USE A PAN, WHEN TO USE A DISH

Most of the recipes in this book call for a 9×13 pan or dish interchangeably. But when a recipe specifies one or the other, you'll want to choose accordingly to get the best results. Silicone pans are another alternative for using in the microwave, oven, and freezer. Follow the manufacturer's directions when using silicone pans.

BREAKFAST & BRUNCH

When you're in the mood to wake up to more than a cup of coffee and a commute, try opening your eyes to the beauty of these breakfasts. This chapter brings you a big bouquet of morning glories—from yeasty sweet rolls to make-ahead egg casseroles—and each is the kind of homey and wholesome stick-to-the-ribs nourishment that will make your whole family rise and shine.

CRESPELLE WITH ORANGE SAUCE

Crespelle [cress-PELL-lay]

is the Italian

word for "crepe."

Prep: 1 hour   **Bake:** 15 minutes   **Oven:** 375°F

- ⅓ **cup sugar**
- 3 **tablespoons all-purpose flour**
- 1 **teaspoon finely shredded orange peel**
- ¼ **teaspoon salt**
- 1¼ **cups milk**
- 1 **egg, lightly beaten**
- 1 **tablespoon butter**
- 1 **teaspoon vanilla**
- 2 **eggs, lightly beaten**
- 1½ **cups milk**
- 1 **cup all-purpose flour**
- 2 **tablespoons sugar**
- 1 **tablespoon vegetable oil**
- ¼ **teaspoon salt**
- ¼ **cup sugar**
- 2 **teaspoons cornstarch**
- 1 **cup orange juice**
- ⅓ **cup golden raisins**

1 Grease a 9×13-inch baking dish; set aside. For filling: In a medium saucepan combine the ⅓ cup sugar, the 3 tablespoons flour, ½ teaspoon of the orange peel, and ¼ teaspoon salt. Stir in the 1¼ cups milk. Cook and stir on medium heat until thickened and bubbly. Cook and stir for 2 minutes more. Gradually stir half of the hot mixture into the 1 egg. Return egg mixture to saucepan. Cook and stir just until bubbly. Immediately transfer to a medium bowl. Stir in butter and vanilla. Cover surface with plastic wrap; cool without stirring.

2 For crespelle: In a medium bowl combine the 2 eggs, the 1½ cups milk, the 1 cup flour, the 2 tablespoons sugar, the oil, and ¼ teaspoon salt. Beat with a rotary beater until combined. Heat a lightly greased 6-inch nonstick skillet on medium heat. Remove from heat. Spoon in 2 tablespoons of the batter; lift and tilt skillet to spread batter. Return to heat; brown on one side only. (Or cook on a crepemaker according to the manufacturer's directions.) Invert crespelle onto a paper towel. Repeat with the remaining batter to make 16 to 18 crespelle, greasing skillet occasionally.

3 Preheat oven to 375°F. For orange sauce: In a small saucepan combine the ¼ cup sugar, the cornstarch, and the remaining ½ teaspoon orange peel. Stir in orange juice and raisins. Cook and stir on medium heat until thickened and bubbly.

4 Spread about 1 tablespoon of the filling over unbrowned side of each crespelle, spreading to within ¼ inch of the edge. Roll up crespelle. Place, seam sides down, in prepared baking dish. Pour orange sauce evenly over crespelle. Bake, uncovered, about 15 minutes or until heated through.

Makes 8 servings.

Per Serving: 273 cal., 7 g total fat (3 g sat. fat), 90 mg chol., 218 mg sodium, 45 g carbo., 1 g fiber, 8 g pro.

Note: *If you prefer, substitute eight 9-inch ready-to-use crepes for the homemade crespelle. Fill each purchased crepe with about 3 tablespoons of the filling and plan to serve only 1 crepe to each person.*

Crespelle with Berries: *Prepare as directed, except when making the orange sauce, omit raisins. Before serving top crespelle with ⅓ cup fresh raspberries and sprinkle with powdered sugar.*

FRENCH TOAST CASSEROLE

Keeping traditional French toast warm while preparing it for several people can be difficult. This problem-solving dish provides eight servings in one pan.

Prep: 20 minutes   Chill: 4 to 24 hours   Bake: 40 minutes   Stand: 15 minutes   Oven: 350°F

- 1 cup packed brown sugar
- ½ cup butter
- 2 tablespoons light-color corn syrup
- 1 1-pound loaf unsliced cinnamon bread, cut into 1-inch slices
- 8 eggs, beaten
- 3 cups half-and-half or light cream
- 2 teaspoons vanilla
- ½ teaspoon salt
- 1 tablespoon orange liqueur (optional)

1 In a medium saucepan combine brown sugar, butter, and corn syrup; cook and stir until boiling. Boil, uncovered, for 1 minute. Pour into a 9×13-inch baking dish.

2 Arrange bread slices on top of brown sugar mixture. In a large bowl combine eggs, half-and-half, vanilla, and salt; pour over bread slices. Cover and chill in the refrigerator for at least 4 or up to 24 hours.

3 Preheat oven to 350°F. Let baking dish stand at room temperature while oven preheats. Bake, uncovered, for 40 to 45 minutes or until top is browned and puffed and a knife inserted near center comes out clean. Let stand for 15 minutes before serving. If desired, drizzle with orange liqueur.

Makes 8 servings.

Per Serving: 579 cal., 30 g total fat (16 g sat. fat), 279 mg chol., 692 mg sodium, 65 g carbo., 1 g fiber, 14 g pro.

STRAWBERRY-STUFFED FRENCH TOAST

Using croissants instead of sliced bread makes every portion extra thick, rich, and satisfying.

Prep: 20 minutes   **Bake:** 15 minutes   **Oven:** 375°F

Nonstick cooking spray
4 croissants, split
1 8-ounce tub light cream cheese spread with strawberries
2 eggs, lightly beaten
½ cup milk
½ teaspoon ground cinnamon
Powdered sugar
Fresh strawberries
Maple syrup, warmed

1 Preheat oven to 375°F. Line a 9×13-inch baking pan with foil. Lightly coat the foil with cooking spray; set pan aside.

2 Spread cut sides of croissants with cream cheese. Place cut sides back together. In a shallow dish use a fork to beat together eggs, milk, and cinnamon. Dip each filled croissant in the egg mixture for 30 seconds, turning once. Place in prepared baking pan.

3 Bake, uncovered, about 15 minutes or until browned and heated through. Sprinkle with powdered sugar. Serve warm with fresh strawberries and warm maple syrup.

Makes 4 servings.

Per Serving: 522 cal., 29 g total fat (17 g sat. fat), 209 mg chol., 454 mg sodium, 53 g carbo., 3 g fiber, 13 g pro.

ORANGE BLINTZ CASSEROLE

When grating orange peel, be sure to remove just the thin orange skin. The white membrane beneath it can be bitter.

Prep: 25 minutes **Bake:** 45 minutes **Cool:** 30 minutes **Oven:** 350°F

- 6 eggs
- 2 egg whites
- 1½ cups sour cream
- 2 teaspoons finely shredded orange peel
- ½ cup orange juice
- ¼ cup butter, softened
- 1 cup all-purpose flour
- ½ cup granulated sugar
- 2 teaspoons baking powder
- 2 egg yolks
- 1 12-ounce carton cream-style cottage cheese
- 1 8-ounce package cream cheese, softened and cut up
- 2 tablespoons granulated sugar
- 2 teaspoons vanilla
- ½ cup orange marmalade, melted
- Orange slices (optional)

1 Preheat oven to 350°F. Grease a 9×13-inch baking dish; set aside. For batter: In a blender or food processor combine eggs, egg whites, sour cream, orange peel, orange juice, and butter. Cover and blend or process until smooth. Add flour, the ½ cup granulated sugar, and the baking powder. Cover and blend or process until smooth. Transfer to a bowl; set aside.

2 For filling: In a clean blender or food processor combine egg yolks, cottage cheese, cream cheese, the 2 tablespoons granulated sugar, and the vanilla. Cover and blend or process until smooth.

3 Pour about 2 cups of the batter into prepared baking dish. Spoon filling over batter in dish; swirl filling with a knife. Pour the remaining batter evenly over filling.

4 Bake, uncovered, about 45 minutes or until puffed and lightly browned. Cool in pan on a wire rack for 30 minutes (edges may fall during cooling). Drizzle with orange marmalade. If desired, garnish with orange slices.

Makes 12 servings.

Per Serving: 338 cal., 20 g total fat (10 g sat. fat), 189 mg chol., 304 mg sodium, 31 g carbo., 0 g fiber, 10 g pro.

13

BAGEL, LOX, AND EGG STRATA

> Lox is a luscious form of brined,
> cold-smoked salmon that is especially popular
> in American-Jewish cuisine.

Prep: 30 minutes **Chill:** 4 to 24 hours **Bake:** 45 minutes **Stand:** 10 minutes **Oven:** 350°F

¼ **cup butter or margarine, melted**

8 **cups plain bagels cut into bite-size pieces (4 to 6 bagels)**

1 **3-ounce package thinly sliced smoked salmon (lox-style), cut into small pieces**

2 **cups shredded Swiss cheese or Monterey Jack cheese (8 ounces)**

¼ **cup snipped fresh chives**

8 **eggs, beaten**

2 **cups milk**

1 **cup cottage cheese**

¼ **teaspoon black pepper**

1 Pour melted butter into a 9×13-inch baking dish, spreading to cover the bottom. Spread bagel pieces evenly in prepared baking dish. Sprinkle lox, cheese, and chives evenly over bagel pieces. In a large bowl combine eggs, milk, cottage cheese, and pepper. Pour over layers in baking dish.

2 Press gently with the back of a wooden spoon to moisten all of the ingredients. Cover and chill for at least 4 or up to 24 hours.

3 Preheat oven to 350°F. Bake, uncovered, about 45 minutes or until set and the edges are puffed and golden. Let stand for 10 minutes before serving.

Makes 12 servings.

Per Serving: 267 cal., 14 g total fat (8 g sat. fat), 176 mg chol., 497 mg sodium, 16 g carbo., 1 g fiber, 17 g pro.

POTATO-AND-CHEESE-STUFFED CHILES

> Choose your chiles. Use squat, dark poblanos for rich, complex flavor or Anaheims for fresh, sprightly flavor and elegant, graceful shape.

Prep: 40 minutes   **Bake:** 25 minutes   **Oven:** 350°F

Nonstick cooking spray

- **3** large fresh Anaheim or poblano chiles or 3 small sweet green or red peppers
- **1½** cups chopped sweet potatoes or potatoes
- **1** to 3 tablespoons milk
- **⅓** cup finely chopped green onions
- **2** teaspoons chili powder
- **1** clove garlic, minced
- **½** cup shredded asadero, queso quesadilla, Chihuahua, or Monterey Jack cheese
- **1** egg white, beaten

1 Preheat oven to 350°F. Lightly coat a 9×13-inch baking dish with cooking spray; set aside.

2 Cut the peppers in half lengthwise.* Remove seeds and membranes. In a large saucepan cook the peppers in boiling water about 5 minutes or until crisp-tender. Drain well.

3 Meanwhile, in a covered medium saucepan cook potatoes in boiling lightly salted water for 15 to 20 minutes or until tender; drain. Mash the potatoes, adding the milk 1 tablespoon at a time, until potato mixture is fluffy. Stir in green onions, chili powder, and garlic. Stir in half of the shredded cheese and the egg white. Spoon potato mixture into peppers. Place stuffed peppers close together in prepared baking dish.

4 Cover with foil. Bake for 25 to 30 minutes or until heated through. Sprinkle with the remaining shredded cheese.

Makes 6 servings.

Per Serving: 79 cal., 2 g total fat (1 g sat. fat), 9 mg chol., 118 mg sodium, 11 g carbo., 2 g fiber, 4 g pro.

*****Note:** *Because chiles contain volatile oils that can burn your skin and eyes, avoid direct contact with them as much as possible. When working with chiles, wear plastic or rubber gloves. If your bare hands do touch the chiles, wash your hands and nails well with soap and warm water.*

BREAKFAST BREAD PUDDING

Why limit bread pudding to dessert? This one contains breakfast items—eggs, bread, and juice—and it starts the day in a wonderful way.

Prep: 30 minutes **Bake:** 30 minutes **Stand:** 15 minutes **Oven:** 325°F

5 to 6 slices whole wheat cinnamon-swirl bread or cinnamon-raisin bread

Nonstick cooking spray

1½ cups fat-free milk

3 eggs

2 tablespoons sugar

1 teaspoon vanilla

¼ teaspoon ground nutmeg

1 5.5-ounce can (⅔ cup) apricot nectar or peach nectar

2 teaspoons cornstarch

1 | Preheat oven to 325°F. Cut enough of the bread into cubes to make 4 cups. Place bread cubes in a 9×13-inch baking pan. Bake, uncovered, about 10 minutes or until bread is dry, stirring once. Cool on a wire rack.

2 | Lightly coat six 6-ounce soufflé dishes or custard cups with cooking spray. Divide bread cubes among the prepared dishes. In a medium bowl combine milk, eggs, sugar, vanilla, and nutmeg; beat with a rotary beater or wire whisk. Pour milk mixture evenly over bread cubes. Press gently with the back of a spoon to thoroughly moisten bread.

3 | Place soufflé dishes in a 9×13-inch baking pan. Place baking pan on oven rack. Carefully pour hot tap water into the baking pan around dishes to a depth of 1 inch.

4 | Bake, uncovered, for 30 to 35 minutes or until a knife inserted near centers comes out clean. Transfer dishes to a wire rack. Let stand for 15 minutes before serving.

5 | Meanwhile, for sauce: In a small saucepan gradually stir apricot nectar into cornstarch until combined. Cook and stir over medium heat until thickened and bubbly. Reduce heat. Cook and stir for 2 minutes more.

6 | If desired, remove puddings from soufflé dishes. Spoon sauce over warm puddings.

Makes 6 servings.

Per Serving: 178 cal., 4 g total fat (1 g sat. fat), 107 mg chol., 179 mg sodium, 27 g carbo., 3 g fiber, 9 g pro.

EASY HUEVOS RANCHEROS CASSEROLE

This Latin-inpired concoction is
a people pleaser that you
will make time and time again.

Prep: 15 minutes   Bake: 38 minutes   Stand: 10 minutes   Oven: 375°F

Nonstick cooking spray
- 1 **32-ounce package frozen fried potato nuggets**
- 12 **eggs**
- 1 **cup milk**
- 1½ **teaspoons dried oregano, crushed**
- 1½ **teaspoons ground cumin**
- ½ **teaspoon chili powder**
- ¼ **teaspoon garlic powder**
- 1 **8-ounce package shredded Mexican cheese blend**
- 1 **16-ounce jar thick and chunky salsa**
- 1 **8-ounce carton sour cream**

1 Preheat oven to 375°F. Lightly coat a 9×13-inch baking dish with cooking spray. Arrange frozen potato nuggets in prepared baking dish.

2 In a large bowl whisk together eggs, milk, oregano, cumin, chili powder, and garlic powder. Pour egg mixture over potato nuggets.

3 Bake, uncovered, for 35 to 40 minutes or until a knife inserted near the center comes out clean. Sprinkle cheese over egg mixture. Bake, uncovered, about 3 minutes more or until cheese melts. Let stand for 10 minutes before serving. Serve with salsa and sour cream.

Makes 12 servings.

Per Serving: 343 cal., 21 g total fat (9 g sat. fat), 238 mg chol., 823 mg sodium, 26 g carbo., 2 g fiber, 14 g pro.

BREAKFAST ENCHILADAS COLORADAS

**Asadero is a Mexican cow's
milk cheese with amazing melting properties.
It is often labeled "Oaxaca" as well.**

Prep: 40 minutes   **Bake:** 15 minutes   **Cook:** 30 minutes (sauce)   **Oven:** 350°F

½   cup chopped green onions (4)

1   tablespoon butter

6   eggs

1   tablespoon milk or water

¼   teaspoon salt

½   cup grape tomatoes, quartered

4   ounces asadero cheese or Monterey Jack cheese, shredded (1 cup)

1   14-ounce can refried beans

2   to 3 tablespoons vegetable oil

12   6-inch corn tortillas

1   recipe Colorado Sauce or 2¾ cups canned enchilada sauce

Shredded lettuce (optional)

1 In a large skillet cook green onions in hot butter about 1 minute or until tender. For scrambled eggs: In a large bowl whisk together eggs, milk, and salt. Pour egg mixture into skillet with onion; cook, stirring often, just until eggs are set. Remove from heat. Add tomatoes and sprinkle with half of the cheese. Set aside. Place refried beans in a microwave-safe medium bowl. Microwave, uncovered, on high about 2 minutes or until heated through, stirring once.

2 For tortillas: In a medium or large skillet heat 2 tablespoons of the oil on medium heat. Using tongs, dip tortillas, 1 at a time, into the oil; cook for 15 to 20 seconds or just until hot, turning once. Drain on paper towels (do not stack). Add additional oil as needed.

3 Preheat oven to 350°F. Spread ½ cup of the Colorado Sauce in a 9×13-inch baking dish. Divide refried beans among tortillas, spreading evenly. Divide scrambled eggs among tortillas. Spoon about 1 tablespoon of the Colorado Sauce over each. Roll up tortillas. Place rolled tortillas, seam sides down, in prepared baking dish. Spoon the remaining Colorado Sauce over. Top with the remaining cheese.

4 Bake, uncovered, for 15 minutes. If desired, serve on top of lettuce.

Makes 6 servings.

Per Serving: 452 cal., 20 g total fat (7 g sat. fat), 237 mg chol., 1,376 mg sodium, 51 g carbo., 11 g fiber, 20 g pro.

19

Colorado Sauce: *Remove stems and seeds from 4 dried New Mexico chiles or ancho chiles.* In a medium saucepan combine the chiles; one 14-ounce can chicken broth; 2 cloves garlic, minced; 1 teaspoon ground cumin; 1 teaspoon dried oregano, crushed; and ½ teaspoon salt. Bring to boiling; reduce heat. Simmer, covered, for 20 minutes. Cool slightly. Transfer mixture to a blender or food processor. Cover and blend or process until smooth. Return to saucepan. Stir in one 15-ounce can tomato puree and 1 tablespoon packed brown sugar. Bring to boiling; reduce heat. Simmer, uncovered, about 10 minutes or until slightly thickened. Use immediately. (The sauce can be made ahead and chilled for up to 3 days. Or transfer to a freezer container; cover and freeze for up to 6 months. Thaw and reheat before using.)*

---

*Note: *Because chiles contain volatile oils that can burn your skin and eyes, avoid direct contact with them as much as possible. When working with chiles, wear plastic or rubber gloves. If your bare hands do touch the chiles, wash your hands and nails well with soap and warm water.*

CINNAMON ROLLS

Cinnamon rolls are not something
you make every day, but that is what
makes them so special.

Prep: 45 minutes   **Rise:** 1½ hours   **Stand:** 10 minutes   **Bake:** 25 minutes   **Cool:** 5 minutes   **Oven:** 375°F

- **4** to 4½ cups all-purpose flour
- **1** package active dry yeast
- **1** cup milk
- **⅓** cup granulated sugar
- **⅓** cup butter
- **½** teaspoon salt
- **2** eggs
- **¾** cup packed brown sugar
- **¼** cup all-purpose flour
- **1** tablespoon ground cinnamon
- **⅓** cup butter
- **½** cup golden raisins (optional)
- **½** cup chopped pecans, toasted (optional)
- **1** recipe Vanilla Icing

1 In a large bowl combine 2 cups of the flour and the yeast; set aside. In a small saucepan heat and stir milk, granulated sugar, ⅓ cup butter, and salt just until warm (120°F to 130°F) and butter almost melts. Add milk mixture to flour mixture along with eggs. Beat with an electric mixer on low to medium for 30 seconds, scraping sides of bowl constantly. Beat on high for 3 minutes. Using a wooden spoon, stir in as much of the remaining 2 to 2½ cups flour as you can.

2 Turn out dough onto a lightly floured surface. Knead in enough of the remaining flour to make a moderately soft dough that is smooth and elastic (3 to 5 minutes total). Shape dough into a ball. Place dough in a lightly greased bowl, turning once to grease surface. Cover; let dough rise in a warm place until double in size (1 to 1½ hours).

3 Punch down dough. Turn out dough onto a lightly floured surface; divide dough in half. Cover and let rest for 10 minutes.

4 Meanwhile, lightly grease a 9×13-inch baking pan; set aside. For filling: Stir together brown sugar, the ¼ cup flour, and the cinnamon. Using a pastry blender, cut in ⅓ cup butter until the mixture resembles coarse crumbs. If desired, stir in raisins and pecans.

5 Roll each dough half into an 8×12-inch rectangle. Sprinkle filling over dough, leaving a 1-inch border on 1 of the long sides. Press filling lightly into dough with your fingers. Moisten the 1-inch border with water. Roll up each rectangle, starting from the filled long side. Pinch dough to seal seam. Slice each rolled rectangle into 9 equal pieces (18 pieces total). Arrange in prepared baking pan. Cover; let rise in a warm place until nearly double in size (about 30 minutes).

6 Preheat oven to 375°F. Bake about 25 minutes or until golden brown and done in center. Cool in pan on a wire rack for 5 minutes; invert onto the wire rack. Invert again onto serving platter. Drizzle with Vanilla Icing. If desired, serve warm.

Makes 18 rolls.

Per Roll: 268 cal., 8 g total fat (5 g sat. fat), 43 mg chol., 130 mg sodium, 45 g carbo., 1 g fiber, 4 g pro.

Vanilla Icing: *In a small bowl stir together 1¼ cups powdered sugar, 1 teaspoon light-color corn syrup, and ½ teaspoon vanilla. Stir in enough half-and-half or light cream (1 to 2 tablespoons) to make drizzling consistency.*

GINGERBREAD CINNAMON BUNS

Whip up a batch of these warm,
gooey wonders for the kids you love most.
They'll adore them.

Prep: 30 minutes   Rise: 1³/₄ hours   Stand: 15 minutes   Bake: 22 minutes   Cool: 5 minutes   Oven: 350°F

- 2 packages active dry yeast
- ¼ cup warm water (105°F to 115°F)
- ½ cup evaporated milk
- ⅓ cup molasses
- ¼ cup packed brown sugar
- 1 egg, lightly beaten
- 2 tablespoons vegetable oil
- ½ teaspoon salt
- 3³/₄ to 4 cups all-purpose flour
- ¼ cup packed brown sugar
- 2 tablespoons granulated sugar
- 1 teaspoon ground cinnamon
- ½ teaspoon ground ginger
- ¼ teaspoon ground cloves
- 2 tablespoons butter, softened
- 1 recipe Spiced Glaze
- Sugared cranberries* (optional)

1. In a large bowl combine yeast and the warm water. Let stand for 5 minutes. Stir in evaporated milk, molasses, ¼ cup brown sugar, the egg, oil, and salt. Stir in as much of the flour as you can with a wooden spoon. Turn out dough onto a floured surface. Knead in enough of the remaining flour to make a moderately soft dough that is smooth and elastic (3 to 5 minutes total). Shape dough into a ball. Place dough in a lightly greased bowl, turning once to grease surface. Cover; let rise in a warm place until double in size (1 to 1½ hours).

2. Punch down dough. Turn out onto a lightly floured surface. Cover; let rest for 10 minutes. Lightly grease a 9×13-inch baking pan; set aside.

3. For filling: In a small bowl combine ¼ cup brown sugar, the granulated sugar, cinnamon, ginger, and cloves. Roll dough into an 8×12-inch rectangle. Spread butter over dough. Sprinkle with filling, leaving 1 inch unfilled along 1 of the long sides. Starting from the filled long side, roll up rectangle into a spiral. Pinch dough to seal seams. Slice into 12 equal pieces. Arrange in prepared baking pan. Cover and let rise in a warm place until nearly double in size (about 45 minutes).

4. Preheat oven to 350°F. Bake, uncovered, for 22 to 25 minutes or until golden brown and nicely set on the tops. Cool in pan on a wire rack for 5 minutes; invert onto a serving platter. Drizzle with Spiced Glaze. If desired, serve warm and top with sugared cranberries.

Makes 12 buns.

Per Bun: 332 cal., 6 g total fat (2 g sat. fat), 26 mg chol., 136 mg sodium, 64 g carbo., 1 g fiber, 6 g pro.

Spiced Glaze: *In a medium bowl whisk together 1½ cups powdered sugar, ½ teaspoon ground cinnamon, and ½ teaspoon vanilla. Whisk in enough milk (4 to 5 teaspoons total) to make drizzling consistency.*

*Note: *To make sugared cranberries, roll frozen cranberries in sugar.*

CRANBERRY-MAPLE CINNAMON ROLLS

Pure maple syrup is expensive, but worth every penny. Do splurge on a bottle if you can— it will make these rolls magnificent.

Prep: 30 minutes   Rise: 1½ hours   Stand: 20 minutes   Bake: 25 minutes   Cool: 5 minutes   Oven: 375°F

- 1 **cup fat-free milk**
- 2 **tablespoons pure maple syrup or maple-flavor syrup**
- 2 **tablespoons butter**
- 1 **teaspoon salt**
- ¼ **cup warm water (110°F to 115°F)**
- 1 **package active dry yeast**
- 1 **egg, lightly beaten**
- 1¼ **cups white whole wheat flour or whole wheat flour**
- 2½ **to 3 cups all-purpose flour**
- ⅓ **cup packed brown sugar**
- 2 **teaspoons ground cinnamon**
- ¼ **cup snipped dried cranberries**
- ¼ **cup chopped pecans, toasted**
- 1 **recipe Maple-Brown Sugar Icing (optional)**

1 In a small saucepan heat and stir milk, maple syrup, butter, and salt just until warm (110°F to 115°F) and butter almost melts; set aside. In a large bowl combine the warm water and yeast; let stand for 10 minutes. Add egg and milk mixture to yeast mixture. Stir in whole wheat flour. Stir in as much of the all-purpose flour as you can with a wooden spoon.

2 Turn out dough onto a lightly floured surface. Knead in enough of the remaining all-purpose flour to make a moderately soft dough that is smooth and elastic (3 to 5 minutes total). Shape dough into a ball. Place in a lightly greased bowl, turning once to grease surface. Cover and let rise in a warm place until double in size (about 1 hour). Punch down dough. Turn out onto a lightly floured surface. Cover; let rest for 10 minutes.

3 Meanwhile, lightly grease a 9×13-inch baking pan; set aside. In a small bowl combine brown sugar and cinnamon. Stir in dried cranberries and pecans.

4 Roll dough into an 8×15-inch rectangle. Sprinkle with pecan mixture, leaving 1 inch unfilled along one of the long sides. Starting from the filled long side, roll up rectangle into a spiral. Pinch dough to seal seams. Slice into 15 equal pieces. Arrange pieces, cut sides up, in prepared baking pan. Cover and let rise in a warm place until nearly double in size (about 30 minutes).

5 Preheat oven to 375°F. Bake, uncovered, for 25 to 30 minutes or until golden brown. Cool in pan on a wire rack for 5 minutes. Invert pan onto a baking sheet. Lift off pan. Invert rolls onto a serving platter. If desired, drizzle with Maple-Brown Sugar Icing. Serve warm.

Makes 15 rolls.

Per Roll: 180 cal., 4 g total fat (1 g sat. fat), 18 mg chol., 180 mg sodium, 33 g carbo., 2 g fiber, 5 g pro.

Maple-Brown Sugar Icing: *In a small bowl combine 2 tablespoons packed brown sugar and 1 tablespoon very hot water; stir to dissolve brown sugar. Stir in ¾ cup powdered sugar and ¼ teaspoon maple flavoring. Stir in enough fat-free milk (1 to 2 teaspoons) to make drizzling consistency.*

CHERRY COFFEE CAKE

Invite the kids into the kitchen
to make this simple yet
scrumptious coffee cake.

Prep: 25 minutes   **Stand:** 45 minutes   **Bake:** 30 minutes   **Cool:** 30 minutes   **Oven:** 375°F

Nonstick cooking spray
- 1 **package 2-layer-size yellow cake mix**
- 1 **cup all-purpose flour**
- 2/3 **cup warm water (120°F to 130°F)**
- 2 **eggs**
- 1 **package active dry yeast**
- 1/3 **cup butter, melted**
- 1/3 **cup sliced almonds**
- 1 **teaspoon ground cinnamon**
- 1 **12-ounce jar cherry preserves**
- 1 **recipe Lemon Icing**

1 Lightly coat a 9×13-inch baking pan with cooking spray; set aside. In a large bowl combine 1½ cups of the dry cake mix, the flour, the water, eggs, and yeast. Beat with an electric mixer on low just until combined. Beat on medium for 2 minutes, scraping sides of bowl occasionally (mixture will be thick).

2 Spread batter into prepared baking pan; cover loosely and let stand at room temperature for 45 minutes.

3 Preheat oven to 375°F. For streusel: In a medium bowl stir together the remaining cake mix, the butter, almonds, and cinnamon until combined. Spoon the cherry preserves in small mounds evenly over batter in pan. Crumble the streusel evenly over preserves.

4 Bake, uncovered, for 30 to 35 minutes or until top is golden brown. Cool in pan on a wire rack for 30 minutes. Drizzle with Lemon Icing. Serve warm.

Makes 12 to 16 servings.

Per Serving: 390 cal., 11 g total fat (5 g sat. fat), 49 mg chol., 338 mg sodium, 71 g carbo., 1 g fiber, 4 g pro.

Lemon Icing: *In a small bowl stir together ¾ cup powdered sugar, 2 teaspoons lemon juice, and enough water (1 to 2 teaspoons) to make drizzling consistency.*

BLUEBERRY STREUSEL COFFEE CAKE

26

**Try other seasonal fruits,
such as sliced peeled apples or pears,
in this moist, tender quick bread.**

Prep: 30 minutes   **Bake:** 35 minutes   **Oven:** 350°F

1½	cups packed brown sugar
1	cup coarsely chopped nuts
4	teaspoons ground cinnamon
1	8-ounce carton sour cream
1	teaspoon baking soda
¾	cup granulated sugar
½	cup butter, softened
3	eggs
1	teaspoon vanilla
2	cups all-purpose flour
1½	teaspoons baking powder
2	cups fresh or frozen blueberries, thawed
1	recipe Powdered Sugar Icing

1 Preheat oven to 350°F. Grease a 9×13-inch baking pan; set aside. For topping: In a small bowl stir together brown sugar, nuts, and cinnamon. In another small bowl stir together sour cream and baking soda.

2 In a large bowl combine granulated sugar and butter. Beat with an electric mixer on medium until light and fluffy. Add eggs and vanilla; beat until combined. Add the flour and baking powder; beat until combined. Beat in the sour cream mixture.

3 Pour half of the batter into prepared baking pan, spreading evenly. Sprinkle with blueberries and half of the topping. Carefully pour remaining batter over layers in pan, spreading evenly. Sprinkle with the remaining topping.

4 Bake, uncovered, for 35 to 40 minutes or until a toothpick inserted near center comes out clean. Drizzle with Powdered Sugar Icing. Serve warm or cool completely.

Makes 16 servings.

Per Serving: 345 cal., 14 g total fat (6 g sat. fat), 61 mg chol., 184 mg sodium, 51 g carbo., 2 g fiber, 4 g pro.

Powdered Sugar Icing: *In a small bowl stir together ½ cup powdered sugar, 2 teaspoons milk, and ¼ teaspoon vanilla. Stir in enough additional milk, 1 teaspoon at a time, to reach drizzling consistency.*

ORANGE BREAKFAST GRANOLA

This healthful and gorgeous
granola packed in a jar and tied with a pretty
ribbon makes a welcome gift.

Prep: 15 minutes   Bake: 30 minutes   Oven: 325°F

3 cups regular rolled oats

½ cup toasted wheat germ

½ cup coarsely chopped hazelnuts (filberts) or sliced almonds

⅓ cup honey

½ teaspoon finely shredded orange peel

⅓ cup orange juice

½ teaspoon ground cinnamon

Nonstick cooking spray

1 cup flaked or shredded coconut

1 Preheat oven to 325°F. In a large bowl stir together the oats, wheat germ, and hazelnuts; set aside.

2 In a small saucepan stir together honey, orange peel, orange juice, and cinnamon. Bring just to boiling. Pour honey mixture over oat mixture; toss gently to coat.

3 Lightly coat a 9×13-inch baking pan with cooking spray. Spread oat mixture evenly in prepared baking pan.

4 Bake, uncovered, for 15 minutes. Stir the coconut into the oat mixture. Bake, uncovered, for 15 to 20 minutes more or until light brown, stirring once.

5 Immediately turn out onto a large piece of foil; cool. Break apart. Store in an airtight container at room temperature for up to 2 weeks or in the freezer for up to 3 months.

Makes about 5 cups.

Per ½-cup Serving: 224 cal., 8 g total fat (3 g sat. fat), 0 mg chol., 3 mg sodium, 33 g carbo., 1 g fiber, 7 g pro.

BAKED GRAPEFRUIT HALVES

**A colorful combination of fruit and a
splash of orange liqueur makes these grapefruit
halves perfect for a holiday brunch, .**

Prep: 20 minutes **Bake:** 12 minutes **Oven:** 450°F

- 3 red grapefruit
- 1 medium orange, peeled and sectioned
- 1 medium banana, sliced
- 1/3 cup dried cherries
- 2 tablespoons orange liqueur or orange juice
- 1 tablespoon canola oil
- 2 tablespoons packed brown sugar
- 1/2 teaspoon ground cinnamon

1 Preheat oven to 450°F. Cut each grapefruit in half horizontally; cut a very thin slice from the bottom of each half so the halves will sit flat. Using a grapefruit knife or other small knife, cut around the outer edge to loosen fruit from shell. Cut between each segment and membrane to loosen the segment.

2 In a medium bowl combine orange sections, banana, cherries, and orange liqueur. Place grapefruit halves, cut sides up, in a 9×13-inch baking dish. Mound the orange mixture on top of grapefruit halves. Drizzle with oil. In a small bowl combine brown sugar and cinnamon; sprinkle over orange mixture.

3 Bake fruit, uncovered, for about 12 minutes or until grapefruit halves are warm and the topping is completely heated through.

Makes 6 servings.

Per Serving: 154 cal., 3 g total fat (0 g sat. fat), 0 mg chol., 4 mg sodium, 32 g carbo., 3 g fiber, 2 g pro.

29

BRUNCH BAKED APPLES WITH
GREEK YOGURT

Greek yogurt, as thick as
sour cream, can now be found in most
American grocery stores.

Prep: 30 minutes   **Bake:** 1 hour   **Oven:** 350°F

- 6 to 8 medium baking apples (such as McIntosh, Rome Beauty, or Granny Smith)
- 1 cup orange juice
- 1 cup rolled oats
- ½ cup packed brown sugar
- ⅓ cup slivered almonds, toasted
- 1 tablespoon all-purpose flour
- ¾ teaspoon ground cinnamon
- ¼ teaspoon ground nutmeg
- ⅓ cup butter, melted
- Cinnamon sticks, broken (optional)
- ⅓ cup honey
- 1 6- to 7-ounce carton Greek yogurt or other creamy-style yogurt

1 Preheat oven to 350°F. Remove a ½-inch slice from the top of each apple. Using a melon baller, remove core, stopping about ½ inch from the bottom of the apple. Arrange apples in a 9×13-inch baking dish. (If necessary, remove a thin slice from the bottom of each apple so the apples sit flat.) Brush with 1 tablespoon of the orange juice.

2 In a medium bowl combine oats, brown sugar, almonds, flour, ground cinnamon, and nutmeg. Stir in melted butter. Fill and top apples with oat mixture. Pour the remaining orange juice around apples.

3 Cover with foil. Bake for 50 minutes. If desired, place pieces of cinnamon stick in oat mixture to resemble stems. Bake, uncovered, for 10 to 15 minutes more or until apples are tender. Cool slightly. Drizzle apples with honey. Serve with yogurt.

Makes 6 to 8 servings.

Per Serving: 487 cal., 18 g total fat (9 g sat. fat), 32 mg chol., 89 mg sodium, 78 g carbo., 7 g fiber, 8 g pro.

EVERYTHING BREAKFAST BARS

What a great alternative to packaged
granola bars—and these chewy squares
are every bit as portable.

Prep: 25 minutes **Bake:** 22 minutes **Oven:** 350°F

Nonstick cooking spray
- ½ **cup refrigerated egg product or 2 eggs, beaten**
- ¼ **cup vegetable oil**
- ¼ **cup water**
- 1 **14-ounce package fat-free banana muffin mix**
- 1¾ **cups crisp rice cereal**
- 1½ **cups low-fat granola**
- ⅔ **cup cinnamon-flavor pieces**
- ½ **cup dried cranberries**
- ½ **cup sliced almonds, toasted**

1. Preheat oven to 350°F. Line a 9×13-inch baking pan with foil, extending foil over edges of pan. Lightly coat foil with cooking spray; set pan aside.

2. In a large bowl stir together eggs, oil, and the water. Add muffin mix, cereal, granola, cinnamon pieces, cranberries, and almonds; stir to combine. Spoon into prepared baking pan. Using the back of a spoon, press mixture evenly into the pan.

3. Bake, uncovered, for 22 to 25 minutes or until edges start to brown. Cool in pan on a wire rack. Using edges of foil, lift uncut bars out of pan. Cut into bars.

4. Store bars in a covered container at room temperature for up to 3 days or in the freezer for up to 3 months.

Makes 24 bars.

Per Bar: 171 cal., 6 g total fat (1 g sat. fat), 0 mg chol., 196 mg sodium, 27 g carbo., 2 g fiber, 3 g pro.

BEEF, PORK & LAMB

They're all here—the dinners you've been dreaming of—from fondly remembered dishes to those with new and exciting dimensions. Each of these exceptionally hearty, wholly satisfying recipes is blessed with oven-to-table convenience. Take your pick: You'll be proud to serve these meaty dishes anytime, in any season and for any reason.

BEEF TENDERLOIN WITH TOMATO JAM

Fire-roasting imbues
tomatoes with
unexpected sweetness.

Prep: 35 minutes **Roast:** 35 minutes **Stand:** 15 minutes **Oven:** 425°F

- 1 **medium onion, cut into 1-inch wedges**
- 3 **cloves garlic, peeled**
- 2 **tablespoons olive oil**
- 2 **14.5-ounce cans fire-roasted diced tomatoes, drained**
- ½ **teaspoon sugar**
- ½ **teaspoon kosher salt**
- ½ **teaspoon finely shredded orange peel**
- 1 **2½-pound center-cut beef tenderloin roast**
- 1 **tablespoon olive oil**
- 1 **teaspoon kosher salt**
- 1 **teaspoon freshly ground black pepper**
  Fresh thyme sprigs (optional)

1 Preheat oven to 425°F. For tomato jam: In a 9×13-inch baking pan combine onion and garlic. Drizzle with the 2 tablespoons oil; toss gently to coat. Spread in a single layer. Roast, uncovered, for 15 minutes. Using a slotted spoon, remove garlic; set aside. Roast onion, uncovered, about 10 minutes more or until onion starts to brown. Cool slightly. Coarsely chop onion and garlic. In a medium bowl stir together roasted onion and garlic, tomatoes, sugar, the ½ teaspoon salt, and the orange peel. Set aside.

2 Meanwhile, trim fat from meat. Brush meat with the 1 tablespoon oil; sprinkle with the 1 teaspoon salt and the pepper. Place meat on a rack in a shallow roasting pan. If desired, insert an oven-going meat thermometer into the center of the meat.

3 Roast, uncovered, for 35 to 40 minutes for medium rare (135°F) or 45 to 50 minutes for medium (150°F). Remove tenderloin from oven. Cover with foil; let stand for 15 minutes before slicing. Temperature of meat after standing should be 145°F for medium rare or 160°F for medium.

4 To serve, cut meat into ½-inch slices. Serve with tomato jam. If desired, garnish with thyme sprigs.

Makes 8 servings.

Per Serving: 308 cal., 17 g total fat (5 g sat. fat), 87 mg chol., 657 mg sodium, 7 g carbo., 0 g fiber, 30 g pro.

Make-Ahead Directions: *Prepare tomato jam as directed. Transfer to an airtight container; cover. Store in the refrigerator for up to 3 days.*

SPICE-RUBBED BEEF TENDERLOIN

Consider making a double batch
of this aromatic rub—it's
perfect for grilled steaks too.

Prep: 10 minutes   **Roast:** 30 minutes   **Stand:** 15 minutes   **Oven:** 425°F

- ½ to ¾ teaspoon chili powder
- ½ teaspoon kosher salt
- ¼ teaspoon coarsely ground black pepper
- ⅛ teaspoon ground cumin
- ⅛ teaspoon dried oregano, crushed
- 1 1- to 1½-pound beef tenderloin roast

1 Preheat oven to 425°F. For rub: In a small bowl combine chili powder, salt, pepper, cumin, and oregano. Sprinkle rub evenly over all sides of roast; rub in with your fingers. Place meat on a rack in a 9×13-inch baking pan. Insert a meat thermometer into center of meat. Roast, uncovered, for 30 to 40 minutes for medium rare (135°F) or 40 to 50 minutes for medium (150°F).

2 Cover meat with foil. Let stand for 15 minutes before slicing. Temperature of the meat after standing should be 145°F for medium rare or 160°F for medium.

Makes 4 servings.

Per Serving: 175 cal., 7 g total fat (3 g sat. fat), 76 mg chol., 308 mg sodium, 0 g carbo., 0 g fiber, 25 g pro.

BASIL-GARLIC SIRLOIN ROAST

A regal cut of beef like this one needs only simple seasonings as enhancements.

Prep: 15 minutes   **Roast:** 50 minutes   **Stand:** 15 minutes   **Oven:** 425°F/350°F

- 1   3- to 3½-pound boneless beef sirloin roast, cut 1¾ inches thick
- ¼   teaspoon salt
- ¼   teaspoon black pepper
- 2   cups lightly packed fresh basil leaves, snipped
- 8   to 10 cloves garlic, minced, or 2 tablespoons bottled minced garlic
- 2   teaspoons olive oil

1 Preheat oven to 425°F. Make five or six 5-inch-long slits along the top of the roast, cutting almost through it. Sprinkle roast with salt and pepper. In a small bowl combine basil and garlic; stuff into slits in roast. Tie roast with 100%-cotton kitchen string to hold slits closed. Drizzle roast with oil.

2 Place meat on a rack in a 9×13-inch baking pan. Insert an oven-going meat thermometer into center of meat. Roast, uncovered, for 15 minutes. Reduce oven temperature to 350°F. Roast, uncovered, for 35 to 45 minutes more or until thermometer registers 160°F (medium). Cover roast with foil. Let stand for 15 minutes before slicing.

Makes 10 to 12 servings.

Per Serving: 255 cal., 13 g total fat (5 g sat. fat), 91 mg chol., 121 mg sodium, 1 g carbo., 0 g fiber, 31 g pro.

SLOW-ROASTED BEEF TENDERLOIN

Slow roasting in the beginning of the cooking time makes this tenderloin incredibly tender.

Prep: 20 minutes **Roast:** 50 minutes **Stand:** 15 minutes **Oven:** 250°F/425°F

- 1 2½- to 3-pound beef tenderloin
- 2 tablespoons vegetable oil
- 1 to 2 cloves garlic, minced
- 1 teaspoon cracked black pepper
- ½ teaspoon sea salt or kosher salt or ¼ teaspoon regular salt
- 4 sprigs fresh rosemary
- 4 sprigs fresh oregano
- 4 sprigs fresh thyme
- 1 recipe Mushroom Tumble or Horseradish Cream

   Fresh thyme sprigs

1 Preheat oven to 250°F. Drizzle tenderloin with vegetable oil. Rub minced garlic evenly over the surface of the meat. Sprinkle with pepper and salt.

2 Place rosemary, oregano, and the 4 thyme sprigs in a 9×13-inch baking pan. Add a roasting rack. Place meat on rack.

3 Roast, uncovered, for 20 minutes. Increase oven temperature to 425°F. Roast, uncovered, for 30 to 40 minutes more or until an instant-read thermometer inserted in thickest part of the meat registers 135°F. Cover loosely with foil. Let stand for 15 minutes. Temperature of meat after standing should be 145°F for medium rare.

4 Slice meat. Serve with Mushroom Tumble or Horseradish Cream; sprinkle with additional fresh thyme sprigs.

Makes 8 to 10 servings.

Per Serving: 316 cal., 20 g total fat (5 g sat. fat), 87 mg chol., 238 mg sodium, 3 g carbo., 1 g fiber, 32 g pro.

Mushroom Tumble: *In an extra-large bowl toss together 6 cups assorted fresh mushrooms (such as chanterelle, portobello, shiitake, and oyster); halve any large mushrooms and, if necessary, remove stems. Add 3 tablespoons olive oil, 2 tablespoons lemon juice, and 1 teaspoon reduced-sodium soy sauce; gently toss to coat mushrooms. In a very large skillet cook mushroom mixture on medium heat about 10 minutes or until tender. Sprinkle with coarse sea salt and cracked black pepper.*

Horseradish Cream: *In a small bowl stir together one 7- to 8-ounce carton crème fraîche or sour cream and 2 tablespoons prepared horseradish. Stir in ⅛ teaspoon salt and ⅛ teaspoon black pepper.*

BEEF STROGANOFF CASSEROLE

With this incredibly
rich casserole, all you need
is a crisp green salad.

Prep: 35 minutes **Bake:** 30 minutes **Oven:** 350°F

- 12 ounces dried campanelle or penne pasta
- 1 17-ounce package refrigerated cooked beef roast au jus
- 2 large fresh portobello mushrooms, stems removed, coarsely chopped (about 4 cups)
- 1 medium sweet onion (such as Vidalia, Walla Walla, or Maui), cut into thin wedges
- 2 cloves garlic, minced
- 2 tablespoons butter
- 3 tablespoons all-purpose flour
- 2 tablespoons tomato paste
- 1 14-ounce can beef broth
- 1 tablespoon Worcestershire sauce
- 1 teaspoon smoked paprika or Spanish paprika
- ¼ teaspoon salt
- ¼ teaspoon black pepper
- 1 8-ounce carton sour cream
- 1 tablespoon prepared horseradish
- 1 teaspoon snipped fresh dill or ¼ teaspoon dried dill

  Fresh dill sprigs (optional)

1. Preheat oven to 350°F. Cook pasta according to package directions; drain. Return to hot pan.

2. Meanwhile, remove meat from container, reserving juices. Using 2 forks, shred meat into bite-size pieces. Set aside.

3. In a large skillet cook mushrooms, onion, and garlic in hot butter on medium heat for 4 to 5 minutes or until tender. Stir in flour and tomato paste. Gradually stir in reserved meat juices, broth, Worcestershire sauce, paprika, salt, and pepper. Cook and stir until thickened and bubbly. Remove from heat. Stir in ½ cup of the sour cream.

4. Stir shredded meat and mushroom mixture into cooked pasta. Spoon meat mixture into a 9×13-inch baking dish. Cover with foil. Bake about 30 minutes or until heated through.

5. Meanwhile, in a small bowl combine the remaining sour cream, the horseradish, and snipped or dried dill. Serve with meat mixture. If desired, garnish with dill sprigs.

Makes 6 servings.

Per Serving: 485 cal., 18 g total fat (10 g sat. fat), 72 mg chol., 770 mg sodium, 56 g carbo., 4 g fiber, 26 g pro.

41

SOUTHWESTERN TRI-TIP ROAST

Tri-tip—also called "triangle" steak or roast—is a superlatively flavorful yet economical cut.

Prep: 15 minutes **Chill:** 6 to 24 hours **Roast:** 30 minutes **Stand:** 15 minutes **Oven:** 425°F

- 1 tablespoon dried chipotle chiles, seeded and finely chopped* (about 2 teaspoons)
- 1 tablespoon snipped fresh oregano or 1 teaspoon dried oregano, crushed
- 1 tablespoon olive oil
- 1 teaspoon ground cumin
- ½ teaspoon salt
- 2 cloves garlic, minced
- 1 1½- to 2-pound boneless beef tri-tip roast (bottom sirloin)

1 For rub: In a small bowl combine chipotle chiles, oregano, oil, cumin, salt, and garlic. Spread over surface of meat, rubbing in with glove-covered hands. Cover and chill for at least 6 or up to 24 hours.

2 Preheat oven to 425°F. Place meat on a rack in a 9×13-inch baking pan. Insert an oven-going meat thermometer into center of roast. Roast, uncovered, for 30 to 35 minutes for medium rare (135°F) or 40 to 45 minutes for medium (150°F). Cover with foil. Let stand for 15 minutes. Temperature of meat after standing should be 145°F for medium rare or 160°F for medium.

Makes 6 to 8 servings.

Per Serving: 156 cal., 7 g total fat (2 g sat. fat), 45 mg chol., 248 mg sodium, 1 g carbo., 0 g fiber, 21 g pro.

Note: *Because chiles contain volatile oils that can burn your skin and eyes, avoid direct contact with them as much as possible. When working with chiles, wear plastic or rubber gloves. If your bare hands do touch the chiles, wash your hands and nails well with soap and warm water.*

SHREDDED BEEF AND CHILE ENCHILADAS

**Mexican-inspired dishes like this
are a smart choice for company—
almost everyone loves Latin flavors.**

Prep: 35 minutes **Roast:** 3 hours **Stand:** 15 minutes **Bake:** 40 minutes **Oven:** 325°F/350°F

1	3-pound fresh beef brisket
4½	teaspoons chili powder
1	tablespoon ground cumin
1	teaspoon dried oregano, crushed
2	medium onions, thinly sliced
1	14-ounce can beef broth
¼	cup white wine vinegar
2	4-ounce cans diced green chiles, undrained
1	tablespoon all-purpose flour
1	8-ounce carton sour cream
2	cups shredded Monterey Jack cheese (8 ounces)
12	7- to 8-inch flour tortillas
1	cup salsa verde or desired salsa

1 Preheat oven to 325°F. Trim fat from brisket. In a small bowl combine 4 teaspoons of the chili powder, the cumin, and oregano. Sprinkle spice mixture evenly over all sides of the brisket; rub in with your fingers.

2 Place brisket in a shallow roasting pan. Top with sliced onions; pour broth and vinegar over meat. Roast, covered, about 3 hours or until meat is fork tender. Let meat stand in pan juices about 15 minutes or until cool enough to handle. Remove meat from pan. Using a slotted spoon, remove onions; reserve pan juices. Halve meat crosswise. Using 2 forks, pull meat apart into shreds. Stir onions into shredded meat; stir in enough of the reserved pan juices to moisten (½ to 1 cup). Set meat mixture aside. Discard remaining pan juices.

3 In a medium saucepan combine undrained chiles and the remaining ½ teaspoon chili powder; cook about 1 minute or until heated through. Stir in flour. Cook and stir for 1 minute more. Remove from heat. Stir in sour cream and ½ cup of the cheese.

4 Increase oven temperature to 350°F. Grease a 9×13-inch baking dish; set aside. Divide shredded meat mixture among tortillas. Top with sour cream mixture. Roll up tortillas (tortillas will be full). Arrange rolled tortillas, seam sides down, in prepared baking dish.

5 Cover with foil. Bake for 30 minutes. Spoon salsa verde over; sprinkle with the remaining 1½ cups cheese. Bake, uncovered, about 10 minutes more or until cheese is melted and enchiladas are heated through.

Makes 12 enchiladas.

Per Enchilada: 559 cal., 38 g total fat (17 g sat. fat), 118 mg chol., 716 mg sodium, 23 g carbo., 3 g fiber, 29 g pro.

MEXICAN BEEF AND MACARONI
CASSEROLE

This is the kind
of casserole that brings family
to the table fast.

Prep: 20 minutes **Bake:** 30 minutes **Oven:** 350°F

- 2 cups dried elbow macaroni
- 1½ pounds lean ground beef
- 2½ cups picante sauce or salsa
- 1 15-ounce can black beans, rinsed and drained
- 2 teaspoons dried oregano, crushed
- 1 teaspoon ground cumin
- 1 teaspoon chili powder
- ¾ teaspoon garlic powder
- 1 16-ounce carton sour cream
- ¾ cup sliced green onions (6)
- 1 2.25-ounce can sliced pitted ripe olives, drained
- 1 cup shredded Monterey Jack cheese (4 ounces)
  Snipped fresh parsley (optional)

1 Preheat oven to 350°F. In a large Dutch oven cook macaroni according to package directions; drain. Return to hot Dutch oven.

2 Meanwhile, in a large skillet cook ground beef on medium heat until browned, stirring to break up meat as it cooks. Drain off fat. Stir meat into cooked macaroni. Stir in picante sauce, beans, oregano, cumin, chili powder, and garlic powder. Spoon into a 9×13-inch baking dish. Cover with foil. Bake about 25 minutes or until heated through.

3 In a medium bowl stir together sour cream, green onions, and olives. Spoon the sour cream mixture over top of mixture in baking dish; sprinkle with cheese. Bake, uncovered, about 5 minutes more or until cheese is melted. If desired, sprinkle with snipped fresh parsley.

Makes 8 servings.

Per Serving: 500 cal., 27 g total fat (14 g sat. fat), 93 mg chol., 744 mg sodium, 36 g carbo., 5 g fiber, 31 g pro.

44

ENCHILADA GRANDE CASSEROLE

Enchiladas are traditionally made with corn tortillas, but this one uses the flour variety.

Prep: 30 minutes **Bake:** 30 minutes **Stand:** 10 minutes **Oven:** 350°F

- 1 **pound lean ground beef**
- 1 **16-ounce can refried beans**
- 1 **15-ounce can low-sodium tomato sauce**
- ½ **cup water**
- 1 **1.375-ounce package enchilada sauce mix**
- 8 **7- to 8-inch flour tortillas**
- 2 **cups shredded cheddar cheese (8 ounces)**
  Sour cream (optional)
  Sliced green onions (optional)

1 Preheat oven to 350°F. Grease a 9×13-inch baking dish; set aside. In a large skillet cook ground beef on medium heat until browned, stirring to break up meat as it cooks. Drain off fat. Stir refried beans, tomato sauce, the water, and enchilada sauce mix into meat in skillet. Bring to boiling; reduce heat. Simmer, uncovered, for 15 minutes, stirring occasionally.

2 Arrange 4 of the tortillas in prepared baking dish, cutting to fit and overlapping as necessary. Spoon half of the meat mixture over tortillas in dish. Sprinkle with 1 cup of the cheese. Repeat layers with the remaining 4 tortillas and the remaining meat mixture.

3 Bake, uncovered, for 20 minutes. Sprinkle with the remaining 1 cup cheese. Bake, uncovered, about 10 minutes more or until heated through. Let stand for 10 minutes before serving. If desired, top with sour cream and green onions.

Makes 8 to 10 servings.

Per Serving: 442 cal., 20 g total fat (10 g sat. fat), 60 mg chol., 1,227 mg sodium, 41 g carbo., 8 g fiber, 24 g pro.

SICILIAN MEAT ROLL

> This Italian-style meat loaf is packed full of mozzarella cheese, prosciutto, and Italian herbs. When sliced, it displays an attractive swirl for a dazzling presentation.

Prep: 25 minutes   **Bake:** 70 minutes   **Stand:** 10 minutes   **Oven:** 350°F

- **2** eggs
- **¾** cup soft bread crumbs (1 slice)
- **½** cup tomato juice
- **2** tablespoons snipped fresh parsley
- **½** teaspoon dried oregano, crushed
- **¼** teaspoon salt
- **¼** teaspoon black pepper
- **1** small clove garlic, minced
- **2** pounds lean ground beef
- **6** ounces thinly sliced prosciutto
- **1½** cups shredded mozzarella cheese (6 ounces)

1 Preheat oven to 350°F. In a large bowl beat eggs with a fork. Stir in bread crumbs, tomato juice, parsley, oregano, salt, pepper, and garlic. Add ground beef; mix well.

2 On a large piece of foil pat meat mixture into a 10×12-inch rectangle. Arrange prosciutto slices on the meat, leaving a ¾-inch border around all edges. Sprinkle 1¼ cups of the mozzarella cheese over the prosciutto. Starting from a short end, carefully roll up meat rectangle, using foil to lift; seal edges and ends. Place meat roll, seam side down, in a 9×13-inch baking pan.

3 Bake, uncovered, about 65 minutes or until an instant-read thermometer inserted in the center registers 160°F and juices run clear. (Center of meat roll will be pink due to prosciutto.) Sprinkle the remaining ¼ cup mozzarella cheese over top of meat roll. Bake, uncovered, about 5 minutes more or until cheese melts. Let stand for 10 to 15 minutes before slicing.

Makes 8 servings.

Per Serving: 312 cal., 17 g total fat (7 g sat. fat), 152 mg chol., 878 mg sodium, 4 g carbo., 0 g fiber, 33 g pro.

ALFREDO BEEF SANDWICHES

Make your own bread crumbs
for pennies by simply giving dry,
leftover bread a whirl in the food processor.

Prep: 20 minutes **Bake:** 21 minutes **Oven:** 350°F

1   egg, lightly beaten
½   cup fine dry bread crumbs
½   teaspoon garlic salt
¼   teaspoon black pepper
1   pound lean ground beef
6   hoagie buns
1   16-ounce jar Alfredo or marinara pasta sauce
6   slices provolone cheese (about 6 ounces)

1   Preheat oven to 350°F. In a large bowl combine egg, bread crumbs, garlic salt, and pepper. Add ground beef; mix well. Shape mixture into twenty-four 1¼-inch meatballs. Arrange in a 9×13-inch baking pan. Bake, uncovered, for 15 minutes.

2   Split hoagie buns nearly all the way through but leave a long side attached. Spread 2 tablespoons of the Alfredo sauce over the bottom of each bun. Fill buns with meatballs and cheese.

3   Place sandwiches on a large baking sheet. Bake, uncovered, for 6 to 8 minutes or until buns are toasted and cheese is melted.

4   Meanwhile, heat the remaining Alfredo sauce and serve with sandwiches for dipping.

Makes 6 sandwiches.

Per Sandwich: 733 cal., 41 g total fat (21 g sat. fat), 152 mg chol., 1,405 mg sodium, 57 g carbo., 2 g fiber, 33 g pro.

POTLUCK CHEESY MOCK SHEPHERD'S PIE

This potluck favorite makes
two casseroles, which is
perfect for large groups.

Prep: 45 minutes **Bake:** 20 minutes **Oven:** 350°F

- 2 pounds lean ground beef
- 1 cup finely chopped onion (1 large)
- 1 10.75-ounce can condensed tomato soup
- ¼ cup water
- 1 tablespoon Worcestershire sauce
- 2 teaspoons dried Italian seasoning, crushed
- 2 cloves garlic, minced
- ¼ teaspoon black pepper
- 3 pounds potatoes (such as russet or red), peeled and quartered
- 6 tablespoons butter or margarine
- ⅔ cup milk

  Salt

  Black pepper
- 3 cups chopped zucchini (2 medium)
- 2 16-ounce packages frozen mixed vegetables
- 2 10.75-ounce cans condensed cheddar cheese soup
- ⅓ cup water

1 In a large skillet cook ground beef and onion on medium heat until beef is browned and onion is tender, stirring to break up meat as it cooks. Drain off fat. Stir tomato soup, the ¼ cup water, the Worcestershire sauce, Italian seasoning, garlic, and the ¼ teaspoon pepper into meat in skillet. Simmer, covered, for 15 to 20 minutes or until thickened.

2 Meanwhile, in a covered 4- to 6-quart Dutch oven cook potatoes in enough boiling water to cover for 20 to 25 minutes or until tender; drain. Using a potato masher or an electric mixer on low, mash potatoes. Stir in butter and milk. Season to taste with salt and additional pepper.

3 Preheat oven to 350°F. In a large saucepan combine zucchini, frozen mixed vegetables, cheese soup, and the ⅓ cup water. Cover and cook until heated through. Transfer hot meat mixture to a very large bowl. Stir in vegetable mixture.

4 Divide meat-vegetable mixture between two 9×13-inch baking dishes (or one 9×13-inch baking dish and one 3-quart casserole). Top with spoonfuls of the potato mixture, smoothing to make an even layer of potatoes. If desired, sprinkle with additional pepper.

5 Bake, uncovered, for 20 to 25 minutes or until potatoes are golden brown and meat mixture is bubbly.

Makes 12 to 16 servings.

Per Serving: 429 cal., 20 g total fat (9 g sat. fat), 72 mg chol., 791 mg sodium, 43 g carbo., 7 g fiber, 22 g pro.

BAKED PENNE WITH MEAT SAUCE

> Crushing dried oregano
> between your fingers just before
> adding releases the herb's flavor.

Prep: 30 minutes **Bake:** 25 minutes **Oven:** 350°F

8	ounces dried penne pasta
1	pound lean ground beef
½	cup chopped onion (1 medium)
1	14.5-ounce can diced tomatoes, undrained
½	of a 6-ounce can (⅓ cup) Italian-style tomato paste
⅓	cup dry red wine or tomato juice
⅓	cup water
½	teaspoon sugar
½	teaspoon dried oregano, crushed, or 2 teaspoons snipped fresh oregano
¼	teaspoon salt
¼	teaspoon black pepper
¼	cup sliced pitted ripe olives
1	cup shredded reduced-fat mozzarella cheese (4 ounces)

1 Preheat oven to 350°F. Cook pasta according to package directions; drain well.

2 Meanwhile, in a large skillet cook ground beef and onion on medium heat until meat is browned, stirring to break up meat as it cooks. Drain off fat. Stir undrained tomatoes, tomato paste, wine, the water, sugar, dried oregano (if using), salt, and pepper into meat in skillet. Bring to boiling; reduce heat. Simmer, covered, for 10 minutes. Stir in pasta, fresh oregano (if using), and olives. Spoon into a 9×13-inch baking dish.

3 Cover with foil. Bake about 20 minutes or until heated through. Sprinkle with mozzarella cheese. Bake, uncovered, about 5 minutes more or until cheese melts.

Makes 6 servings.

Per Serving: 342 cal., 10 g total fat (4 g sat. fat), 51 mg chol., 465 mg sodium, 37 g carbo., 2 g fiber, 22 g pro.

SHORTCUT LASAGNA

Nobody will ever guess
that making this homey lasagna
is so simple.

Prep: 30 minutes **Bake:** 40 minutes **Stand:** 5 minutes **Oven:** 350°F

- **8** ounces ground beef
- **8** ounces bulk Italian sausage
- **1** 26-ounce jar tomato-basil pasta sauce
- **1** egg
- **1** 15-ounce carton low-fat ricotta cheese or cream-style cottage cheese
- **1** 2.25-ounce can sliced pitted ripe olives
- **9** no-boil lasagna noodles
- **1** 8-ounce package sliced mozzarella cheese
- **¼** cup grated Parmesan cheese (1 ounce)

1 Preheat oven to 350°F. In a large saucepan cook beef and sausage until browned, stirring to break up meat as it cooks. Drain off fat. Stir pasta sauce into meat in saucepan; bring to boiling.

2 Meanwhile, in a medium bowl beat egg slightly with a fork. Stir in ricotta cheese and olives.

3 To assemble lasagna, spread about 1 cup of the hot meat mixture into a 9×13-inch baking pan or baking dish. Cover with 3 of the uncooked lasagna noodles, breaking noodles as necessary to fit and making sure that noodles do not touch the edge of the pan or dish. Cover with one-third of the ricotta mixture, one-third of the remaining meat mixture, and one-third of the mozzarella cheese. Repeat with 2 more layers of noodles, meat mixture, ricotta cheese mixture, and mozzarella cheese. (Make sure that noodles are covered with sauce.) Sprinkle with Parmesan cheese.

4 Cover with foil. Bake for 30 minutes. Uncover. Bake for 10 to 15 minutes more or until cheese is golden brown and noodles are tender. Let stand for 5 minutes before serving.

Makes 8 servings.

Per Serving: 492 cal., 26 g total fat (12 g sat. fat), 109 mg chol., 987 mg sodium, 34 g carbo., 2 g fiber, 31 g pro.

RED PEPPER LASAGNA

Italian sausage is available in both mild "sweet" and hot versions. Choose whichever variety suits your family's taste.

Prep: 40 minutes **Bake:** 55 minutes **Stand:** 15 minutes **Oven:** 350°F

- 8 ounces bulk Italian sausage
- 1 28-ounce can crushed tomatoes
- 4 cloves garlic, minced
- ½ teaspoon black pepper
- ¼ teaspoon salt
- 1 cup bottled roasted sweet red peppers, drained and cut into thin strips
- ½ cup snipped fresh basil
- ⅓ cup butter
- ⅓ cup all-purpose flour
- ½ teaspoon ground nutmeg
- ¼ teaspoon salt
- 3 cups milk
- 12 no-boil lasagna noodles
- 1¼ cups finely shredded Parmesan cheese (5 ounces)

1 Preheat oven to 350°F. Lightly grease a 9×13-inch baking pan or baking dish; set aside. For meat sauce: In a large saucepan cook sausage until browned, stirring to break up meat as it cooks. Drain off fat. Stir crushed tomatoes, garlic, black pepper, and ¼ teaspoon salt into meat in saucepan. Bring to boiling; reduce heat. Simmer, covered, for 10 minutes, stirring occasionally. Remove from heat. Stir in roasted peppers and basil; set aside.

2 Meanwhile, for white sauce: In a medium saucepan melt butter on medium heat. Stir in flour, nutmeg, and ¼ teaspoon salt. Gradually stir in milk. Cook and stir until thickened and bubbly.

3 To assemble, arrange 3 of the uncooked noodles in prepared baking pan or dish. Spread with about 1 cup of the meat sauce and about ¾ cup of the white sauce. Sprinkle with ¼ cup of the Parmesan cheese. Repeat layering noodles, meat sauce, white sauce, and cheese three more times, making sure the top layer of noodles is completely covered with sauce. Sprinkle with the remaining Parmesan cheese.

4 Cover pan with foil. Bake for 40 minutes. Uncover. Bake about 15 minutes more or until edges are bubbly and top is lightly browned. Cover and let stand for 15 minutes before serving.

Makes 8 servings.

Per Serving: 420 cal., 16 g total fat (9 g sat. fat), 45 mg chol., 745 mg sodium, 49 g carbo., 3 g fiber, 21 g pro.

STUFFED PIZZA PEPPERS

Using both red and yellow sweet peppers
and placing them alternately in the pan
makes this family favorite oh-so-pretty.

Prep: 40 minutes **Bake:** 45 minutes **Oven:** 350°F

- **4** medium sweet red and/or yellow peppers (6 to 8 ounces each)
- **8** ounces bulk Italian sausage or sweet Italian sausage
- **1** cup chopped fresh mushrooms
- **1** cup marinara pasta sauce
- **⅓** cup sliced pitted ripe or kalamata olives
- **¼** teaspoon black pepper
- **1** cup soft bread crumbs*
- **¼** cup shredded mozzarella cheese (1 ounce)
- **¼** cup shredded Parmesan cheese (1 ounce)
- **3** tablespoons pine nuts

1 Preheat oven to 350°F. Grease a 9×13-inch baking dish; set aside. Cut tops from peppers; chop tops and set aside. Halve peppers lengthwise. Remove seeds. Set the pepper halves, cut sides up, in prepared baking dish.

2 In a large skillet cook sausage until browned, stirring to break up meat as it cooks. Drain off fat. Stir chopped sweet pepper and mushrooms into meat in skillet; cook and stir until vegetables are tender. Stir in marinara sauce, olives, and black pepper; heat through. Remove from heat. Stir in bread crumbs. Spoon about ⅓ cup of the sausage mixture into each pepper half.

3 Cover with foil. Bake for 40 to 45 minutes or until peppers are tender. Sprinkle with mozzarella cheese, Parmesan cheese, and pine nuts. Bake, uncovered, about 5 minutes more or until cheese melts.

Makes 4 to 6 servings.

Per Serving: 365 cal., 23 g total fat (8 g sat. fat), 49 mg chol., 837 mg sodium, 22 g carbo., 4 g fiber, 18 g pro.

*Note: *Use a blender or food processor to make fluffy soft bread crumbs. One slice yields ¾ cup crumbs.*

MEAT-STUFFED MANICOTTI

Make moving slippery
cooked manicotti simple by slipping
a chopstick through their openings.

Prep: 30 minutes   **Bake:** 35 minutes   **Oven:** 350°F

- **12** dried manicotti pasta
- **8** ounces lean ground beef
- **8** ounces bulk Italian sausage
- **2** cups shredded mozzarella cheese (8 ounces)
- **½** of a 15-ounce carton (about 1 cup) ricotta cheese
- **½** cup finely shredded Parmesan cheese (2 ounces)
- **1½** teaspoons dried Italian seasoning, crushed
- **3** cups marinara pasta sauce
- Shredded mozzarella cheese (optional)
- Finely shredded Parmesan cheese (optional)
- Snipped fresh rosemary, oregano, and/or parsley (optional)

1 Preheat oven to 350°F. Cook manicotti according to package directions; drain. Place manicotti in a single layer on a sheet of greased foil.

2 Meanwhile, in a large skillet cook ground beef and sausage on medium heat until browned, stirring to break up meat as it cooks. Drain off fat. In a medium bowl combine 1 cup of the mozzarella cheese, the ricotta cheese, the ½ cup Parmesan cheese, and the Italian seasoning. Stir in meat mixture.

3 Using a small spoon, fill manicotti with meat-cheese mixture. Arrange filled manicotti in a 9×13-inch baking dish. Pour marinara sauce over manicotti. Sprinkle with the remaining 1 cup mozzarella cheese.

4 Cover with foil. Bake for 25 minutes. Uncover. Bake about 10 minutes more or until heated through and cheese melts. If desired, sprinkle with additional mozzarella cheese, additional Parmesan cheese, and fresh herbs.

Makes 6 servings.

Per Serving: 584 cal., 34 g total fat (15 g sat. fat), 96 mg chol., 1,258 mg sodium, 38 g carbo., 3 g fiber, 34 g pro.

STUFFED CHILES IN TWO SAUCES

These festive stuffed chiles are inspired by *chiles en nogada*, a special-occasion dish in Puebla, Mexico.

Prep: 45 minutes **Bake:** 25 minutes **Oven:** 350°F

- 1 **pound ground pork, uncooked ground turkey, or uncooked ground chicken**
- 1/3 **cup chopped onion (1 small)**
- 1 **clove garlic, minced**
- 2 **cups chopped peeled apples and/or pears (2 large)**
- 1 **8-ounce can tomato sauce**
- 1/4 **cup raisins**
- 1/2 **teaspoon salt**
- 1/4 **teaspoon ground cinnamon**
- 1/4 **teaspoon ground cumin**
- 1/4 **cup slivered almonds, toasted**
- 6 **large fresh poblano chiles**
- 1 **recipe Walnut Sauce**
- 1 **recipe Mole**

1 For filling: In a large skillet cook ground pork, onion, and garlic until meat is browned and onion is tender, stirring to break up meat as it cooks. Drain off fat. Stir apples, tomato sauce, raisins, salt, cinnamon, and cumin into meat mixture in skillet. Bring to boiling; reduce heat. Simmer, covered, for 10 minutes. Stir in almonds.

2 Meanwhile, cut a lengthwise slit in a side of each chile and remove seeds and membranes.* In a large saucepan cook chiles in boiling water about 5 minutes or until crisp-tender. Drain well. Cool slightly.

3 Preheat oven to 350°F. Spoon meat mixture into the chiles. Place stuffed chiles in a 9×13-inch baking dish. Cover with foil. Bake about 25 minutes or until heated through. Meanwhile, prepare the sauces.

4 To serve, spoon Walnut Sauce and Mole onto 6 dinner plates. Place stuffed chiles on top of the sauces.

Makes 6 servings.

Per Serving: 373 cal., 23 g total fat (7 g sat. fat), 52 mg chol., 629 mg sodium, 29 g carbo., 4 g fiber, 17 g pro.

Walnut Sauce: *In a blender or food processor combine ½ cup walnuts; one 3-ounce package cream cheese, cut up; ⅓ cup milk; ¼ teaspoon ground cinnamon; and ⅛ teaspoon salt. Cover and blend or process until smooth.*

Mole: *In a small saucepan cook ½ cup finely chopped onion (1 medium) and 1 clove garlic, minced, in 1 tablespoon hot vegetable oil over medium heat for 4 to 5 minutes or until onion is tender. Stir in 1 large tomato, chopped; 3 tablespoons canned diced green chiles; 2 teaspoons unsweetened cocoa powder; 1 teaspoon chili powder; and ¼ teaspoon salt. Bring to boiling; reduce heat. Simmer, covered, for 10 minutes. Cool slightly. Puree in a blender or food processor until smooth.*

---

*Note: *Because chiles contain volatile oils that can burn your skin and eyes, avoid direct contact with them as much as possible. When working with chiles, wear plastic or rubber gloves. If your bare hands do touch the chiles, wash your hands and nails well with soap and warm water.*

WHOLE WHEAT PIZZA WITH THE WORKS

If rolling bread dough is difficult,
cover dough with a towel and allow it to relax
for about 10 minutes before continuing.

Prep: 30 minutes   **Bake:** 30 minutes   **Oven:** 375°F

Nonstick cooking spray

1 **16-ounce loaf frozen whole wheat bread dough, thawed**

½ **cup pizza sauce**

½ **of a 6-ounce package pizza-style Canadian bacon or thinly sliced cooked turkey pepperoni**

1½ **cups thinly sliced fresh mushrooms**

1 **cup shredded 4-cheese Italian-blend cheese or mozzarella cheese**

2 **tablespoons snipped fresh Italian (flat-leaf) parsley**

1. Preheat oven to 375°F. Lightly coat a 9×13-inch baking pan with cooking spray. On a lightly floured surface roll bread dough into a 12½-inch circle. Transfer dough circle to prepared baking pan; build up edges. Prick the dough several times with a fork.

2. Bake, uncovered, for 10 minutes. Spread pizza sauce over hot crust. Top with Canadian bacon and mushrooms. Sprinkle with cheese.

3. Bake, uncovered, for 20 to 25 minutes or until cheese melts and edge of crust is brown. Sprinkle with snipped parsley.

Makes 8 servings.

Per Serving: 216 cal., 6 g total fat (2 g sat. fat), 13 mg chol., 661 mg sodium, 30 g carbo., 3 g fiber, 14 g pro.

DIJON PORK SALAD

Brush the pork with the same
bottled salad dressing
you toss with the greens.

Prep: 10 minutes **Roast:** 25 minutes **Stand:** 15 minutes **Oven:** 425°F

1	1-pound pork tenderloin
	Salt
	Black pepper
$^2/_3$	cup bottled Dijon lime salad dressing or oil and vinegar salad dressing
8	cups torn mixed salad greens
2	ounces Gouda cheese or white cheddar cheese, cut into bite-size strips
12	cherry tomatoes, quartered

1 Preheat oven to 425°F. Trim fat from tenderloin. Place tenderloin on a rack in a 9×13-inch baking pan. Sprinkle with salt and pepper. Brush tenderloin with 2 tablespoons of the salad dressing. Roast, uncovered, for 25 to 35 minutes or until an instant-read thermometer inserted in center of tenderloin registers 155°F. Cover with foil. Let stand for 15 minutes. Temperature of meat after standing should be 160°F.

2 Meanwhile, arrange salad greens on four salad plates. Top with cheese and tomatoes. Thinly slice pork; arrange pork slices on salads. Serve with the remaining salad dressing.

Makes 4 servings.

Per Serving: 336 cal., 24 g total fat (5 g sat. fat), 71 mg chol., 535 mg sodium, 5 g carbo., 2 g fiber, 23 g pro.

PORK AND NOODLE SALAD

Bean threads, also called cellophane or glass noodles, are made from mung bean starch. They require no boiling, just a short soak in warm water.

Prep: 25 minutes   **Roast:** 25 minutes   **Stand:** 15 minutes   **Chill:** 1 to 24 hours   **Oven:** 425°F

- 1 12- to 16-ounce pork tenderloin
-    Salt
-    Black pepper
- 1 recipe Ginger-Soy Dressing
- 1 3.75-ounce package bean threads or cellophane noodles
- 2 cups shredded napa cabbage
- 1 cup shredded carrots (2 medium)
- 1 cup thinly sliced radishes
- 2 cups torn bok choy or baby bok choy
- ½ cup fresh cilantro leaves
- 1 recipe Wonton Crisps

1 Preheat oven to 425°F. Line a 9×13-inch baking pan with foil; set pan aside. Trim fat from tenderloin; place tenderloin in prepared baking pan. Sprinkle with salt and pepper. Roast, uncovered, about 25 minutes or until an instant-read thermometer inserted in center of tenderloin registers 155°F, brushing with 1 tablespoon of the Ginger-Soy Dressing during the last 5 minutes of roasting. Cover with foil. Let stand for 15 minutes. Temperature of meat after standing should be 160°F. Thinly slice tenderloin.

2 Meanwhile, prepare noodles according to package directions. Rinse with cold water to cool; drain well. Using scissors, snip noodles into short lengths. Add cabbage; toss.

3 In a 9×13-inch baking dish layer noodle mixture, carrots, pork, and radishes. Drizzle with half of the remaining Ginger-Soy dressing. Top with bok choy and cilantro. Cover and chill for 1 to 24 hours. Serve salad with Wonton Crisps; pass the remaining dressing.

Makes 6 servings.

Per Serving: 351 cal., 17 g total fat (2 g sat. fat), 38 mg chol., 529 mg sodium, 35 g carbo., 2 g fiber, 15 g pro.

Ginger-Soy Dressing: *In screw-top jar combine ⅓ cup vegetable oil, 3 tablespoons lime juice, 3 tablespoons rice vinegar, 1 tablespoon packed brown sugar, 1 tablespoon grated fresh ginger, 1 tablespoon soy sauce, 1 tablespoon honey, 1 teaspoon toasted sesame oil, ¼ teaspoon salt, and ¼ teaspoon crushed red pepper. Cover; shake well. Refrigerate for up to 3 days.*

Wonton Crisps: *Preheat oven to 425°F. Line a baking sheet with foil. Lightly coat with nonstick cooking spray. Place 12 wonton wrappers on a baking sheet. Brush tops of wrappers with 1 tablespoon toasted sesame oil or peanut oil. Bake, uncovered, for 5 to 6 minutes or until golden brown (wontons will continue to brown after removed from oven). When cool, break into pieces.*

ROASTED PORK TENDERLOIN WITH
BLACKBERRY SAUCE

If pressed for time, piercing the tenderloin in several places with a fork will allow the marinade to work its magic more quickly.

Prep: 20 minutes **Marinate:** 2 to 5 hours **Roast:** 35 minutes **Stand:** 15 minutes **Oven:** 425°F

1	1½-pound pork tenderloin
¼	cup blackberry preserves, melted and cooled
¼	cup dry white wine or apple juice
2	tablespoons balsamic vinegar
2	tablespoons olive oil
2	tablespoons Dijon mustard
3	cloves garlic, minced
1	teaspoon soy sauce
1	teaspoon finely shredded orange peel
½	teaspoon snipped fresh rosemary
	Shredded orange peel (optional)

1 Place tenderloin in a resealable plastic bag set in a shallow dish. For marinade: In a medium bowl whisk together the preserves, wine, vinegar, olive oil, mustard, garlic, soy sauce, the 1 teaspoon orange peel, and the rosemary. Pour marinade over tenderloin; seal bag. Marinate in the refrigerator for at least 2 or up to 5 hours, turning bag occasionally. Drain; reserving marinade.

2 Preheat oven to 425°F. Place tenderloin on a rack in a 9×13-inch baking pan. Roast, uncovered, for 35 to 45 minutes or until an instant-read thermometer inserted in center of tenderloin registers 155°F. Cover with foil. Let stand for 15 minutes. Temperature of meat after standing should be 160°F.

3 Meanwhile, for sauce: In a small saucepan bring the reserved marinade to boiling; reduce heat. Simmer, uncovered, about 5 minutes or until desired consistency. Slice pork diagonally. Serve with sauce. If desired, garnish with additional orange peel.

Makes 6 servings.

Per Serving: 221 cal., 7 g total fat (1 g sat. fat), 74 mg chol., 244 mg sodium, 11 g carbo., 0 g fiber, 24 g pro.

PORK LOIN WITH VEGETABLES

If you don't usually keep apricot preserves
on hand, make this succulent pork dish with
peach or pineapple preserves instead.

Prep: 15 minutes   **Roast:** 35 minutes   **Stand:** 15 minutes   **Oven:** 425°F

12 ounces packaged peeled baby carrots (2½ cups)

12 ounces small new potatoes, quartered

1 12- to 16-ounce pork tenderloin

⅔ cup apricot preserves

¼ cup white wine vinegar or white vinegar

1 Preheat oven to 425°F. In a covered medium saucepan cook carrots and potatoes in a small amount of boiling water for 4 minutes; drain. Meanwhile, place the tenderloin in a 9×13-inch baking pan. Arrange carrots and potatoes around meat. Roast, uncovered, for 20 minutes.

2 Meanwhile, in a small bowl stir together preserves and vinegar; brush some of the preserves mixture over tenderloin. Drizzle the remaining preserves mixture over vegetables; toss to coat. Roast, uncovered, about 15 minutes more or until an instant-read thermometer inserted in center of tenderloin registers 155°F. Stir vegetables.

3 Cover meat and vegetables with foil. Let stand for 15 minutes. Temperature of meat after standing should be 160°F. Transfer meat to a serving platter; slice meat. Using a slotted spoon, transfer vegetables to the platter. Drizzle pan juices over meat and vegetables.

Makes 4 servings.

Per Serving: 365 cal., 2 g total fat (1 g sat. fat), 50 mg chol., 84 mg sodium, 62 g carbo., 5 g fiber, 23 g pro.

CRUSTED FENNEL-LAVENDER PORK TENDERLOIN

67

You can find culinary lavender
in natural food stores
and some produce markets.

Prep: 25 minutes   **Roast:** 25 minutes   **Stand:** 15 minutes   **Oven:** 425°F

1	**1-pound pork tenderloin**
1	**tablespoon fennel seeds, crushed**
2	**teaspoons dried lavender**
½	**teaspoon salt**
¼	**teaspoon black pepper**
1	**tablespoon butter**
1	**small shallot, chopped**
1	**clove garlic, minced**
1	**14-ounce can chicken broth**
¼	**cup whipping cream**
2	**tablespoons dry white wine (optional)**
1	**tablespoon butter, softened**
1	**tablespoon cornstarch**
	Hot cooked rice or hot cooked wild rice

1 Preheat oven to 425°F. Trim fat from tenderloin. In a shallow dish combine fennel seeds, lavender, salt, and pepper; set aside 2 teaspoons of the seed mixture. Sprinkle the remaining seed mixture evenly over tenderloin; pat in with your fingers. Place tenderloin on a rack in a 9×13-inch baking pan.

2 Roast, uncovered, for 25 to 35 minutes or until an instant-read thermometer inserted in the center of the tenderloin registers 155°F. Cover with foil and let stand for 15 minutes. Temperature of meat after standing should be 160°F.

3 Meanwhile, in a large skillet melt butter on medium heat. Add shallot and garlic; cook and stir until shallot is tender. Add broth, whipping cream, wine, and the reserved 2 teaspoons seed mixture; bring to boiling. Boil gently, uncovered, for 5 minutes. In a small bowl combine softened butter and cornstarch; add to skillet. Cook and stir until thickened and bubbly. Cook and stir for 2 minutes more. Strain sauce and serve with pork and hot cooked rice.

Makes 4 servings.

Per Serving: 315 cal., 14 g total fat (8 g sat. fat), 110 mg chol., 798 mg sodium, 18 g carbo., 1 g fiber, 26 g pro.

PECAN-PARMESAN PORK WITH PORT SAUCE

Restaurants would hate for you to know how simple it is to prepare a gourmet crusted pork entrée like this one.

Prep: 25 minutes **Roast:** 25 minutes **Stand:** 15 minutes **Oven:** 425°F

- 2 **1-pound pork tenderloins**
- 1 **cup broken pecans**
- ²/₃ **cup finely shredded Parmesan cheese**
- 3 **tablespoons yellow mustard**
- 1 **tablespoon Worcestershire sauce or soy sauce**
- 2 **cups port or dry Marsala**
- 1 **cup snipped dried Calimyrna or Mission figs (5½ to 6 ounces)**
- 2 **tablespoons packed brown sugar**
  Kumquats (optional)

1 Preheat oven to 425°F. Trim fat from tenderloins; set tenderloins aside. In a blender or food processor combine pecans, cheese, mustard, and Worcestershire sauce. Cover and blend or process until pecans are finely chopped. Press mixture onto all sides of the tenderloins to coat with a thin layer.

2 Place tenderloins, side by side, on a rack in a 9×13-inch baking pan. Roast, uncovered, for 25 to 35 minutes or until an instant-read thermometer inserted in centers of tenderloins registers 155°F. Cover with foil; let stand for 15 minutes. Temperature of meat after standing should be 160°F.

3 Meanwhile, for sauce: In a medium saucepan stir together port, figs, and brown sugar. Bring to boiling; reduce heat. Simmer, uncovered, for 10 to 15 minutes or until mixture is reduced to 2¼ cups. Cool slightly.

4 Transfer half of the sauce to the blender or processor. Cover and blend or process until nearly smooth. Pour mixture through a sieve over a bowl, pressing solids to release juices. Discard solids. Repeat with the remaining sauce. Return all of the sauce to saucepan. Cook and stir over low heat just until heated through.

5 To serve, slice meat. Serve with warm sauce. If desired, garnish with kumquats.

Makes 8 servings.

Per Serving: 428 cal., 15 g total fat (3 g sat. fat), 78 mg chol., 253 mg sodium, 31 g carbo., 4 g fiber, 29 g pro.

PORK LOIN WITH APPLES AND PEARS

**Prepare this succulent roast
in the autumn, when fresh apples and pears
are at their finest.**

Prep: 25 minutes   **Roast:** 65 minutes   **Stand:** 15 minutes   **Oven:** 425°F

Olive oil

2   teaspoons black pepper

1   teaspoon salt

1   teaspoon garlic powder

1   3-pound boneless pork top loin roast (single loin)

1/3   cup molasses

2   tablespoons red wine vinegar

1   tablespoon reduced-sodium soy sauce

3   apples, cut into halves, wedges, or slices

2   red pears, cut into halves, wedges, or slices

2   tablespoons sugar

1 Preheat oven to 425°F. Line a 9×13-inch baking pan with heavy foil; brush foil lightly with olive oil. Place roasting rack in pan; set aside.

2 In a small bowl combine pepper, salt, and garlic powder. Brush pork with 1 tablespoon olive oil. Sprinkle pepper mixture evenly over pork; rub in with your fingers. Place pork on rack in prepared baking pan. Roast, uncovered, for 35 minutes.

3 For glaze: In a small skillet combine molasses, vinegar, and soy sauce. Bring to boiling; reduce heat. Simmer, uncovered, for 1 minute. Pour glaze into a small bowl; set aside 2 tablespoons of the glaze and the skillet.

4 Brush pork with the remaining glaze. Roast, uncovered, for 10 minutes more; brush again with glaze. Discard the remainder of the glaze used to brush pork.

5 Roast, uncovered, about 20 minutes more or until an instant-read thermometer inserted in center of roast registers 150°F. Cover with foil. Let stand for 15 minutes. Temperature of meat after standing should be 160°F.

6 Meanwhile, in the skillet used for the glaze heat 1 tablespoon olive oil on medium heat. In a large bowl toss fruit with sugar. Add fruit to skillet; cover and cook for 2 minutes. Uncover. Cook about 3 minutes more or until crisp-tender. Add the 2 tablespoons reserved glaze; heat through. Slice pork. Serve pork with fruit and drizzle with pan juices.

Makes 8 servings.

Per Serving: 361 cal., 10 g total fat (3 g sat. fat), 107 mg chol., 444 mg sodium, 28 g carbo., 3 g fiber, 39 g pro.

CHILI-GLAZED PORK ROAST

Leftovers of this spicy roast
(if you're lucky enough to have any)
make terrific tacos.

Prep: 20 minutes   **Roast:** 1¼ hours   **Stand:** 15 minutes   **Oven:** 325°F

- **1** **tablespoon packed brown sugar**
- **1** **tablespoon snipped fresh thyme or 1 teaspoon dried thyme, crushed**
- **1** **teaspoon chili powder**
- **1** **teaspoon snipped fresh rosemary or ¼ teaspoon dried rosemary, crushed**
- **⅛** **teaspoon cayenne pepper**
- **1** **2- to 2½-pound boneless pork top loin roast (single loin)**
  Fresh rosemary sprigs (optional)

1 Preheat oven to 325°F. In a small bowl combine brown sugar, thyme, chili powder, rosemary, and cayenne pepper. Sprinkle mixture evenly over roast; rub in with your fingers.

2 Place roast on a rack in a 9×13-inch baking pan. Insert an oven-going meat thermometer into center of roast. Roast, uncovered, for 1¼ to 1¾ hours or until meat thermometer registers 150°F. Cover with foil. Let stand for 15 minutes before slicing. Temperature of the meat after standing should be 160°F. If desired, garnish with rosemary sprigs.

Makes 8 to 10 servings

Per Serving: 134 cal., 4 g total fat (2 g sat. fat), 50 mg chol., 37 mg sodium, 2 g carbo., 0 g fiber, 20 g pro.

CRANBERRY-AND-CITRUS-GLAZED PORK ROAST

This holiday-perfect
---
pork roast is as easy as can
---
be to prepare.

Prep: 15 minutes   **Roast:** 1½ hours   **Stand:** 15 minutes   **Oven:** 325°F

¼   **teaspoon salt**
¼   **teaspoon black pepper**
½   **teaspoon ground sage**
1   **2½- to 3-pound boneless pork top loin roast (single loin)**
1   **16-ounce can whole or jellied cranberry sauce**
½   **teaspoon finely shredded orange peel**
⅓   **cup orange juice**

1 Preheat oven to 325°F. For rub: In a small bowl stir together salt, pepper, and ¼ teaspoon of the sage. Sprinkle rub evenly all over roast; rub in with your fingers. Place roast on rack in a 9×13-inch baking pan. Roast, uncovered, for 1 hour.

2 Meanwhile, for sauce: In a medium saucepan stir together cranberry sauce, orange peel, orange juice, and the remaining ¼ teaspoon sage. Bring to boiling; reduce heat. Simmer, uncovered, about 10 minutes or until slightly thickened.

3 Spoon about ¼ cup of the sauce over meat. Roast, uncovered, for 30 to 45 minutes more or until an instant-read thermometer inserted in center registers 150°F. Cover loosely with foil. Let stand for 15 minutes before slicing. Temperature of meat after standing should be 160°F.

4 In small saucepan bring the remaining sauce to boiling; boil for 1 minute. Serve with sliced meat.

Makes 8 to 10 servings.

Per Serving: 290 cal., 7 g total fat (2 g sat. fat), 77 mg chol., 132 mg sodium, 23 g carbo., 1 g fiber, 31 g pro.

RHUBARB-GLAZED PORK ROAST

To choose rhubarb for this rosy-hued roast, look for crisp stalks with cherry red color.

Prep: 25 minutes   **Roast:** 1¼ hours   **Stand:** 15 minutes   **Oven:** 325°F

- 1   **2- to 3-pound boneless pork top loin roast (single loin)**
- 4   **cups fresh or frozen sliced rhubarb**
- ½   **of a 12-ounce can frozen apple-cranberry juice concentrate**
- 2   **tablespoons cornstarch**
- 2   **tablespoons cold water**
- ⅓   **cup honey**
- 2   **tablespoons Dijon mustard**
- 1   **tablespoon wine vinegar**

1 Preheat oven to 325°F. Place roast on a rack in a 9×13-inch baking pan. Insert an oven-going meat thermometer into center of roast. Roast, uncovered, for 1¼ hours to 1¾ hours or until the thermometer registers 150°F.

2 Meanwhile, for rhubarb glaze: In a medium saucepan combine rhubarb and apple-cranberry juice concentrate. Bring to boiling; reduce heat. Simmer, covered, for 10 to 15 minutes or until rhubarb is very tender. Strain mixture into a 2-cup liquid measure, pressing out liquid with the back of a spoon; discard pulp. If necessary, add enough water to liquid to equal 1⅓ cups.

3 In the saucepan stir together cornstarch and the cold water. Stir in the rhubarb liquid. Cook and stir on medium heat until thickened and bubbly. Cook and stir for 2 minutes more. Stir in honey, mustard, and vinegar. Heat through.

4 Brush some of the glaze onto the meat during the last 30 minutes of roasting. Cover meat with foil. Let stand for 15 minutes. Temperature of the meat after standing should be 160°F. In a small saucepan bring the remaining glaze to boiling; boil for 1 minute. Serve warm glaze with meat.

Makes 6 to 8 servings.

Per Serving: 336 cal., 8 g total fat (3 g sat. fat), 83 mg chol., 85 mg sodium, 32 g carbo., 0 g fiber, 33 g pro.

Apricot-Glazed Pork Roast: *Prepare roast as directed through Step 1. Omit rhubarb glaze. For apricot glaze: In a small saucepan combine ⅔ cup apricot preserves, 4 teaspoons lime juice, 2 teaspoons soy sauce, ¼ teaspoon grated fresh ginger or ⅛ teaspoon ground ginger, and dash cayenne pepper. Cook and stir until bubbly. Continue as directed in Step 4.*

Per Serving: *309 cal., 7 g total fat (3 g sat. fat), 83 mg chol., 168 mg sodium, 25 g carbo., 0 g fiber, 33 g pro.*

HOT-SPICED PORK AND RICE

> Chili paste is made from fermented fava beans, hot red chiles, and garlic. Look for it in the Asian section of your supermarket.

Prep: 45 minutes   **Bake:** 1 hour   **Stand:** 10 minutes   **Oven:** 375°F

2   to 2¼ pounds boneless pork shoulder roast

2   to 3 tablespoons vegetable oil

2   cups thinly sliced carrots (4 medium)

1   medium sweet yellow pepper, cut into thin strips

1   8-ounce can sliced water chestnuts, drained

1   cup chopped onion (1 large)

1   cup long grain rice

1   14-ounce can reduced-sodium chicken broth

½   cup water

¼   cup soy sauce

2   tablespoons molasses

2   tablespoons light-color corn syrup

1   to 2 teaspoons red chili paste

1   teaspoon five-spice powder

⅓   cup sliced green onions

1 Preheat oven to 375°F. Trim fat from roast. Cut roast into ¾-inch pieces. In an extra-large skillet heat 2 tablespoons of the oil on medium-high heat. Cook meat, half at a time, in hot oil until brown. Transfer meat to a 9×13-inch baking dish. Stir in carrots, sweet pepper, and water chestnuts.

2 If needed, add the remaining 1 tablespoon oil to skillet. Add onion; cook just until tender. Add uncooked rice; cook and stir for 1 minute. Stir in broth, the water, soy sauce, molasses, corn syrup, chili paste, and five-spice powder. Cook and stir just until boiling. Carefully add to meat mixture; stir to combine.

3 Cover with foil. Bake about 1 hour or until meat and rice are tender. Let stand, covered, for 10 minutes before serving. Stir gently. Sprinkle with green onions.

Makes 6 servings.

Per Serving: 439 cal., 14 g total fat (3 g sat. fat), 91 mg chol., 980 mg sodium, 47 g carbo., 3 g fiber, 34 g pro.

OVEN-FRIED PORK CHOPS

Your family will love the crunchy
coating on these moist,
flavorful, and supersimple chops.

Prep: 10 minutes **Bake:** 20 minutes **Oven:** 425°F

- 4 **bone-in pork loin chops, cut ³/₄ inch thick**
- 2 **tablespoons butter, melted**
- 1 **egg, beaten**
- 2 **tablespoons milk**
- ¼ **teaspoon black pepper**
- 1 **cup herb-seasoned stuffing mix, finely crushed**

1 Preheat oven to 425°F. Trim fat from chops. Pour butter into a 9×13-inch baking pan, tilting pan to coat the bottom. In a shallow dish combine egg, milk, and pepper. Place stuffing mix in a second shallow dish. Dip chops into egg mixture, turning to coat. Coat both sides of each chop with stuffing mix. Place in prepared baking pan.

2 Bake, uncovered, for 10 minutes. Turn chops. Bake, uncovered, for 10 to 15 minutes more or until an instant-read thermometer inserted in center of chops registers 160°F and juices run clear.

Makes 4 servings.

Per Serving: 289 cal., 13 g total fat (6 g sat. fat), 141 mg chol., 342 mg sodium, 12 g carbo., 1 g fiber, 29 g pro.

INDIAN-STYLE LAMB CURRY

If you do not cook with curry powder often, purchase it in small jars—the spice mixture loses its fragrance and potency quickly.

Prep: 30 minutes   **Bake:** 25 minutes   **Oven:** 350°F

1½   pounds ground lamb

1   large red onion, halved and thinly sliced

2   cloves garlic, minced

2   medium potatoes (12 ounces), cut into ½-inch pieces

2   cups cauliflower florets

1   cup apple juice

½   cup sliced carrot (1 medium)

1   tablespoon curry powder

1   teaspoon salt

¼   teaspoon ground ginger

¼   cup cold water

2   tablespoons cornstarch

1   medium zucchini, halved lengthwise and sliced (about 1¼ cups)

1   cup frozen peas

⅓   cup golden raisins

3   cups hot cooked rice

Chutney (optional)

1 Preheat oven to 350°F. Grease a 9×13-inch baking dish; set aside. In an extra-large skillet or Dutch oven cook ground lamb, onion, and garlic on medium heat until meat is brown and onion is tender, stirring to break up meat as it cooks. Drain off fat. Stir potatoes, cauliflower, apple juice, carrot, curry powder, salt, and ginger into meat mixture in skillet. Bring to boiling; reduce heat. Simmer, covered, for 10 minutes.

2 In a small bowl combine the cold water and cornstarch; stir into meat mixture. Cook and stir just until mixture comes to boiling. Stir in zucchini, peas, and raisins. Spoon into prepared baking dish.

3 Cover with foil. Bake for 25 to 30 minutes or until the potatoes and cauliflower are tender. Serve over hot cooked rice. If desired, serve with chutney.

Makes 8 servings.

Per Serving: 337 cal., 12 g total fat (5 g sat. fat), 57 mg chol., 378 mg sodium, 39 g carbo., 3 g fiber, 19 g pro.

77

GREEK-INSPIRED MEAT LOAF ROLL

All you need to serve with this company-special spiral is a simple cucumber-onion salad. Leftover meat loaf slices make delicious sandwiches.

Prep: 25 minutes **Bake:** 1¼ hours **Stand:** 10 minutes **Oven:** 350°F

- 2   eggs, lightly beaten
- ¼   cup tomato juice
- ¾   cup soft bread crumbs
- 1   teaspoon Greek seasoning
- ½   teaspoon salt
- 1   pound ground lamb or ground beef
- 1   pound uncooked ground turkey
- ½   of a 10-ounce package frozen chopped spinach, thawed and well drained
- 2   ounces feta cheese, crumbled (½ cup)
- ¼   cup oil-pack dried tomatoes, patted dry and chopped
   Chopped fresh tomato (optional)
   Crumbled feta cheese (optional)

1 Preheat oven to 350°F. In a large bowl stir together eggs, tomato juice, bread crumbs, Greek seasoning, and salt. Add ground lamb and turkey; mix well. On a piece of parchment paper or foil pat meat mixture into an 8×12-inch rectangle. Leaving a ½-inch border, sprinkle meat with spinach, the 2 ounces feta, and the dried tomatoes. Starting from a short side, carefully roll up meat, using paper or foil to lift; seal edges and ends. Place meat roll, seam side down, in a 9×13-inch baking pan, reshaping roll as necessary.

2 Bake, uncovered, about 1¼ hours or until an instant-read thermometer inserted into center registers 165°F.* Cover with foil. Let stand for 10 minutes.

3 To serve, slice meat roll. If desired, sprinkle slices with chopped fresh tomato and additional crumbled feta cheese.

Makes 8 servings.

Per Serving: 303 cal., 21 g total fat (7 g sat. fat), 145 mg chol., 403 mg sodium, 4 g carbo., 1 g fiber, 23 g pro.

*Note: *The internal color of a meat loaf is not a reliable doneness indicator. A lamb or beef and turkey loaf cooked to 165°F is safe, regardless of color. To measure the doneness of a meat loaf, insert an instant-read thermometer into the center of the loaf.*

POULTRY

This chapter features a captivating collection of poultry recipes ready to flock straight into your oven. Whether you favor chicken, turkey, or game hens—and seek ideas for simple suppers or special-occasion fare—these poultry-packed dishes flown in from as close as the Midwest and as far as Asia give unexpectedly enticing multiethnic twists to this all-American family favorite.

TEXAS-STYLE CASSEROLE

To save prep time, you may use
packaged tostada shells instead of
frying corn tortillas.

Prep: 45 minutes **Bake:** 35 minutes **Stand:** 10 minutes **Oven:** 350°F

1½ **pounds skinless, boneless chicken breast halves**

2 **cups water**

1 **bay leaf**

1 **teaspoon snipped fresh thyme or ½ teaspoon dried thyme, crushed**

½ **teaspoon salt**

1 **clove garlic, minced**

   Dash black pepper

2 **tablespoons vegetable oil**

1 **cup chopped onion (1 large)**

2 **tomatillos, husks removed, rinsed, and finely chopped (about ½ cup) (optional)**

1 **clove garlic, minced**

2 **4-ounce jars diced pimiento, drained**

2 **4-ounce cans diced green chiles, undrained**

2 **fresh jalapeños, seeded and finely chopped***

   Vegetable oil

12 **6-inch corn tortillas**

¼ **cup butter**

¼ **cup all-purpose flour**

4 **teaspoons chili powder**

¼ **teaspoon salt**

   Dash black pepper

1 **8-ounce carton sour cream**

2 **cups shredded mozzarella cheese (8 ounces)**

   Pico de gallo or salsa (optional)

1 In a large saucepan combine chicken, the water, bay leaf, thyme, the ½ teaspoon salt, 1 clove garlic, and dash black pepper. Bring to boiling; reduce heat. Simmer, covered, about 15 minutes or until chicken is tender and no longer pink (170°F). Drain, reserving 2 cups broth. Strain broth through a double thickness of 100%-cotton cheesecloth. Chop chicken. Set aside.

2 Meanwhile, preheat oven to 350°F. In a medium saucepan heat the 2 tablespoons oil on medium heat. Add onion, tomatillos (if desired), and 1 clove garlic; cook until onion is tender. Remove from heat. Stir in pimiento, green chiles, and jalapeños. Set aside.

3 In a medium skillet heat ¼ inch oil on medium heat. Cook tortillas, 1 at a time, in hot oil until crisp, turning once. Drain on paper towels.

4 In a small saucepan melt butter on medium heat. Stir in flour, chili powder, the ¼ teaspoon salt, and dash black pepper. Gradually stir in the reserved 2 cups broth. Cook and stir until thickened and bubbly. Cook and stir for 1 minute more. Remove from heat. Stir in sour cream.

5 In a 9×13-inch baking dish arrange 6 of the tortillas, overlapping slightly. Top with half of the chicken, half of the onion mixture, half of the sour cream mixture, and half of the cheese. Repeat layers.

6 Cover loosely with foil. Bake for 35 to 40 minutes or until heated through. Let stand for 10 minutes before serving. If desired, serve with pico de gallo or salsa.

Makes 12 servings.

Per Serving: 462 cal., 33 g total fat (10 g sat. fat), 63 mg chol., 577 mg sodium, 22 g carbo., 2 g fiber, 21 g pro.

***Note:** Because chiles contain volatile oils that can burn your skin and eyes, avoid direct contact with them as much as possible. When working with chiles, wear plastic or rubber gloves. If your bare hands do touch the chiles, wash your hands and nails well with soap and warm water.*

CHIPOTLE CHILE CHICKEN WITH BLUEBERRY PEPPER SALSA

> Blueberries flavor more than muffins.
> Try the antioxidant-packed berries in savory
> preparations too—like this healthful salsa.

Start to Finish: 25 minutes **Oven:** 400°F

Nonstick cooking spray

2 tablespoons honey

1 tablespoon butter, melted

2 teaspoons finely chopped chipotle chile in adobo sauce

1 teaspoon dried oregano, crushed

½ teaspoon salt

4 skinless, boneless chicken breast halves (1¼ to 1½ pounds total)

1½ cups frozen blueberries, thawed, drained

1 11-ounce can mandarin oranges, drained

3 tablespoons finely chopped red onion

1 teaspoon finely shredded lime peel

2 teaspoons lime juice

1 Preheat oven to 400°F. Coat a 9×13-inch baking pan with cooking spray; set aside. In a small bowl stir together 1 tablespoon of the honey, the melted butter, 1 teaspoon of the chipotle chile, the oregano, and salt. Brush both sides of each chicken breast half with chipotle mixture. Arrange chicken in prepared baking pan.

2 Bake chicken, uncovered, for 15 to 20 minutes or until chicken is tender and no longer pink (170°F).

3 Meanwhile, for salsa: In a medium bowl combine blueberries, mandarin oranges, red onion, lime peel, lime juice, the remaining 1 tablespoon honey, and the remaining 1 teaspoon chipotle chile. Serve salsa with chicken.

Makes 4 servings.

Per Serving: 279 cal., 5 g total fat (2 g sat. fat), 90 mg chol., 420 mg sodium, 25 g carbo., 2 g fiber, 34 g pro.

APRICOT-CHICKEN ROLL-UPS

These tantalizing chicken bundles have honey-sweetened
apricots and cranberries on the inside
and a crispy Parmesan cheese coating on the outside.

Prep: 40 minutes   Bake: 35 minutes   Oven: 350°F

Nonstick cooking spray

1   6- or 7-ounce package dried apricots, snipped (about 1⅓ cups)

½   cup dried cranberries

3   tablespoons honey

1½   teaspoons ground ginger

⅔   cup fine dry bread crumbs

2   tablespoons snipped fresh parsley

1   tablespoon all-purpose flour

1   tablespoon finely shredded Parmesan cheese

1   teaspoon paprika

½   teaspoon sugar

½   teaspoon salt

½   teaspoon dried oregano, crushed

¼   teaspoon garlic powder

¼   teaspoon onion powder

¼   teaspoon black pepper

2   tablespoons shortening

2   eggs

6   skinless, boneless chicken breast halves (about 2 pounds total)

1 Preheat oven to 350°F. Lightly coat a 9×13-inch baking dish with cooking spray; set aside. In a small bowl stir together dried apricots, cranberries, honey, and ginger; set aside.

2 In a medium bowl stir together bread crumbs, parsley, flour, cheese, paprika, sugar, salt, oregano, garlic powder, onion powder, and pepper. Using a pastry blender, cut in shortening until mixture resembles fine crumbs. Transfer mixture to a shallow dish; set aside. Place eggs in another shallow dish; beat lightly with a fork and set aside.

3 Place each chicken breast between 2 pieces of plastic wrap. Using the flat side of a meat mallet, lightly pound each to make a rectangle slightly less than ¼ inch thick. Discard plastic wrap. Spoon a scant ¼ cup of the apricot mixture onto the center of each chicken breast. Fold in bottom and sides; roll up. Secure with toothpicks. Dip each chicken roll in egg, then coat with bread crumb mixture. Place chicken rolls in prepared baking dish.

4 Bake, uncovered, for 35 to 40 minutes or until chicken is tender and no longer pink (170°F). Remove toothpicks before serving.

Makes 6 servings.

Per Serving: 405 cal., 9 g total fat (2 g sat. fat), 159 mg chol., 546 mg sodium, 43 g carbo., 4 g fiber, 40 g pro.

BAKED CHICKEN CORDON BLEU

Bring this classic French dish to your
American table the next time you need to prepare
an elegant and impressive dinner.

Prep: 50 minutes **Bake:** 40 minutes **Oven:** 350°F

- 2 **6-ounce packages long grain and wild rice mix**
- 2 **cups sliced fresh mushrooms**
- ¼ **cup sliced green onions**
- 2 **cloves garlic, minced**
- 2 **tablespoons butter or margarine**
- 2 **tablespoons all-purpose flour**
- 2 **cups half-and-half or light cream**
- ½ **cup shredded Gruyère cheese (2 ounces)**
- 2 **tablespoons dry sherry (optional)**
- 6 **skinless, boneless chicken breast halves (about 2½ pounds total)**
- 3 **ounces Gruyère cheese, cut into 3×1½×½-inch sticks**
- 6 **very thin slices Black Forest ham or country ham**
- ½ **teaspoon salt**
- ¼ **teaspoon black pepper**
- ⅓ **cup all-purpose flour**
- 2 **eggs, lightly beaten**
- 2 **tablespoons water**
- 1½ **cups panko (Japanese-style bread crumbs)**
- ¼ **cup vegetable oil**

1 Prepare rice mixes according to package directions. Spread cooked rice in a 9×13-inch baking dish.

2 Meanwhile, for sauce: In a medium saucepan cook mushrooms, green onions, and garlic in hot butter on medium heat until tender. Stir in the 2 tablespoons flour. Gradually stir in half-and-half. Cook and stir until thickened and bubbly. Stir in shredded cheese until melted. If desired, stir in sherry. Spoon sauce over rice; cover and keep warm.

3 Preheat oven to 350°F. Starting from the thickest side of each chicken breast half, make a horizontal slit to, but not through, the other side. Wrap each cheese stick in a slice of ham and insert into a slit. Secure with toothpicks. Sprinkle chicken with salt and pepper.

4 Place the ⅓ cup flour in a shallow dish. In a second shallow dish combine eggs and the water. Place panko in a third shallow dish. Dip chicken in flour, shaking off excess; dip in egg, then in panko, turning to coat.

5 In an extra-large skillet heat 2 tablespoons of the oil on medium heat. Cook chicken, half at a time, in hot oil about 4 minutes or until browned on both sides, adding the remaining 2 tablespoons oil with the second batch. Remove toothpicks. Place chicken on top of sauce in baking dish.

6 Cover with foil. Bake for 40 to 45 minutes or until chicken is no longer pink (170°F).

Makes 6 servings.

Per Serving: 862 cal., 36 g total fat (15 g sat. fat), 256 mg chol., 1,586 mg sodium, 66 g carbo., 3 g fiber, 68 g pro.

APRICOT AND CRANBERRY STUFFED CHICKEN

Another time try these plump
stuffed chicken rolls with peach or strawberry
jam instead of apricot.

Prep: 30 minutes   **Bake:** 25 minutes   **Oven:** 400°F

6   skinless, boneless chicken breast halves (about 2 pounds total)

1½   cups herb-seasoned stuffing mix

½   cup apricot jam

⅓   cup dried cranberries

¼   cup butter or margarine, melted

1 Preheat oven to 400°F. Grease a 9×13-inch baking dish; set aside. Place each chicken breast half, boned side up, between 2 pieces of plastic wrap. Using the flat side of a meat mallet, lightly pound chicken to make rectangles about ⅛ inch thick. Discard plastic wrap. Set chicken aside.

2 In a medium bowl combine stuffing mix, ⅓ cup of the jam, ¼ cup of the cranberries, and 3 tablespoons of the melted butter. Stir until moistened; set aside.

3 For glaze: In a small bowl stir together the remaining jam, the remaining cranberries, and the remaining 1 tablespoon melted butter. Set glaze aside.

4 Place about ⅓ cup of the stuffing mixture on each chicken piece. Fold in bottom and sides and roll up. Secure with toothpicks. Place chicken rolls in prepared baking dish.

5 Bake, uncovered, for 15 minutes. Brush glaze over chicken rolls. Bake, uncovered, for 10 to 15 minutes more or until chicken is tender and no longer pink (170°F). Remove toothpicks before serving; discard.

Makes 6 servings.

Per Serving: 393 cal., 11 g total fat (6 g sat. fat), 109 mg chol., 374 mg sodium, 35 g carbo., 2 g fiber, 37 g pro.

CHEESE-STUFFED CHICKEN BREASTS

If you like, serve these cheese-stuffed chicken breasts on a bed of pasta draped with warm marinara sauce.

Prep: 20 minutes   Bake: 45 minutes   Oven: 375°F

- **6** bone-in chicken breast halves
- **½** cup ricotta cheese
- **½** cup shredded fontina cheese or mozzarella cheese (2 ounces)
- **⅓** cup grated Parmesan cheese or Romano cheese
- **2** teaspoons snipped fresh basil or ½ teaspoon dried basil, crushed
- **1** teaspoon snipped fresh oregano or ¼ teaspoon dried oregano, crushed
- **¼** teaspoon lemon-pepper seasoning
- **2** tablespoons butter or margarine, melted

1. Preheat oven to 375°F. Using your fingers, gently separate the chicken skin from the meat of the breast halves along the rib edge of each.

2. For stuffing: In a small bowl combine ricotta cheese, fontina cheese, Parmesan cheese, basil, oregano, and lemon-pepper seasoning.

3. Spoon a rounded tablespoon of the stuffing under the skin of each breast half. Place chicken, bone sides down, in a 9×13-inch baking dish. Brush chicken with melted butter.

4. Bake, uncovered, for 45 to 55 minutes or until no longer pink (170°F).

Makes 6 servings.

Per Serving: 346 cal., 22 g total fat (10 g sat. fat), 116 mg chol., 356 mg sodium, 1 g carbo., 0 g fiber, 35 g pro.

DUTCH CHICKEN DELIGHT

Besides wooden shoes the Dutch are famed for exceptionally rich and especially homey cuisine. This ridiculously yummy recipe is a perfect example.

Prep: 30 minutes   **Bake:** 40 minutes   **Oven:** 350°F

12	ounces dried egg noodles
3	slices bacon, halved crosswise
1½	pounds skinless, boneless chicken breast halves, cut into 1-inch pieces
1	10.75-ounce can condensed cream of mushroom soup
1¼	cups milk
1	8-ounce carton sour cream
½	of a 4.5-ounce jar sliced dried beef, coarsely chopped (about ¾ cup)
	Celery leaves

1 Preheat oven to 350°F. Cook noodles according to package directions; drain. Spoon noodles into a 9×13-inch baking dish.

2 Meanwhile, in a large skillet cook bacon on medium heat until crisp. Drain on paper towels, reserving drippings in skillet. Cook and stir chicken, half at a time, in the reserved drippings about 4 minutes or until no longer pink. Drain off fat.

3 In a medium bowl combine cream of mushroom soup, milk, and sour cream. Add cooked chicken, soup mixture, and dried beef to cooked noodles in dish; stir gently to combine.

4 Cover with foil. Bake about 40 minutes or until heated through, stirring once halfway through baking. Sprinkle with bacon and celery leaves.

Makes 6 to 8 servings.

Per Serving: 588 cal., 25 g total fat (10 g sat. fat), 158 mg chol., 920 mg sodium, 48 g carbo., 2 g fiber, 43 g pro.

CHICKEN, SPINACH, AND RICE CASSEROLE

To drain spinach well, press it firmly into a sieve with the back of a spoon. For good measure, squeeze it in your fist as well.

Prep: 20 minutes **Bake:** 1¼ hours **Oven:** 375°F

Nonstick cooking spray

1 10-ounce package frozen chopped spinach, thawed and well drained

½ of an 8-ounce tub cream cheese spread with chives and onion

1 10.75-ounce can condensed cream of chicken soup

1 cup milk

¼ cup snipped fresh oregano

¼ cup grated Parmesan cheese

2 cloves garlic, minced

¼ teaspoon crushed red pepper

1 cup long grain rice

6 small bone-in chicken breast halves, skin removed

Salt

Black pepper

1 Preheat oven to 375°F. Lightly coat a 9×13-inch baking dish with cooking spray. In a medium bowl combine spinach and cream cheese; spread into prepared baking dish.

2 In a medium bowl combine cream of chicken soup, milk, 3 tablespoons of the oregano, 3 tablespoons of the Parmesan cheese, the garlic, and crushed red pepper; set aside ½ cup of the soup mixture. Stir uncooked rice into the remaining soup mixture. Spoon rice mixture on top of the spinach. Place chicken, bone sides down, on top of the rice mixture. Sprinkle chicken with salt and black pepper. Spoon the reserved ½ cup soup mixture over chicken.

3 Cover tightly with foil. Bake about 1¼ hours or until rice is tender and chicken is no longer pink (170°F). Sprinkle with the remaining 1 tablespoon oregano and the remaining 1 tablespoon Parmesan cheese.

Makes 6 servings.

Per Serving: 470 cal., 13 g total fat (6 g sat. fat), 137 mg chol., 743 mg sodium, 33 g carbo., 2 g fiber, 51 g pro.

GERMAN-STYLE CHICKEN

Dusseldorf, Germany's most famous mustard, has a sweet-and-sour flavor. It's equally delicious on chicken, sausage, and cold meats.

Prep: 15 minutes **Bake:** 45 minutes **Oven:** 375°F°

¼ cup Dusseldorf or horseradish mustard

2 tablespoons dry sherry

½ teaspoon sweet Hungarian paprika or ¼ teaspoon hot Hungarian paprika

4 large bone-in chicken breast halves (about 2½ pounds total), skin removed

½ cup soft rye bread crumbs

1 Preheat oven to 375°F. In a small bowl combine mustard, sherry, and paprika. Transfer 2 tablespoons of the mustard mixture to another small bowl and brush evenly over tops of chicken breast halves. Set aside the remaining mustard mixture. Place chicken breast halves, mustard sides up, in a 9×13-inch baking dish. Sprinkle with bread crumbs. Lightly pat onto chicken.

2 Bake, uncovered, for 45 to 50 minutes or until chicken is tender and no longer pink (170°F). Serve with the reserved mustard mixture.

Makes 4 servings.

Per Serving: 243 cal., 4 g total fat (1 g sat. fat), 107 mg chol., 363 mg sodium, 4 g carbo., 1 g fiber, 44 g pro.

CHEESE-AND-BACON-STUFFED CHICKEN BREASTS

The contrast among the melty cheeses, crisp bacon, and crunchy peanuts imbues these chicken breasts with an incredibly enticing texture.

Prep: 25 minutes   **Bake:** 50 minutes   **Oven:** 350°F

4	medium bone-in chicken breast halves (2 to 2½ pounds total)
¾	cup shredded mozzarella cheese (3 ounces)
½	cup crumbled feta cheese
¼	cup chopped peanuts
2	slices bacon, crisp-cooked, drained, and crumbled, or ¼ cup cooked bacon pieces
	Salt
	Black pepper
	Paprika
	Bottled ranch salad dressing (optional)

1 Preheat oven to 350°F. If desired, skin chicken. Using a sharp knife, make a pocket in each chicken breast half by cutting horizontally from one side, cutting to but not through the opposite side and leaving edges intact.

2 For filling: In a medium bowl combine mozzarella cheese, feta cheese, peanuts, and bacon. Spoon filling into pockets, packing lightly (pockets will be full). Place chicken, bone sides down, in a 9×13-inch baking dish. Lightly sprinkle chicken breasts with salt, pepper, and paprika.

3 Bake, uncovered, for 50 to 55 minutes or until chicken is no longer pink (170°F). If desired, drizzle salad dressing over chicken.

Makes 4 servings.

Per Serving: 457 cal., 29 g total fat (10 g sat. fat), 136 mg chol., 587 mg sodium, 3 g carbo., 1 g fiber, 44 g pro.

OVEN-FRIED BUTTERMILK CHICKEN

It's easy to add a wow factor to oven-fried chicken with a coating of rye crackers. It lends a rich brown color and an appealing flavor.

Prep: 25 minutes **Marinate:** 4 to 24 hours **Bake:** 45 minutes **Oven:** 400°F

5 to 6 pounds meaty chicken pieces (breast halves,* thighs, and/or drumsticks)

2 cups buttermilk

1½ teaspoons salt

1 8-ounce package crisp rye crackers**

2 tablespoons Greek seasoning**

½ cup butter or margarine, melted

3 eggs, beaten

2 tablespoons water

1 If desired, skin chicken. Place chicken in a resealable plastic bag set in a bowl. For marinade: In a small bowl stir together buttermilk and salt. Pour over chicken. Seal bag; turn to coat chicken. Marinate in the refrigerator for at least 4 or up to 24 hours, turning bag occasionally.

2 Drain chicken, discarding marinade. In a blender or food processor combine half of the crackers and half of the Greek seasoning. Blend or process until crackers are crushed; transfer to a shallow dish. Repeat with the remaining crackers and the remaining Greek seasoning.

3 Preheat oven to 400°F. Lightly grease two 9×13-inch baking pans (or two 9×13-inch disposable foil baking pans); set aside. Add melted butter to crushed crackers; toss together. In another shallow dish combine eggs and the water. Dip chicken pieces, 1 at a time, in egg mixture, then roll in cracker mixture

to coat. Arrange chicken in prepared baking pans, making sure pieces do not touch.

4 Bake, uncovered, for 45 to 50 minutes or until chicken pieces are tender and no longer pink (170°F for breasts; 180°F for thighs and drumsticks). Serve warm. (Or cover and chill for up to 24 hours.)

Makes 12 servings.

Per Serving: 388 cal., 20 g total fat (8 g sat. fat), 162 mg chol., 476 mg sodium, 18 g carbo., 5 g fiber, 33 g pro.

---

*Note: *If breast halves are large, cut them in half again before marinating.*

**Note: *You can substitute two 4.25-ounce packages water crackers with cracked pepper for the crisp rye crackers and the Greek seasoning. Continue as directed above.*

COQ AU VIN

If this is your first time making coq au vin, don't be surprised—the wine not only turns your chicken purple but also infuses it with luscious flavor.

Prep: 20 minutes **Bake:** 45 minutes **Cook:** 20 minutes **Oven:** 350°F

2½ to 3 pounds chicken drumsticks and/or thighs, skin removed

2 tablespoons vegetable oil

Salt

Black pepper

2 tablespoons butter or margarine

3 tablespoons all-purpose flour

1¼ cups Pinot Noir or Burgundy wine

¼ cup chicken broth or water

1 cup whole fresh mushrooms

1 cup very thinly sliced carrots (2 medium)

18 frozen small whole onions, thawed (²/₃ cup)

1½ teaspoons snipped fresh marjoram or ½ teaspoon dried marjoram, crushed

1½ teaspoons snipped fresh thyme or ½ teaspoon dried thyme, crushed

2 cloves garlic, minced

2 slices bacon, crisp-cooked, drained, and crumbled

Snipped fresh parsley (optional)

Hot cooked noodles (optional)

1 Preheat oven to 350°F. In an extra-large skillet cook chicken, half at a time, in hot oil on medium heat for 10 to 15 minutes or until browned, turning occasionally. Transfer chicken to a 9×13-inch baking dish. Sprinkle chicken with salt and pepper. Set aside.

2 In the same skillet melt butter on medium heat. Stir in flour until smooth. Gradually stir in wine and broth. Cook and stir until boiling. Halve any large mushrooms. Stir mushrooms, carrots, onions, marjoram, thyme, and garlic into wine mixture. Return just to boiling. Pour vegetable mixture over chicken.

3 Cover with foil. Bake about 45 minutes or until chicken is no longer pink (180°F). Transfer chicken and vegetable mixture to a serving platter. Sprinkle with bacon. If desired, sprinkle with parsley and serve with hot cooked noodles.

Makes 6 servings.

Per Serving: 286 cal., 13 g total fat (4 g sat. fat), 95 mg chol., 321 mg sodium, 8 g carbo., 1 g fiber, 24 g pro.

SPINACH AND CHICKEN PIE

Feta cheese is available in a variety of herb-enhanced flavors, any of which would work well in this dish.

Prep: 35 minutes **Bake:** 45 minutes **Oven:** 375°F

Nonstick cooking spray

2½ pounds uncooked ground chicken

1 cup chopped onion (1 large)

2 tablespoons butter or margarine

3 10-ounce packages frozen chopped spinach, thawed and squeezed dry

1 teaspoon black pepper

½ teaspoon salt

½ teaspoon ground nutmeg

¼ teaspoon crushed red pepper

4 eggs, lightly beaten

1½ cups crumbled feta cheese (6 ounces)

1 tablespoon snipped fresh oregano

16 sheets frozen phyllo dough (9×14-inch rectangles), thawed

1 Preheat oven to 375°F. Lightly coat a 9×13-inch baking dish with cooking spray; set aside. In an extra-large skillet cook ground chicken and onion in hot butter on medium-high heat about 8 minutes or until chicken is browned and onion is tender, stirring to break up chicken as it cooks. Drain. Stir spinach, black pepper, salt, nutmeg, and crushed red pepper into chicken mixture in skillet. Cook and stir for 5 minutes. Spoon mixture into a large bowl. Stir in eggs, cheese, and oregano.

2 Unfold phyllo dough. Using a sharp knife, cut a 1-inch strip off one of the short ends of the phyllo stack; discard. Remove 1 sheet of the phyllo dough. (As you work, cover the remaining phyllo dough with plastic wrap to prevent it from drying out.) Place the phyllo sheet in prepared baking dish. Lightly coat phyllo sheet with cooking spray. Top with 7 more sheets, coating each sheet with cooking spray.

3 Spread chicken mixture over phyllo in baking dish. Top with the remaining 8 phyllo sheets, coating each sheet with cooking spray. Cut the top layer of phyllo sheets into 8 portions.

4 Bake, uncovered, about 45 minutes or until heated through and top is browned. Recut along scored lines before serving.

Makes 8 servings.

Per Serving: 530 cal., 29 g total fat (13 g sat. fat), 273 mg chol., 1,024 mg sodium, 29 g carbo., 4 g fiber, 41 g pro.

TEX-MEX CHICKEN ROLL-UPS

This substantial, kid-friendly
dish takes just minutes
to prepare.

Prep: 20 minutes **Bake:** 25 minutes **Oven:** 350°F

1	**3-ounce package cream cheese, softened**
¼	**cup snipped dried tomatoes**
1	**tablespoon snipped fresh cilantro**
6	**7- to 8-inch flour tortillas**
1	**4.5-ounce can whole green chiles, drained and cut into thin strips**
1½	**cups cooked chicken strips**
½	**cup shredded Monterey Jack cheese (2 ounces)**
	Salsa

1 Preheat oven to 350°F. Lightly grease a 9×13-inch baking dish; set aside. In a small bowl stir together cream cheese, dried tomatoes, and cilantro. Spread mixture over tortillas. Place some of the chile strips near an edge of each tortilla. Top each tortilla with chicken and cheese. Roll up tortillas. Place tortilla rolls in prepared baking dish.

2 Cover with foil. Bake for 25 to 30 minutes or until heated through. Serve with salsa.

Makes 6 servings.

Per Serving: 252 cal., 13 g total fat (6 g sat. fat), 55 mg chol., 377 mg sodium, 17 g carbo., 1 g fiber, 16 g pro.

HOT AND CHEESY CHICKEN CASSEROLE

"Hot" and "cheesy"—aren't those words
the ones that bring the
family to the table the fastest?

Prep: 25 minutes   **Bake:** 40 minutes   **Oven:** 350°F

- 3 cups chopped cooked chicken
- 1 14-ounce package frozen broccoli florets
- 2 cups cooked white rice
- 1½ cups frozen peas
- 1 10.75-ounce can condensed cream of chicken soup
- 1 10.75-ounce can condensed nacho cheese soup
- 1 10-ounce can diced tomatoes and green chiles, undrained
- ½ cup milk
- ½ teaspoon crushed red pepper (optional)
- ½ cup shredded cheddar cheese (2 ounces)
- ½ cup shredded mozzarella cheese (2 ounces)
- 1 cup crushed rich round crackers

1 Preheat oven to 350°F. Place chicken in a 9×13-inch baking dish or oval 3-quart casserole dish. In a large bowl combine broccoli, cooked rice, and peas. Spread broccoli mixture over chicken.

2 In a medium bowl combine chicken soup, cheese soup, undrained tomatoes, milk, and, if desired, crushed red pepper. Stir in ¼ cup of the cheddar cheese and ¼ cup of the mozzarella cheese. Pour soup mixture over broccoli mixture. Sprinkle with crackers, the remaining ¼ cup cheddar cheese, and the remaining ¼ cup mozzarella cheese.

3 Bake, uncovered, for 40 to 50 minutes or until heated through.

Makes 8 to 10 servings.

Per Serving: 354 cal., 15 g total fat (6 g sat. fat), 65 mg chol., 886 mg sodium, 29 g carbo., 4 g fiber, 26 g pro.

CHICKEN CHILE RELLENOS

These boat-shape peppers brim with a luscious chicken, cheese, and cilantro filling and are topped with a fiery cumin-spiced tomato sauce.

Prep: 45 minutes   **Bake:** 22 minutes   **Oven:** 350°F

- 6 **fresh poblano chiles (3 to 4 ounces each)***
- 2 **cups shredded or chopped cooked chicken (10 ounces)**
- 1 **cup shredded Monterey Jack cheese (4 ounces)**
- ½ **cup frozen corn, thawed**
- ½ **of an 8-ounce tub cream cheese with chives**
- 2 **tablespoons snipped fresh cilantro**
- 1 **tablespoon olive oil**
- 1 **cup thinly sliced sweet onion (such as Vidalia, Walla Walla, or Maui)**
- 3 **cloves garlic, thinly sliced**
- 1 **15-ounce can tomato sauce**
- 1½ **teaspoons ground cumin**
- ½ **teaspoon ground coriander**
- ¼ **teaspoon salt**
- ¼ **teaspoon cayenne pepper**
- 2 **tablespoons snipped fresh cilantro**

1 Preheat oven to 350°F. Grease a 9×13-inch baking dish; set aside. Lay each chile on its side and cut a lengthwise slice from 1 side, leaving the stem intact on the chile.* (The chile will now be a boat shape.) Chop chile slices that were just removed; set aside. Remove seeds and membranes from chile boats.

2 In a large saucepan cook the chile boats, half at a time, in boiling water for 2 minutes. Drain well; set aside.

3 For filling: In a medium bowl combine chicken, ½ cup of the shredded cheese, the corn, cream cheese, and 2 tablespoons cilantro. Spoon filling into chile boats. Place filled chiles in prepared baking dish.

4 For sauce: In a large skillet heat oil on medium-low heat. Add onion, the reserved chopped chile, and the garlic. Cook about 5 minutes or until tender, stirring occasionally. Stir in tomato sauce, cumin, coriander, salt, and cayenne pepper. Cook and stir until bubbly. Spoon sauce over filled chiles in baking dish.

5 Cover with foil. Bake for 20 to 25 minutes or until heated through. Sprinkle with the remaining ½ cup shredded cheese. Bake, uncovered, about 2 minutes more or until cheese is melted. Sprinkle with 2 tablespoons cilantro.

Makes 6 servings.

Per Serving: 329 cal., 18 g total fat (8 g sat. fat), 78 mg chol., 658 mg sodium, 20 g carbo., 2 g fiber, 23 g pro.

***Note:** Because chiles contain volatile oils that can burn your skin and eyes, avoid direct contact with them as much as possible. When working with chiles, wear plastic or rubber gloves. If your bare hands do touch the chiles, wash your hands and nails well with soap and warm water.*

QUICK CHICKEN TORTILLA BAKE

It's a 15-minute trip from cupboard and refrigerator to oven for this layered casserole. While it bakes toss a simple salad to go with it.

Prep: 15 minutes **Bake:** 45 minutes **Oven:** 350°F

- 2 10.75-ounce cans condensed cream of chicken soup
- 1 10-ounce can diced tomatoes with green chiles, undrained
- 12 6- or 7-inch corn tortillas, cut into thin bite-size strips
- 3 cups cubed cooked chicken (about 1 pound)
- 1 cup shredded Mexican-blend cheese (4 ounces)

1 Preheat oven to 350°F. In a medium bowl combine cream of chicken soup and undrained tomatoes; set aside. Sprinkle one-third of the tortilla strips into a 9×13-inch baking dish. Layer half of the chicken over tortilla strips; spoon half of the soup mixture on top. Repeat layers. Sprinkle with the remaining tortilla strips.

2 Cover with foil. Bake about 40 minutes or until bubbly around edges and hot in the center. Sprinkle with cheese. Bake, uncovered, about 5 minutes more or until cheese melts.

Makes 8 servings.

Per Serving: 325 cal., 14 g total fat (6 g sat. fat), 66 mg chol., 819 mg sodium, 26 g carbo., 4 g fiber, 23 g pro.

CHICKEN FLORENTINE ARTICHOKE BAKE

> When you drain oil-packed dried tomatoes,
> save the flavorful oil and use it later for making
> vinaigrettes or as the fat for scrambling eggs.

Prep: 35 minutes   **Bake:** 30 minutes   **Oven:** 350°F

- 8 ounces dried bow tie pasta
- 1 tablespoon butter or margarine
- 1/3 cup chopped onion (1 small)
- 2 eggs, lightly beaten
- 1 1/4 cups milk
- 1 teaspoon dried Italian seasoning, crushed
- 1/2 teaspoon salt
- 1/4 to 1/2 teaspoon crushed red pepper (optional)
- 1/4 teaspoon black pepper
- 2 cups chopped cooked chicken
- 2 cups shredded Monterey Jack cheese (8 ounces)
- 1 14-ounce can artichoke hearts, drained and quartered
- 1 10-ounce package frozen leaf or chopped spinach, thawed and well drained
- 1/2 cup oil-packed dried tomatoes, drained and chopped
- 1/4 cup grated Parmesan cheese
- 1/2 cup soft bread crumbs
- 1/2 teaspoon paprika (optional)
- 1 tablespoon butter or margarine, melted

1 Preheat oven to 350°F. Cook pasta according to package directions; drain. Meanwhile, in a medium skillet melt 1 tablespoon butter on medium heat. Add onion; cook for 4 to 5 minutes or until tender.

2 In a large bowl combine eggs, milk, Italian seasoning, salt, crushed red pepper (if desired), and black pepper. Stir in cooked onion, chicken, Monterey Jack cheese, artichoke hearts, spinach, dried tomatoes, and half of the Parmesan cheese. Stir in cooked pasta. Spoon into a 9×13-inch baking dish.

3 Cover with foil. Bake for 20 minutes. In a small bowl combine bread crumbs, paprika (if desired), and the remaining Parmesan cheese; stir in the melted butter. Sprinkle over pasta mixture. Bake, uncovered, about 10 minutes more or until heated through and crumbs are golden brown.

Makes 6 to 8 servings.

Per Serving: 531 cal., 24 g total fat (13 g sat. fat), 163 mg chol., 897 mg sodium, 41 g carbo., 5 g fiber, 36 g pro.

SMASHED POTATO-CHICKEN POTPIE

Comfort food was never as easy as this quick-to-fix potpie. It gets a jumpstart from ready-to-go mashed potatoes, vegetables, and chicken.

Prep: 25 minutes   **Bake:** 30 minutes   **Stand:** 5 minutes   **Oven:** 375°F

3 tablespoons butter or margarine

⅓ cup all-purpose flour

½ teaspoon seasoned pepper

¼ teaspoon salt

1 14-ounce can reduced-sodium chicken broth

¾ cup milk

2½ cups chopped cooked chicken or turkey (about 12 ounces)

2 cups frozen peas and carrots, thawed

2 cups frozen cut green beans, thawed

1 24-ounce package refrigerated mashed potatoes (about 2⅔ cups)

2 tablespoons grated Parmesan cheese

1 clove garlic, minced

1 Preheat oven to 375°F. In a large saucepan melt butter on medium heat. Stir in flour, ¼ teaspoon of the seasoned pepper, and the salt. Add broth and milk all at once. Cook and stir until thickened and bubbly. Stir in cooked chicken and thawed vegetables. Pour into a 9×13-inch baking dish.

2 In a medium bowl combine mashed potatoes, Parmesan cheese, garlic, and the remaining ¼ teaspoon seasoned pepper. Using a spoon, drop potato mixture in large mounds over chicken mixture in baking dish.

3 Bake, uncovered, for 30 to 40 minutes or until heated through. Let stand for 5 minutes before serving.

Makes 6 servings.

Per Serving: 330 cal., 13 g total fat (6 g sat. fat), 72 mg chol., 616 mg sodium, 29 g carbo., 4 g fiber, 25 g pro.

CHICKEN LASAGNA ROLLS WITH CHIVE-CREAM SAUCE

Individual lasagna rolls make this dish fun and easy to eat—no messy cutting. Just add crusty Italian bread or breadsticks and you have a whole meal!

Prep: 40 minutes   **Bake:** 35 minutes   **Oven:** 350°F

- 6 dried lasagna noodles
- 1 8-ounce package reduced-fat cream cheese (Neufchâtel), softened
- ½ cup milk
- ¼ cup grated Romano cheese or Parmesan cheese
- 1 tablespoon snipped fresh chives
- 1½ cups chopped cooked chicken
- ½ of a 10-ounce package frozen chopped broccoli, thawed and drained (1 cup)
- ½ cup bottled roasted sweet red peppers, drained and sliced
- ⅛ teaspoon black pepper
- 1 cup marinara pasta sauce

1 Cook lasagna noodles according to package directions; drain. Rinse with cold water; drain again. Cut each noodle in half crosswise. Place noodle halves in a single layer on a sheet of foil; set aside.

2 Meanwhile, for white sauce: In a medium bowl beat cream cheese with an electric mixer on medium to high for 30 seconds. Slowly add milk, beating until smooth. Stir in Romano cheese and chives.

3 Preheat oven to 350°F. For filling: In a medium bowl stir together ½ cup of the white sauce, the chicken, broccoli, roasted sweet red peppers, and black pepper. Place about ¼ cup of the filling at an end of each cooked noodle. Roll up noodles around filling. Arrange rolls, seam sides down, in a 9×13-inch baking dish.

4 Spoon the marinara sauce over the rolls. Spoon remaining white sauce over marinara sauce. Cover with foil. Bake for 35 to 40 minutes or until heated through.

Makes 6 servings.

Per Serving: 288 cal., 13 g total fat (7 g sat. fat), 65 mg chol., 412 mg sodium, 22 g carbo., 2 g fiber, 19 g pro.

105

Quick-Cooked Chicken: *If you need cooked chicken for a recipe but don't have any leftovers, one solution is to purchase a roasted chicken or poach chicken breasts. For 1½ cups chopped cooked chicken, in a large skillet combine 8 ounces skinless, boneless chicken breast halves and 1½ cups water. Cover and simmer for 12 to 14 minutes or until tender and no longer pink. Drain and chop chicken.*

CHICKEN, GOAT CHEESE, AND GREENS

If the people who gather at your table
turn up their noses at goat cheese,
substitute rich, tangy feta instead.

Prep: 15 minutes   **Bake:** 15 minutes   **Oven:** 350°F

1½ pounds Swiss chard, beet greens, and/or mustard greens, trimmed and washed

1 2- to 2½-pound purchased roasted chicken

3 tablespoons olive oil

2 tablespoons lemon juice

2 tablespoons snipped fresh dill, oregano, and/or sage

¼ teaspoon sea salt, kosher salt, or regular salt

¼ teaspoon cracked black pepper

1 3- to 4-ounce log goat cheese (chèvre), sliced into rounds or coarsely crumbled

1 Preheat oven to 350°F. Set aside 1 or 2 small leaves of the chard. Tear the remaining chard and place in a 9×13-inch baking dish. Remove string from chicken; use string to tie chicken legs together. Place chicken on top of the chard in baking dish.

2 In a small bowl combine olive oil and lemon juice. Drizzle olive oil mixture over chicken and chard in baking dish. Sprinkle 1 tablespoon of the snipped herbs over the chicken and chard. Sprinkle salt and ⅛ teaspoon of the pepper over chard only.

3 Cover baking dish loosely with foil. Bake for 15 to 20 minutes or until chard is tender. Meanwhile, sprinkle cheese with the remaining 1 tablespoon snipped herbs and the remaining ⅛ teaspoon pepper.

4 Transfer chicken to a serving platter. Place several goat cheese rounds on top of the chicken. Tear reserved chard leaves and scatter over chicken. Toss cooked chard in dish to evenly coat with cooking liquid. Serve chard and the remaining goat cheese with chicken.

Makes 4 servings.

Per Serving: 542 cal., 36 g total fat (10 g sat. fat), 143 mg chol., 620 mg sodium, 7 g carbo., 3 g fiber, 48 g pro.

FIVE-SPICE CHICKEN

Five-spice powder is a mixture of cinnamon, cloves, fennel seeds, star anise, and Chinese peppercorns that makes this simple dish sweet and spicy.

Prep: 15 minutes **Bake:** 15 minutes **Oven:** 400°F

⅓   **cup bottled hoisin sauce**

1   **to 1½ teaspoons five-spice powder**

    Orange juice

1   **2- to 2½-pound purchased roasted chicken**

2   **3-ounce packages ramen noodles**

1 Preheat oven to 400°F. In a small bowl stir together hoisin sauce, five-spice powder, and enough orange juice (1 to 2 tablespoons) to make a mixture for brushing. Place chicken on a rack in a 9×13-inch baking pan. Brush about half of the hoisin mixture over all sides of the whole chicken.

2 Bake, uncovered, for 15 to 18 minutes or until heated through and glazed. For sauce: Stir enough additional orange juice (1 to 2 tablespoons) into the remaining hoisin sauce mixture to make mixture easy to drizzle. Place the mixture in a small saucepan; heat through.

3 Remove the seasoning packets from ramen noodles; discard or reserve packets for another use. Cook and drain noodles according to package directions.

4 To serve, carve the chicken. Divide chicken and ramen noodles among 4 dinner plates. Spoon half of the sauce over chicken and noodles on dinner plates; pass the remaining sauce.

Makes 4 servings.

Per Serving: 317 cal., 16 g total fat (4 g sat. fat), 125 mg chol., 926 mg sodium, 20 g carbo., 1 g fiber, 24 g pro.

CHUCKWAGON CHICKEN SHEPHERD'S PIE

Tradition has it that shepherd's pie was the frugal cook's way to use up leftovers from Sunday's dinner. You won't need leftovers for this version.

Prep: 25 minutes   **Bake:** 30 minutes   **Oven:** 350°F

1   **24-ounce package refrigerated mashed potatoes**

¼   **cup snipped fresh parsley**

1   **2- to 2½-pound purchased roasted chicken**

1   **28-ounce can baked beans**

1   **11-ounce can whole kernel corn with sweet peppers, drained**

½   **cup salsa**

1   Preheat oven to 350°F. Heat the mashed potatoes according to package directions. Stir in 2 tablespoons of the parsley; set aside.

2   Remove chicken from bones, discarding skin and bones. Using 2 forks, pull meat apart into shreds. In a large bowl stir together chicken, undrained beans, corn, salsa, and the remaining 2 tablespoons parsley. Spoon into a 9×13-inch baking dish. Spoon potato mixture over chicken mixture; spread evenly.

3   Bake, uncovered, for 30 to 35 minutes or until heated through.

Makes 6 servings.

Per Serving: 437 cal., 15 g total fat (4 g sat. fat), 83 mg chol., 1478 mg sodium, 55 g carbo., 8 g fiber, 28 g pro.

ENCHILADAS SUIZAS

111

Don't worry if the tortillas crack
when you roll them. They will become soft
and pliable in the sauce.

Prep: 30 minutes **Broil:** 14 minutes **Bake:** 25 minutes **Stand:** 10 minutes **Oven:** 350°F

1 2- to 2½-pound purchased roasted chicken

12 ounces fresh tomatillos (4 large), husks removed

½ of a medium onion, cut into thin wedges

2 fresh jalapeños

2 cloves garlic

1 14.5-ounce can diced fire-roasted tomatoes, undrained

¾ cup packed fresh cilantro sprigs

1 cup Mexican crema or one 8-ounce carton crème fraîche or sour cream

1 tablespoon all-purpose flour

¼ teaspoon salt

12 6-inch corn tortillas

2 tablespoons vegetable oil

3 ounces Chihuahua cheese or Monterey Jack cheese, shredded (¾ cup)

Fresh cilantro sprigs (optional)

1 Preheat broiler. Remove chicken from bones, discarding skin and bones. Using 2 forks, pull meat apart into shreds. Measure 2½ cups of the chicken for this recipe. (Save any remaining chicken for another use.)

2 On a large baking sheet combine tomatillos, onion wedges, jalapeños, and garlic. Broil 3 inches from heat about 14 minutes or until onion wedges are tender and skin on jalapeños has black spots and is blistered, turning once during broiling. Cool slightly. With gloved hands, use a paring knife to peel as much skin from the jalapeños as possible; halve and seed jalapeños.* Core tomatillos. Reduce oven temperature to 350°F; adjust oven rack to center of oven.

3 In a blender combine vegetables, undrained fire-roasted tomatoes, and cilantro. Cover and blend until smooth. Add Mexican crema, flour, and salt. Cover and blend briefly until smooth.

4 In a medium bowl combine shredded chicken and ½ cup of the tomatillo-crema mixture. Spread about ½ cup of the remaining tomatillo-crema mixture in a 9×13-inch baking dish; set aside.

5 Wash and dry the baking sheet; lay tortillas on baking sheet. Brush both sides of each tortilla lightly with oil. Bake for 2 to 3 minutes or just until softened. Remove from oven. Stack tortillas and wrap in foil.

6 Removing 1 tortilla at a time, divide chicken-tomatillo mixture among tortillas, spreading evenly over each tortilla. Roll up tortillas. Arrange rolled tortillas, seam sides down, in prepared baking dish. Pour the remaining tomatillo-crema mixture over tortillas. Sprinkle with cheese.

7 Bake, uncovered, about 25 minutes or until heated through and cheese starts to brown lightly. Let stand for 10 minutes before serving. If desired, garnish with additional cilantro sprigs.

Makes 12 servings.

Per Serving: 357 cal., 23 g total fat (9 g sat. fat), 108 mg chol., 736 mg sodium, 18 g carbo., 3 g fiber, 22 g pro.

---

*Note: *Because chiles contain volatile oils that can burn your skin and eyes, avoid direct contact with them as much as possible. When working with chiles, wear plastic or rubber gloves. If your bare hands do touch the chiles, wash your hands and nails well with soap and warm water.*

HERBED CHICKEN AND ORZO

Here pasta and green beans
cook together in the same pan, making one
less pan to wash after dinner.

Prep: 25 minutes   **Bake:** 30 minutes   **Stand:** 5 minutes   **Oven:** 350°F

- 8 ounces dried orzo pasta
- 8 ounces fresh green beans, trimmed and cut into 1-inch pieces (1½ cups)
- 1 2- to 2¼-pound purchased roasted chicken
- 2 5.2-ounce containers semisoft cheese with garlic and herbs
- ½ cup milk
- 1½ cups shredded carrots (3 medium)
- 2 tablespoons snipped fresh Italian (flat-leaf) parsley

1 Preheat oven to 350°F. Grease a 9×13-inch baking dish; set aside.

2 Cook pasta according to package directions, adding green beans for the last 3 minutes of cooking; drain. Meanwhile, cut chicken into 6 pieces; set aside.

3 In a large bowl whisk together cheese and milk until combined. Add cooked pasta mixture; stir gently to coat. Stir in carrots. Spoon into prepared baking dish. Top with chicken.

4 Cover with foil. Bake for 30 to 40 minutes or until heated through. Let stand for 5 minutes before serving. Sprinkle with parsley.

Makes 6 servings.

Per Serving: 566 cal., 32 g total fat (16 g sat. fat), 147 mg chol., 685 mg sodium, 37 g carbo., 3 g fiber, 31 g pro.

DILLED CHICKEN-ORZO CASSEROLE

Nothing adds pungent piquancy
to a dish like capers. Be sure to rinse them
before using to remove excess salt.

Prep: 35 minutes   Bake: 35 minutes   Oven: 350°F

8   ounces dried orzo pasta

1   2- to 2¼-pound purchased roasted chicken

2   tablespoons butter or margarine

2   tablespoons all-purpose flour

1   14-ounce can chicken broth

2   tablespoons capers, drained

2   tablespoons snipped fresh dill

1   tablespoon Dijon mustard

1   teaspoon finely shredded lemon peel

1   tablespoon lemon juice

½   teaspoon salt

¼   teaspoon black pepper

2   cups baby pattypan squash, halved, or 1 medium yellow summer squash, halved lengthwise and sliced (1¼ cups)

1   medium sweet red pepper, cut into bite-size strips

½   of a small red onion, thinly sliced

¼   cup pine nuts, toasted

Fresh dill (optional)

1 Preheat oven to 350°F. Cook pasta according to package directions; drain. Meanwhile, remove chicken from bones, discarding skin and bones. Using 2 forks, pull meat apart into coarse shreds.

2 In a medium saucepan melt butter on medium heat. Stir in flour. Gradually stir in broth. Cook and stir until thickened and bubbly. Stir in capers, the 2 tablespoons dill, the mustard, lemon peel, lemon juice, salt, and black pepper.

3 In a large bowl combine cooked pasta, shredded chicken, the dill mixture, squash, sweet pepper, and onion. Spoon into a 9×13-inch baking dish.

4 Cover with foil. Bake about 35 minutes or until heated through. Sprinkle with pine nuts. If desired, garnish with additional fresh dill.

Makes 6 to 8 servings.

Per Serving: 598 cal., 33 g total fat (11 g sat. fat), 178 mg chol., 1,724 mg sodium, 37 g carbo., 3 g fiber, 42 g pro.

FRUIT-STUFFED ROASTED CHICKEN

Although it may be hard to wait, allowing the chicken to stand for 10 minutes makes its meat much more moist and juicy.

Prep: 45 minutes   Roast: 1³/₄ hours   Stand: 10 minutes   Oven: 325°F

- 1   5- to 6-pound whole roasting chicken
-     Salt
-     Black pepper
- ¼   cup dry sherry
- ¼   cup butter or margarine, melted
- 4½   teaspoons snipped fresh thyme or 1½ teaspoons dried thyme, crushed
- 2   teaspoons finely shredded orange peel
- 2   medium cooking apples (such as Granny Smith or Jonathan), cored and chopped (2 cups)
- ½   cup chopped onion (1 medium)
- ½   cup chopped celery (1 stalk)
- 2   cups cubed French bread (³/₄-inch cubes)
- 10   pitted dried plums (prunes) or dried apricot halves, cut up
- 1   cup seedless green grapes, halved
- 2   tablespoons orange juice

116

1 Preheat oven to 325°F. Season chicken's body cavity with salt and pepper. In a small bowl combine 2 tablespoons of the sherry, 2 tablespoons of the melted butter, 1 tablespoon of the snipped thyme (1 teaspoon of the dried thyme, if using), and 1 teaspoon of the orange peel; mix well. Brush chicken with all of the sherry mixture.

2 For stuffing: In a medium skillet cook apples, onion, and celery in the remaining 2 tablespoons melted butter on medium heat for 4 to 6 minutes or until tender. In a large bowl combine apple mixture, bread cubes, dried plums, grapes, orange juice, the remaining 2 tablespoons sherry, the remaining 1½ teaspoons snipped thyme (½ teaspoon dried thyme), and the remaining 1 teaspoon orange peel; mix well. (Stuffing will become more moist while cooking.)

3 Spoon stuffing loosely into neck and body cavities. Skewer chicken neck skin to back. Using 100%-cotton kitchen string, tie drumsticks to the tail. Twist wing tips under back. Place chicken, breast side up, on a rack in a 9×13-inch baking pan. Insert an oven-going meat thermometer into the center of an inside thigh muscle. (The meat thermometer should not touch bone.)

4 Roast, uncovered, for 1³/₄ to 2½ hours or until drumsticks move easily in their sockets and chicken is no longer pink (the meat thermometer registers 180°F). After 1 hour, cut string between legs so thighs cook evenly.

5 Cover with foil. Let stand for 10 minutes. Transfer chicken to a cutting board. Carve chicken; transfer to a serving platter. Spoon some of the stuffing around the chicken. Pass the remaining stuffing.

Makes 10 servings.

Per Serving: 461 cal., 27 g total fat (9 g sat. fat), 127 mg chol., 315 mg sodium, 21 g carbo., 2 g fiber, 31 g pro.

APPLE-AND-WILD RICE-STUFFED CHICKEN

Wild rice—really the seed of a marsh grass and not a rice at all—is known for its exceptionally nutty flavor and chewy texture.

Prep: 35 minutes   Roast: 1³/4 hours   Stand: 10 minutes   Oven: 325°F

- 1 6-ounce package long grain and wild rice mix
- 3 cups sliced fresh mushrooms (8 ounces)
- 2 medium cooking apples (such as Granny Smith or Jonathan), cored and chopped (2 cups)
- 1 cup shredded carrots (2 medium)
- ½ cup thinly sliced green onions (4)
- ½ teaspoon black pepper
- 1 5- to 6-pound whole roasting chicken
- 2 to 3 tablespoons apple jelly, melted

Apple wedges (optional)

1 Preheat oven to 325°F. For stuffing: Cook rice according to package directions, except add mushrooms, chopped apples, carrots, green onions, and pepper to rice before cooking.

2 Spoon stuffing loosely into neck and body cavities of chicken. Skewer chicken neck skin to back. Using 100%-cotton kitchen string, tie drumsticks to the tail. Twist wing tips under back. Place chicken, breast side up, on a rack in a 9×13-inch baking pan. Insert an oven-going meat thermometer into the center of an inside thigh muscle. (The thermometer should not touch bone.)

3 Roast, uncovered, for 1³/4 to 2½ hours or until drumsticks move easily in their sockets and chicken is no longer pink (meat thermometer registers 180°F). After 1 hour, cut string between legs so thighs cook evenly. Brush chicken with melted jelly once or twice during the last 10 minutes of roasting.

4 Cover with foil. Let stand for 10 minutes. Transfer chicken to a cutting board. Carve chicken; transfer to a serving platter. Spoon some of the stuffing around the chicken. If desired, garnish with apple wedges. Pass the remaining stuffing.

Makes 10 servings.

Per Serving: 426 cal., 22 g total fat (6 g sat. fat), 115 mg chol., 300 mg sodium, 23 g carbo., 2 g fiber, 32 g pro.

CARAWAY-RUBBED CHICKEN

Caraway's intense aroma and bold licoricelike flavor infuse the bird with a delightfully memorable taste.

Prep: 20 minutes Roast: 1¼ hours Stand: 10 minutes Oven: 375°F

- 2 tablespoons caraway seeds
- ¼ teaspoon whole black peppercorns
- 1 teaspoon finely shredded lemon peel
- ½ teaspoon kosher salt or regular salt
- 1 3½- to 4-pound whole broiler-fryer chicken
- 2 tablespoons lemon juice
- Lemon slices (optional)

1 Preheat oven to 375°F. With a mortar and pestle, slightly crush caraway seeds and peppercorns. (Or combine caraway seeds with peppercorns in a blender; cover and blend on high for 30 seconds.) Stir in lemon peel and salt; set aside.

2 Skewer neck skin of chicken to back. Using 100%-cotton kitchen string, tie drumsticks to the tail. Twist wing tips under back. Place chicken, breast side up, on a rack in a 9×13-inch baking pan. Rub caraway mixture over entire bird and under skin of breast. Insert an oven-going meat thermometer into the center of an inside thigh muscle. (The meat thermometer should not touch bone.)

3 Roast, uncovered, for 1¼ to 1½ hours or until drumsticks move easily in their sockets and chicken is no longer pink (meat thermometer registers 180°F).

4 Cover with foil. Let stand for 10 minutes. Carefully drizzle lemon juice over chicken. Transfer chicken to a serving platter. If desired, serve with lemon slices.

Makes 6 servings.

Per Serving: 223 cal., 13 g total fat [3 g sat. fat], 79 mg chol., 251 mg sodium, 2 g carbo., 0 g fiber, 25 g pro.

FRESH GARLIC AND PECAN CHICKEN

Roast chicken gets a crunchy twist

with this buttery

thyme and pecan coating.

Prep: 30 minutes   **Roast:** 1¼ hours   **Stand:** 10 minutes   **Oven:** 375°F

- **1** **3- to 3½-pound whole broiler-fryer chicken**
- **6** **cloves garlic, thinly sliced**
- **²/₃** **cup finely chopped pecans**
- **¼** **cup butter or margarine, melted**
- **1** **tablespoon snipped fresh thyme or 1 teaspoon dried thyme, crushed**
- **½** **teaspoon black pepper**
- **¼** **teaspoon salt**

1 Preheat oven to 375°F. Remove neck and giblets from chicken; discard or save for another use. Skewer neck skin of chicken to back. Using 100%-cotton kitchen string, tie drumsticks to the tail. Twist wing tips under back. Using a small, sharp knife, make numerous slits about 1 inch wide and ½ inch deep in the breast portion of the chicken. Stuff garlic into slits.

2 In a small bowl combine pecans, melted butter, thyme, pepper, and salt. Pat mixture onto top of chicken.

3 Place chicken, breast side up, on a rack in a 9×13-inch baking pan. Insert an oven-going meat thermometer in the center of an inside thigh muscle. (The meat thermometer should not touch bone.)

4 Roast, uncovered, for 1¼ to 1½ hours or until drumsticks move easily in their sockets and chicken is no longer pink (meat thermometer registers 180°F). If necessary to prevent pecans from overbrowning, cover chicken loosely with foil for the last 10 to 15 minutes of roasting.

5 Cover with foil. Let stand for 10 minutes. Transfer chicken to a cutting board. Carve chicken; transfer to a serving platter. If desired, spoon pecans from roasting pan over each serving.

Makes 4 servings.

Per Serving: 725 cal., 59 g total fat (18 g sat. fat), 205 mg chol., 400 mg sodium, 4 g carbo., 2 g fiber, 45 g pro.

CRANBERRY-TURKEY ENCHILADAS

Remember this Latin-inpired recipe
when you're thinking of ways
to use holiday turkey leftovers.

Prep: 30 minutes **Bake:** 50 minutes **Oven:** 350°F

Nonstick cooking spray

2 **to 2½ cups shredded cooked turkey**

1 **16-ounce can whole cranberry sauce**

1 **15-ounce can black beans, rinsed and drained**

1½ **cups salsa**

1 **cup shredded Colby and Monterey Jack cheese (4 ounces)**

½ **cup sour cream**

3 **green onions, sliced**

¼ **cup snipped fresh cilantro**

1 **teaspoon ground cumin**

½ **teaspoon salt**

½ **teaspoon black pepper**

8 **7- to 8-inch whole wheat or regular flour tortillas**

1 **teaspoon bottled hot pepper sauce**

Snipped fresh cilantro (optional)

Sliced green onions (optional)

1 Preheat oven to 350°F. Lightly coat a 9×13-inch baking dish with cooking spray; set aside.

2 For filling: In a large bowl stir together turkey, half of the cranberry sauce, the beans, ½ cup of the salsa, ¾ cup of the cheese, the sour cream, the 3 green onions, the ¼ cup cilantro, the cumin, salt, and pepper. Spoon about ⅔ cup of the filling onto each tortilla. Roll up tortillas around filling. Place, seam sides down, in prepared baking dish; set aside.

3 For sauce: In a medium bowl stir together the remaining cranberry sauce, the remaining 1 cup salsa, and the hot pepper sauce. Spoon over filled tortillas.

4 Cover with foil. Bake for 45 minutes. Sprinkle with the remaining ¼ cup cheese. Bake, uncovered, for 5 to 10 minutes more or until heated through and cheese melts. If desired, sprinkle with additional snipped cilantro and sliced green onions.

Makes 8 servings.

Per Serving: 406 cal., 12 g total fat (6 g sat. fat), 45 mg chol., 963 mg sodium, 57 g carbo., 6 g fiber, 22 g pro.

SMOKIN' TETRAZZINI

Smoked cheeses have a yellowish brown skin
that is a result of the smoke-curing process.
This casserole benefits from their enticing BBQ flavor.

Prep: 30 minutes   Bake: 30 minutes   Stand: 5 minutes   Oven: 350°F

12 ounces dried multigrain, spinach, or whole wheat fettuccine or linguine

3/4 cup dried tomatoes (not oil-packed), snipped

3 cups sliced fresh mushrooms (8 ounces)

2 medium sweet red peppers, cut into bite-size strips (2 cups)

1/2 cup chopped onion (1 medium)

2 tablespoons olive oil

2 tablespoons all-purpose flour

1 1/3 cups milk

1 cup water

2 cups shredded smoked Gouda cheese or smoked cheddar cheese (8 ounces)

Salt

Black pepper

2 cups shredded cooked turkey or chicken

2 tablespoons sliced almonds, toasted

Shredded smoked Gouda cheese or smoked cheddar cheese (optional)

1 Preheat oven to 350°F. Grease a 9×13-inch baking dish; set aside. Cook pasta according to package directions, adding dried tomatoes to boiling water with the pasta; drain.

2 For sauce: In a large skillet cook mushrooms, sweet peppers, and onion in hot oil on medium heat until tender. Stir in flour. Gradually stir in milk and the 1 cup water. Cook and stir until slightly thickened and bubbly. Gradually add the 2 cups cheese, stirring until melted. Season to taste with salt and black pepper.

3 In a large bowl combine cooked pasta mixture, sauce, and turkey. Spoon into prepared baking dish. Sprinkle with almonds.

4 Cover with foil. Bake about 30 minutes or until heated through. Let stand for 5 minutes before serving. If desired, sprinkle each serving with additional cheese.

Makes 6 servings.

Per Serving: 526 cal., 19 g total fat (9 g sat. fat), 70 mg chol., 908 mg sodium, 54 g carbo., 7 g fiber, 36 g pro.

123

PEPPERED MAPLE TURKEY BREAST

The pleasing maple and mustard
sauce is the perfect counterpoint
for the peppery roast turkey.

Prep: 15 minutes **Roast:** 1½ hours **Stand:** 10 minutes **Oven:** 325°F

4½ teaspoons cracked black
    peppercorns

1½ teaspoons kosher salt

1   2- to 2½-pound boneless,
    skinless turkey breast half

½   cup pure maple syrup

2¼ teaspoons Dijon mustard

2   tablespoons butter, cut up

1 Preheat oven to 325°F. In a small bowl combine peppercorns and kosher salt. Sprinkle peppercorn mixture on all sides of turkey breast half; rub in with your fingers. Place turkey on rack in a 9×13-inch baking pan. Roast, uncovered, for 40 minutes.

2 Meanwhile, in a small saucepan combine maple syrup and mustard; heat just until boiling. Brush some of the syrup mixture over turkey; dot with half of the butter.

3 Roast, uncovered, for 30 minutes more. Brush with more of the syrup mixture; dot with the remaining butter. Roast, uncovered, for 20 to 35 minutes more or until an instant-read thermometer inserted in the center registers 170°F. (The juices should run clear.)

4 Cover with foil. Let stand for 10 minutes. Transfer turkey to a cutting board. Carve turkey; transfer to a serving platter. In a small saucepan bring the remaining syrup mixture to boiling; serve over sliced turkey.

Makes 4 or 5 servings.

Per Serving: 514 cal., 21 g total fat (8 g sat. fat), 161 mg chol., 937 mg sodium, 28 g carbo., 1 g fiber, 49 g pro.

TURKEY-ASPARAGUS BAKE

To keep asparagus at its best, slice a half inch from the bottoms of the stalks and refrigerate them standing upright in a shallow bowl of water.

Prep: 30 minutes   **Bake:** 23 minutes   **Oven:** 425°F

- 1 **pound fresh asparagus or one 10-ounce package frozen cut asparagus or cut broccoli**
- 1 **pound uncooked ground turkey**
- 1 **cup chopped onion (1 large)**
- ½ **cup chopped sweet red pepper (1 small)**
- 3 **eggs**
- 2 **cups milk**
- 1 **cup all-purpose flour**
- ¼ **cup grated Parmesan cheese**
- 1 **teaspoon lemon-pepper seasoning**
- ½ **teaspoon dried tarragon, basil, or thyme, crushed**
- 1 **cup shredded Swiss cheese (4 ounces)**

1 Preheat oven to 425°F. Grease a 9×13-inch baking dish; set aside. To cook fresh asparagus, wash and scrape off scales. Break off and discard woody bases of asparagus. Cut asparagus into 1½-inch pieces. In a covered saucepan cook asparagus in a small amount of boiling water for 4 to 8 minutes or until crisp-tender; drain. (For frozen asparagus or broccoli, cook according to package directions; drain.) Set aside.

2 In a large skillet cook turkey, onion, and sweet pepper just until turkey is done and vegetables are tender, stirring to break up meat as it cooks. Remove from heat; drain. Arrange meat mixture in prepared baking dish; top with cooked asparagus.

3 In a large bowl combine eggs, milk, flour, Parmesan cheese, lemon-pepper seasoning, and tarragon; beat with a wire whisk or rotary beater until smooth. (Or combine these ingredients in a blender; cover and blend for 20 seconds.) Pour egg mixture evenly over layers in baking dish.

4 Bake, uncovered, about 20 minutes or until a knife inserted near the center comes out clean. Sprinkle with Swiss cheese. Bake, uncovered, for 3 to 5 minutes more or until cheese melts.

Makes 6 servings.

Per Serving: 355 cal., 17 g total fat (8 g sat. fat), 161 mg chol., 417 mg sodium, 24 g carbo., 2 g fiber, 26 g pro.

POPOVER PIZZA CASSEROLE

Serve up some fun for dinner! A popover batter that puffs while it bakes tops a layer of mozzarella and a saucy ground meat and pepperoni mixture.

Prep: 35 minutes **Bake:** 25 minutes **Oven:** 400°F

- 1 **pound uncooked ground turkey or lean ground beef**
- 1 **cup chopped onion (1 large)**
- 1 **cup chopped sweet green pepper (1 large)**
- 1 **15.5-ounce jar pizza sauce**
- ½ **of a 3.5-ounce package sliced pepperoni, halved**
- 1 **2-ounce can (drained weight) mushroom stems and pieces, drained**
- ½ **teaspoon fennel seeds, crushed**
- ½ **teaspoon dried oregano, crushed**
- ½ **teaspoon dried basil, crushed**
- 2 **eggs**
- 1 **cup milk**
- 1 **tablespoon vegetable oil**
- 1 **cup all-purpose flour**
- 1 **6-ounce package thinly sliced mozzarella cheese**
- ¼ **cup grated Parmesan cheese**

1 In a large skillet cook ground turkey, onion, and sweet pepper until meat is brown and vegetables are tender, stirring to break up meat as it cooks. Drain off fat. Stir pizza sauce, pepperoni, mushrooms, fennel seeds, oregano, and basil into meat mixture in skillet. Bring to boiling; reduce heat. Simmer, uncovered, for 10 minutes, stirring occasionally.

2 Meanwhile, for topping: In a small bowl combine eggs, milk, and oil. Beat with an electric mixer on medium for 1 minute. Add flour; beat about 1 minute more or until smooth.

3 Preheat oven to 400°F. Grease the sides of a 9×13-inch baking dish. Spoon meat-mushroom mixture into prepared baking dish. Arrange cheese slices over meat mixture. Pour topping over cheese slices, covering completely. Sprinkle with Parmesan cheese.

4 Bake, uncovered, for 25 to 30 minutes or until topping is puffed and golden brown. Serve immediately.

Makes 8 servings.

Per Serving: 335 cal., 17 g total fat (6 g sat. fat), 126 mg chol., 686 mg sodium, 22 g carbo., 2 g fiber, 23 g pro.

SPICED GAME HENS

These coriander-seasoned hens
are equally good with
hot-style or sweet paprika.

Prep: 25 minutes **Marinate:** 2 hours **Roast:** 1 hour **Oven:** 375°F

¼ cup lemon juice

2 tablespoons olive oil

1 tablespoon paprika

1 teaspoon salt

1 teaspoon ground coriander

½ teaspoon ground turmeric

¼ teaspoon black pepper

4 cloves garlic, minced

2 1½-pound Cornish game hens

½ cup reduced-sodium chicken broth

Salt

Black pepper

1 In a small bowl combine lemon juice, oil, paprika, the 1 teaspoon salt, the coriander, turmeric, the ¼ teaspoon pepper, and the garlic; set aside.

2 Using a long, heavy knife or kitchen shears, halve Cornish hens lengthwise, cutting through the breast bone of each hen just off center and then through the center of the backbone. If desired, remove backbone of each hen.

3 Place game hen halves in a resealable plastic bag. Pour lemon juice mixture over hen halves. Seal bag; turn to coat hen halves. Marinate in the refrigerator for 2 hours, turning bag once.

4 Preheat oven to 375°F. Remove hen halves from bag, reserving marinade. Place hen halves, cut sides down, in a 9×13-inch baking dish. Pour reserved marinade over. Pour broth around hen halves in baking dish. Sprinkle hen halves with additional salt and pepper.

5 Cover with foil. Roast for 40 minutes. Uncover. Roast for 20 to 35 minutes more or until an instant-read thermometer inserted into the inside thigh muscle of each hen half registers 180°F. (The meat thermometer should not touch bone).

Makes 4 servings.

Per Serving: 410 cal., 30 g total fat (7 g sat. fat), 173 mg chol., 813 mg sodium, 4 g carbo., 1 g fiber, 31 g pro.

FiSH & MEATLESS DiSHES

From gardens and fields, seas and shores come an array of mouthwatering and health-enhancing ingredients—all of which will expand the horizons of your favorite rectangular receptacle. Seafood selections bring maritime taste while still stretching your budget. Veggies—from sun-warmed squash to meaty mushrooms—supply suppers with a variety and a visual appeal that will please even the most ardent meat eaters.

TUNA NOODLE CASSEROLE

Give this childhood comfort food grown-up appeal with Dijon mustard and roma tomatoes. Top with potato chips for a nostalgic touch.

Prep: 25 minutes **Bake:** 20 minutes **Stand:** 5 minutes **Oven:** 375°F

4	cups dried wide noodles (8 ounces)
¼	cup butter or vegetable oil
1	cup chopped celery (2 stalks)
¾	cup chopped onion
¼	cup all-purpose flour
3	tablespoons Dijon mustard
½	teaspoon black pepper
¼	teaspoon salt
3	cups milk
2	12-ounce cans chunk light tuna, drained
⅔	cup chopped roma tomatoes (2 medium)
1	cup whole or crushed potato chips (optional)

1 Preheat oven to 375°F. Lightly grease a 9×13-inch baking dish or 3-quart casserole; set aside. Cook noodles according to package directions. Drain; return noodles to hot pan.

2 For sauce: In a large saucepan melt butter on medium heat. Add celery and onion; cook and stir until vegetables are tender. Stir in flour, mustard, pepper, and salt. Add milk all at once; cook and stir until sauce is thickened and bubbly, whisking to remove any lumps.

3 Gently fold sauce, tuna, and tomatoes into noodles. Spoon into prepared baking dish. If desired, top with chips.

4 Bake, uncovered, about 20 minutes or until heated through. Let stand for 5 minutes before serving.

Makes 8 servings.

Per Serving: 403 cal., 18 g total fat (7 g sat. fat), 91 mg chol., 679 mg sodium, 30 g carbo., 2 g fiber, 27 g pro.

SALSA-SAUCED TUNA TORTILLA ROLLS

Sometimes pineapple salsa is shelved
with a market's gourmet items rather than
next to the chips in the snack food aisle.

Prep: 30 minutes   **Bake:** 40 minutes   **Oven:** 350°F

Nonstick cooking spray

1 **12-ounce can solid white tuna (water pack), drained and flaked**

2 **Granny Smith apples, cored and finely chopped (2 cups)**

¼ **cup chopped green onions (2)**

¾ **cup red or green seedless grapes, halved**

½ **cup mayonnaise or salad dressing**

¼ **teaspoon seasoned salt**

¼ **teaspoon freshly ground black pepper**

12 **7-inch flour tortillas**

1 **16-ounce jar pineapple-flavor salsa**

½ **cup sliced almonds, toasted**

1 **tablespoon snipped fresh cilantro**

1 Preheat oven to 350°F. Coat a 9×13-inch baking dish with cooking spray; set aside.

2 In a large bowl combine tuna, apples, green onions, grapes, mayonnaise, seasoned salt, and pepper; mix well. Spoon tuna mixture along 1 edge of each tortilla. Roll up, starting from the edge with the tuna mixture. Arrange rolls, seam sides down, in prepared baking dish.

3 Spoon salsa evenly over the tortillas. Cover with foil. Bake for 35 minutes. Sprinkle with almonds. Bake, uncovered, about 5 minutes more or until heated through. Sprinkle with cilantro.

Makes 6 servings.

Per Serving: 500 cal., 27 g total fat (5 g sat. fat), 30 mg chol., 679 mg sodium, 45 g carbo., 4 g fiber, 20 g pro.

CREAMY CHEESY SALMON ENCHILADAS

**Salmon fillets or steaks can make a pricey meal.
These spicy-good enchiladas are a budget-friendly
way to enjoy the healthful fish.**

Prep: 20 minutes **Bake:** 35 minutes **Oven:** 375°F

- 2 cups shredded Mexican-style four-cheese blend (8 ounces)
- 1 16-ounce jar salsa
- 1 3-ounce package cream cheese, softened
- 1 4-ounce can diced green chiles, drained
- 2 14.75-ounce cans salmon, drained, flaked, and skin and bones removed
- 6 10- to 12-inch flour tortillas

1 Preheat oven to 375°F. For filling: In a large bowl combine 1 cup of the shredded cheese, 2 tablespoons of the salsa, the cream cheese, and chiles. Gently stir in salmon.

2 Spoon about ¾ cup of the filling across each tortilla slightly below center. Fold in ends and roll up tortillas. Arrange tortillas, seam sides down, in a 9×13-inch baking dish. Top with the remaining salsa and the remaining 1 cup shredded cheese.

3 Cover with foil. Bake for 25 minutes. Uncover. Bake about 10 minutes more or until heated through.

Makes 6 servings.

Per Serving: 546 cal., 28 g total fat (12 g sat. fat), 126 mg chol., 1,824 mg sodium, 30 g carbo., 2 g fiber, 41 g pro.

PISTACHIO-BAKED SALMON

The use of sugar as an ingredient in fish dishes is exceedingly rare, but salmon's rich flesh takes to sweetness like a fish to water.

Prep: 20 minutes **Bake:** 6 to 8 minutes per $1/2$-inch thickness **Oven:** 425°F

4   6-ounce fresh or frozen skinless salmon fillets

Nonstick cooking spray

$2/3$ cup salted dry-roasted pistachio nuts, chopped

$1/3$ cup packed brown sugar

2   tablespoons lemon juice

$3/4$ teaspoon dried dill

$3/4$ teaspoon coarsely ground black pepper

Purchased basil pesto (optional)

1 Thaw salmon, if frozen. Rinse fish; pat dry with paper towels. Preheat oven to 425°F. Line a 9×13-inch baking pan with foil. Coat foil with cooking spray; set pan aside.

2 In a small bowl combine nuts, brown sugar, lemon juice, dill, and pepper; set aside.

3 Place salmon fillets in prepared baking pan. Turn under any thin edges to make fillets a uniform thickness. Measure thickness of fish. Spoon pistachio mixture evenly on top of fillets and gently press to form a crust.

4 Bake, uncovered, for 6 to 8 minutes per ½-inch thickness of fish or until fish flakes easily when tested with a fork. If desired, pass pesto with fish.

Makes 4 servings.

Per Serving: 391 cal., 16 g total fat (2 g sat. fat), 88 mg chol., 208 mg sodium, 25 g carbo., 2 g fiber, 39 g pro.

SALMON WITH TROPICAL RICE

Lemon really makes this dish shine, from the simple lemon-pepper seasoning on the fish and lemon peel in the rice to a squeeze of lemon juice before serving.

Prep: 20 minutes **Bake:** 15 minutes **Oven:** 450°F

- 1 1½-pound fresh or frozen skinless salmon fillet, 1 inch thick
- 2 teaspoons olive oil
- 1 teaspoon lemon-pepper seasoning
- 1 8.8-ounce pouch cooked brown or white rice
- 1 medium mango, peeled, seeded, and chopped*
- 1 tablespoon snipped fresh cilantro
- 1 teaspoon finely shredded lemon peel

  Lemon wedges (optional)

  Fresh cilantro sprigs (optional)

1 Thaw salmon, if frozen. Rinse fish; pat dry with paper towels. Preheat oven to 450°F. Grease a 9×13-inch baking dish; place fish in prepared dish. Drizzle olive oil over fish. Sprinkle with lemon-pepper seasoning.

2 In a medium bowl stir together rice, mango, snipped cilantro, and lemon peel, breaking up rice with a spoon. Spoon rice mixture around fish. Bake, uncovered, about 15 minutes or until fish flakes easily when tested with a fork.

3 To serve, cut fish into 4 serving-size pieces. Serve fish on top of rice mixture. If desired, garnish with lemon wedges and cilantro sprigs.

Makes 4 servings.

Per Serving: 462 cal., 22 g total fat (4 g sat. fat), 99 mg chol., 104 mg sodium, 27 g carbo., 2 g fiber, 36 g pro.

---

*Note: *Because the meat from the mango holds tightly to the seed, this fruit requires a little effort before yielding its fragrant spicy-peach meat. An easy way to remove the meat is to make a cut through the mango, sliding a sharp knife next to the seed along one side. Repeat on other side of the seed, resulting in 2 large pieces. Then cut away all of the meat that remains around the seed. Remove peel on all pieces and cut up the meat.*

CALIFORNIA TUNA PARMESAN

**A simple lemon vinaigrette brightens
the flavor of this fresh, light,
and superhealthy main-dish salad.**

Start to Finish: 20 minutes **Oven:** 450°F

- **4** **4-ounce fresh or frozen tuna steaks**
- **2** **lemons**
- **⅓** **cup olive oil**
- **½** **teaspoon freshly ground black pepper**
- **¼** **teaspoon salt**
- **12** **ounces fresh asparagus, trimmed**
- **1** **5-ounce package mixed baby greens**
- **⅓** **cup finely shaved Parmesan cheese**

1 Thaw fish, if frozen. Rinse fish; pat dry with paper towels. Preheat oven to 450°F. Finely shred 2 teaspoons peel from 1 of the lemons; squeeze juice from that lemon. For dressing: In a small bowl whisk together lemon peel, lemon juice, oil, pepper, and salt; set aside. Cut the remaining lemon into wedges; set aside.

2 Place asparagus in a single layer in a 9×13-inch baking pan. Drizzle with 2 tablespoons of the dressing. Bake, uncovered, for 8 minutes.

3 Meanwhile, in a large skillet heat 1 tablespoon of the dressing. Add fish; cook for 8 to 12 minutes or until browned and center is slightly pink, turning once halfway through cooking.

4 Divide greens among 4 dinner plates; top with tuna and asparagus. Drizzle with the remaining dressing. Sprinkle with Parmesan cheese; pass lemon wedges.

Makes 4 servings.

Per Serving: 377 cal., 26 g total fat (5 g sat. fat), 48 mg chol., 312 mg sodium, 9 g carbo., 4 g fiber, 31 g pro.

ROASTED RED SNAPPER WITH ROSEMARY

This Italian-style snapper—stuffed with fennel, lemon, cipollini, herbs, and garlic—is a simple and elegant dish for entertaining. Serve it with rice and steamed green beans.

Prep: 30 minutes **Bake:** 40 minutes **Oven:** 400°F

Nonstick cooking spray

- 1 **3-pound fresh whole drawn red snapper, rockfish, or whitefish**
- ½ **teaspoon salt**
- ½ **teaspoon black pepper**
- 1 **lemon, sliced**
- 4 **cipollini* or 1 small red onion, very thinly sliced**
- ½ **of a medium fennel bulb, trimmed and chopped**
- 6 **sprigs fresh rosemary**
- 2 **cloves garlic, sliced**
- 1 **tablespoon olive oil**
- ½ **teaspoon salt**
- ½ **teaspoon black pepper**

Lemon slices (optional)

Fresh rosemary sprigs (optional)

Lemon wedges (optional)

1 Preheat oven to 400°F. Line a 9×13-inch baking pan with foil; coat foil with cooking spray. Rinse fish; pat dry with paper towels. Place fish in prepared baking pan.

2 Sprinkle fish cavity with ½ teaspoon salt and ½ teaspoon pepper. Stuff cavity with the slices from 1 lemon, the cipollini, fennel, the 6 sprigs rosemary, and the garlic (cavity will be full). Rub oil over outside of fish; sprinkle with ½ teaspoon salt and ½ teaspoon pepper. If desired, place additional lemon slices and additional rosemary sprigs on top of fish.

3 Bake, uncovered, about 40 minutes or until the flesh near the bone flakes easily when tested with a fork. Using a wide spatula, transfer fish to a serving platter.

4 To serve, loosen and gently pull back skin from top of fish. Cut the top fillet into two portions; lift each portion away from backbone. Discard stuffing mixture. Pull away and discard the backbone and head. Cut the bottom fillet into two portions; remove each portion from the skin underneath. If desired, serve fish with lemon wedges.

Makes 4 servings.

Per Serving: 237 cal., 7 g total fat (1 g sat. fat), 75 mg chol., 713 mg sodium, 0 g carbo., 0 g fiber, 41 g pro.

---

*Note: *Cipollini are tiny, flat onionlike bulbs about 2 inches in diameter, and they have an appealing sharp and sweet flavor.*

CRISPY FISH AND VEGETABLES

This colorful one-pan meal is bound to please.
With a salad of bright, fresh greens, it makes a pretty
and healthful meal.

Prep: 30 minutes   **Bake:** 25 minutes   **Oven:** 450°F

- **4** 6-ounce fresh or frozen skinless white sea bass, catfish, or tilapia fillets, about ½ inch thick
- **4** ounces fresh haricots verts (young green beans)
- **1** small zucchini or yellow squash, cut into bite-size sticks (1 cup)
- **8** ounces cipollini,* quartered and peeled, or 1 cup thinly sliced red onion
- **1** cup cherry tomatoes or grape tomatoes, halved
- **2** tablespoons olive oil
- **¼** teaspoon salt
- **¼** teaspoon black pepper
- **⅓** cup fine dry bread crumbs
- **⅓** cup crushed potato chips
- **¼** cup grated Parmesan cheese
- **½** teaspoon paprika
- **⅛** teaspoon cayenne pepper
- **2** tablespoons butter or margarine, melted

1. Thaw fish, if frozen. Rinse fish; pat dry with paper towels. Preheat oven to 450°F. Trim the beans, if desired. In a small covered saucepan cook haricots verts in a small amount of boiling salted water for 5 minutes; drain.

2. In a 9×13-inch baking dish combine beans, zucchini, cipollini, and tomatoes. Drizzle with oil; sprinkle with salt and pepper. Toss to coat. Spread in an even layer. Place fish fillets on top of vegetables.

3. In a small bowl stir together bread crumbs, potato chips, Parmesan cheese, paprika, and cayenne pepper. Add melted butter; stir to combine. Top fillets evenly with crumb mixture, pressing it into fillets.

4. Bake, uncovered, for 25 to 30 minutes or until fish flakes easily when tested with a fork.

Makes 4 servings.

Per Serving: 491 cal., 26 g total fat (9 g sat. fat), 89 mg chol., 736 mg sodium, 27 g carbo., 4 g fiber, 38 g pro.

140

*Note: Cipollini are tiny, flat onionlike bulbs about 2 inches in diameter and they have an appealing sharp and sweet flavor.

COD WITH POTATOES, PARSNIPS, AND POACHED EGGS

This dish is essentially *brandade*—a simple dish from the South of France that is made most often with salt cod, a fresh cod that has been salted and dried.

Prep: 55 minutes **Soak:** 48 hours **Bake:** 15 minutes **Stand:** 10 minutes **Oven:** 425°F

2	pounds salt cod or fresh cod
4	slices bacon
1	pound russet potatoes, cut into 2-inch pieces
1	pound parsnips, peeled and cut into 2-inch pieces
½	cup milk
¼	cup butter or margarine
½	teaspoon salt
¼	teaspoon ground white pepper
2	medium shallots, sliced
2	cloves garlic, minced
1	cup whipping cream
½	teaspoon finely shredded lemon peel
1	tablespoon lemon juice
¼	teaspoon ground white pepper
	Salt (optional)
6	eggs

1 If using salt cod, in a medium bowl combine salt cod and enough water to cover. Cover and soak in the refrigerator for 48 hours, changing the water 2 or 3 times. Rinse and drain cod. If using fresh cod, omit the soaking step.

2 Preheat oven to 425°F. Fill an extra-large skillet half-full of water. Bring to boiling. Add cod; reduce heat. Simmer gently, covered, for 8 to 10 minutes or until fish flakes easily when tested with a fork. Drain and cool slightly. Remove skin (if present) and bones; break cod into large pieces.

3 Meanwhile, in a large skillet cook bacon on medium heat until crisp. Transfer bacon to paper towels, reserving 2 tablespoons drippings in skillet. Set skillet aside. Crumble bacon; set bacon aside. In a covered large saucepan cook potatoes and parsnips in enough boiling salted water to cover about 20 minutes or until tender; drain. Return to saucepan. Add milk, butter, the ½ teaspoon salt, and ¼ teaspoon white pepper. Using a potato masher, coarsely mash potato mixture. Stir in crumbled bacon. Spoon into a 9×13-inch baking dish; cover and keep warm.

4 Add shallots and garlic to the reserved bacon drippings; cook until tender. Stir in cream; bring just to boiling.

5 In a food processor combine cooked cod, cream mixture, lemon peel, lemon juice, and ¼ teaspoon white pepper. Cover and process until nearly smooth. Season with additional salt, if necessary. Spread cod mixture over potato mixture.

6 Using the bottom of a ladle or glass, make 6 deep indentations in ingredients in dish. Crack an egg into each indentation. Bake, uncovered, for 15 to 20 minutes or until egg whites are set and yolks start to thicken but are not hard. Let stand for 10 minutes before serving.

Makes 6 servings.

Per Serving: 605 cal., 36 g total fat (19 g sat. fat), 363 mg chol., 471 mg sodium, 32 g carbo.,5 g fiber, 40 g pro.

TRUFFLED LOBSTER MACARONI AND CHEESE

A tiny bottle of truffle oil—usually sold for
about $10—lasts a long time and is a clever way to
affordably enjoy the luxurious flavor of truffles.

Prep: 35 minutes   **Bake:** 30 minutes   **Stand:** 10 minutes   **Oven:** 350°F

12	ounces dried tiny bow tie pasta or tiny penne pasta
6	slices applewood-smoked bacon
3	cups sliced fresh cremini mushrooms (8 ounces)
2/3	cup sliced leeks (2 medium)
8	ounces cooked lobster meat,* chopped
8	ounces process Gruyère cheese, cut up
1½	cups half-and-half or light cream
1	cup crumbled blue cheese (4 ounces)
1	tablespoon truffle-flavor oil
⅛	teaspoon cayenne pepper
1½	cups coarse soft bread crumbs (2 slices)
1	tablespoon butter, melted

1 Preheat oven to 350°F. Grease a 9×13-inch baking dish; set aside. Cook pasta according to package directions; drain. Return to hot pan.

2 Meanwhile, in a large skillet cook bacon on medium heat until crisp. Drain bacon on paper towels, reserving 2 tablespoons drippings in skillet. Crumble bacon; set aside. Add mushrooms and leeks to the reserved drippings; cook about 5 minutes or until tender.

3 Stir crumbled bacon, mushroom mixture, lobster meat, Gruyère cheese, half-and-half, blue cheese, truffle oil, and cayenne pepper into cooked pasta. Spoon into prepared baking dish.

4 Cover with foil. Bake for 20 minutes. Stir gently. In a small bowl combine bread crumbs and melted butter; sprinkle over pasta mixture. Bake, uncovered, for 10 to 15 minutes more or until heated through and crumbs are lightly browned. Let stand for 10 minutes before serving.

Makes 6 to 8 servings.

Per Serving: 693 cal., 36 g total fat (19 g sat. fat), 115 mg chol., 996 mg sodium, 56 g carbo., 3 g fiber, 34 g pro.

*****Note:** *For 8 ounces cooked lobster meat, start with two 8-ounce fresh or frozen lobster tails. Thaw lobster, if frozen. Rinse lobster; pat dry with paper towels. Butterfly the lobster tails by cutting through the center of the hard top shells and meat. Spread the tail halves apart. Preheat broiler. Place lobster tails, meat sides up, on the unheated rack of a broiler pan. Broil 4 inches from the heat for 12 to 14 minutes or until lobster meat is opaque. Remove meat from shells.*

SHRIMP RELLENO CASSEROLE

Poblano chiles possess a mildly snappy flavor but not too much heat. Choose dark-color poblanos— their flavor is richer and deeper than light-color chiles.

Prep: 30 minutes   **Bake:** 35 minutes   **Oven:** 350°F

- 1 **pound fresh or frozen peeled and deveined cooked shrimp**
- 3 **tablespoons butter or margarine**
- 4 **large fresh poblano chiles, seeded and chopped* (4 cups)**
- 1 **cup finely chopped onion (1 large)**
- 4 **cloves garlic, minced**
- 1 **8-ounce package cream cheese, cut up**
- 1 **cup chopped roma tomatoes (3 medium)**
- 2 **cups shredded Monterey Jack cheese (8 ounces)**
- 2 **cups shredded cheddar cheese (8 ounces)**
- 1 **cup all-purpose flour**
- 1 **teaspoon baking powder**
- 1 **teaspoon baking soda**
- ½ **teaspoon salt**
- 1 **egg, lightly beaten**
- 1 **cup milk**
- 2 **tablespoons vegetable oil**

1 Thaw shrimp, if frozen. Rinse shrimp; pat dry with paper towels. Preheat oven to 350°F. Grease a 9×13-inch baking dish; set aside.

2 In an extra-large nonstick skillet melt butter on medium heat. Add poblano chiles, onion, and garlic; cook about 5 minutes or until onion is tender. Add cream cheese, stirring until smooth. Stir in shrimp and tomatoes. Remove from heat. Stir in 1 cup of the Monterey Jack cheese and 1 cup of the cheddar cheese. Spoon into prepared baking dish.

3 In a medium bowl stir together flour, baking powder, baking soda, and salt. In a small bowl combine egg, milk, and oil. Add egg mixture to flour mixture; stir just until batter is smooth. Pour batter over shrimp mixture, spreading evenly. Sprinkle with the remaining 1 cup Monterey Jack cheese and the remaining 1 cup cheddar cheese.

4 Bake, uncovered, for 35 to 40 minutes or until top is set and golden brown.

Makes 10 servings.

Per Serving: 449 cal., 30 g total fat (17 g sat. fat), 190 mg chol., 742 mg sodium, 18 g carbo., 1 g fiber, 26 g pro.

---

*Note: *Because chiles contain volatile oils that can burn your skin and eyes, avoid direct contact with them as much as possible. When working with chiles, wear plastic or rubber gloves. If your bare hands do touch the chiles, wash your hands and nails well with soap and warm water.*

VEGETABLE LASAGNA

> Swiss chard is finally making inroads on the American dining scene, and that's a good thing—its mild green leaves are packed with vitamins A and C.

Prep: 30 minutes   **Bake:** 50 minutes   **Stand:** 15 minutes   **Oven:** 375°F

- **1** tablespoon olive oil
- **1½** pounds Swiss chard, trimmed and chopped (8 cups)
- **2** cups chopped onions (2 large)
- **4** cloves garlic, minced
- **¼** teaspoon salt
- **1** large yellow summer squash, halved crosswise and cut lengthwise into ¼-inch slices (2½ cups)
- **1** 26-ounce jar marinara pasta sauce (2½ cups)
- **12** no-boil lasagna noodles
- **1** 15-ounce container light ricotta cheese
- **1** cup shredded mozzarella cheese (4 ounces)

1 Preheat oven to 375°F. In an extra-large nonstick skillet heat oil on medium-high heat. Add chard, onions, garlic, and salt. Cook and stir for 5 minutes. Add squash. Cook and stir for 2 to 3 minutes more or until vegetables are tender.

2 To assemble, spoon half of the marinara sauce into a 9×13-inch baking dish. Top with 3 of the uncooked noodles, placing noodles crosswise in dish. Top with one-third of the vegetable mixture. Spoon one-third of the ricotta cheese in mounds over the vegetable mixture. Repeat layers twice, starting with noodles and ending with ricotta cheese. Top with the remaining 3 noodles and the remaining marinara sauce. Sprinkle with mozzarella cheese.

3 Cover tightly with foil. Bake for 50 to 55 minutes or until noodles are tender when pierced with a fork. Uncover. Let stand for 15 minutes before serving.

Makes 8 to 10 servings.

Per Serving: 261 cal., 8 g total fat (3 g sat. fat), 21 mg chol., 644 mg sodium, 32 g carbo., 3 g fiber, 14 g pro.

BUTTERNUT SQUASH LASAGNA

Roasted squash takes the place of meat
in this lasagna that has autumn written all over it—
but it's a recipe you'll relish year 'round.

Prep: 30 minutes   **Roast:** 25 minutes   **Bake:** 50 minutes   **Stand:** 10 minutes   **Oven:** 425°F/375°F

- **3** pounds butternut squash, peeled, seeded, and cut into ¼- to ½-inch slices
- **3** tablespoons olive oil
- **½** teaspoon salt
- **¼** cup butter or margarine
- **6** cloves garlic, minced
- **¼** cup all-purpose flour
- **½** teaspoon salt
- **4** cups milk
- **1** tablespoon snipped fresh rosemary
- **9** no-boil lasagna noodles
- **1⅓** cups finely shredded Parmesan cheese
- **1** cup whipping cream

1 Lightly grease a 10×15-inch baking pan. Preheat oven to 425°F. Place squash, oil, and ½ teaspoon salt in prepared baking pan; toss gently to coat. Spread in an even layer. Roast, uncovered, for 25 to 30 minutes or until squash is tender, stirring once. Reduce oven temperature to 375°F.

2 Meanwhile, for sauce: In a large saucepan melt butter on medium heat. Add garlic; cook and stir for 1 minute. Stir in flour and ½ teaspoon salt. Gradually stir in milk. Cook and stir until thickened and bubbly. Stir in squash and rosemary.

3 Lightly grease a 9×13-inch baking pan or baking dish. Spread about 1 cup of the sauce evenly into prepared baking pan or dish. Layer 3 of the uncooked noodles in baking pan or dish. Spread with one-third of the remaining sauce. Sprinkle with ⅓ cup of the Parmesan cheese. Repeat layers twice, starting with noodles and ending with cheese. Pour the whipping cream evenly over layers in baking pan or dish. Sprinkle with the remaining ⅓ cup Parmesan cheese.

4 Cover tightly with foil. Bake for 40 minutes. Uncover. Bake about 10 minutes more or until edges are bubbly, noodles are tender when pierced with a fork, and top is lightly browned. Let stand for 10 minutes before serving.

Makes 8 to 10 servings.

Per Serving: 525 cal., 29 g total fat (15 g sat. fat), 76 mg chol., 628 mg sodium, 53 g carbo., 4 g fiber, 16 g pro.

ROASTED VEGETABLE LASAGNA

Roasting vegetables—here accomplished quickly
under the broiler—gives them a subtle sweetness
that enhances most any dish.

Prep: 35 minutes **Broil:** 12 minutes **Bake:** 50 minutes **Stand:** 10 minutes **Oven:** 375°F

12	dried lasagna noodles
4	cups zucchini cut into bite-size pieces
2½	cups thinly sliced carrots (5 medium)
2	cups fresh cremini or button mushrooms, halved
1½	cups coarsely chopped sweet red or green pepper
¼	cup olive oil
1	tablespoon dried Italian seasoning, crushed
½	teaspoon salt
½	teaspoon black pepper
1	12-ounce carton cottage cheese
1	egg, beaten
½	cup grated Parmesan cheese
1	26-ounce jar marinara pasta sauce
3	cups shredded mozzarella cheese (12 ounces)

1 Cook noodles according to package directions; drain. Rinse with cold water; drain again. Place noodles in a single layer on a sheet of foil; set aside.

2 Meanwhile, preheat broiler. In a very large bowl combine zucchini, carrots, mushrooms, and sweet pepper. Drizzle vegetables with olive oil; sprinkle with Italian seasoning, salt, and black pepper. Toss well to combine. Place vegetable mixture in a shallow roasting pan.

3 Broil vegetables 5 to 6 inches from heat for 6 minutes. Stir vegetables. Broil for 6 to 8 minutes more or until light brown and tender. Set vegetables aside.

4 In a medium bowl combine cottage cheese, egg, and ¼ cup of the Parmesan cheese; set aside. Reduce oven temperature to 375°F.

5 Grease a 9×13-inch baking dish. Place one-third of the marinara sauce in prepared baking dish. Layer 4 of the cooked noodles on top of sauce. Top with half of the roasted vegetables, one-third of the sauce, and one-third of the mozzarella cheese. Add 4 more noodles, all of the cottage cheese mixture, and one-third of the mozzarella cheese. Add the remaining 4 noodles, the remaining vegetables, the remaining sauce, and the remaining mozzarella. Sprinkle with the remaining ¼ cup Parmesan cheese.

6 Cover with foil. Bake for 30 minutes. Uncover. Bake about 20 minutes more or until heated through. Let stand for 10 minutes before serving.

Makes 9 servings.

Per Serving: 420 cal., 21 g total fat (8 g sat. fat), 3 mg chol., 1,020 mg sodium, 37 g carbo., 3 g fiber, 22 g pro.

VEGETABLE LASAGNA WITH GRUYÈRE AND WALNUTS

Walnuts supply this plant-based lasagna with a meaty taste and hearty texture that even carnivores will appreciate.

Prep: 35 minutes **Bake:** 55 minutes **Stand:** 10 minutes **Oven:** 350°F

- 2 **cups thinly sliced onions (2 large)**
- 1 **cup shredded carrots (2 medium)**
- 1 **cup chopped celery (2 stalks)**
- ½ **cup chopped sweet green pepper (1 small)**
- 2 **cloves garlic, minced**
- 2 **tablespoons olive oil**
- 2 **10-ounce packages frozen chopped spinach, thawed and well drained**
- 1 **15-ounce can tomato puree**
- 2 **teaspoons dried Italian seasoning, crushed**
- ½ **teaspoon salt**
- 12 **dried lasagna noodles**
- 1 **15-ounce carton ricotta cheese or 1 3/4 cups cottage cheese**
- 2 **eggs, beaten**
- 1 **cup chopped walnuts, toasted**
- 1 **pound Gruyère cheese or Swiss cheese, shredded (4 cups)**

1 Preheat oven to 350°F. In a large skillet cook onions, carrots, celery, sweet pepper, and garlic in hot oil on medium-high heat about 5 minutes or until tender. Stir in spinach. Cook and stir for 1 minute. Stir in tomato puree, Italian seasoning, and salt.

2 Meanwhile, cook lasagna noodles according to package directions; drain. Rinse with cold water; drain again. Place noodles in a single layer on a sheet of foil; set aside.

3 For filling: In a medium bowl combine ricotta cheese, eggs, and walnuts; set aside.

4 Spread about ½ cup of the vegetable mixture into a 9×13-inch baking dish. Layer 4 of the cooked noodles over tomato mixture in baking dish, overlapping as needed. Spread with half of the filling, 1⅓ cups of the vegetable mixture, and 1⅓ cups of the Gruyère cheese. Repeat layers, starting with noodles and ending with Gruyère cheese. Top with the remaining 4 cooked noodles. Spoon any remaining vegetable mixture over the noodles. Sprinkle with any remaining Gruyère cheese.

5 Cover with foil. Bake for 45 minutes. Uncover. Bake about 10 minutes more or until heated through. Let stand for 10 minutes before serving.

Makes 12 servings.

Per Serving: 439 cal., 27 g total fat (11 g sat. fat), 95 mg chol., 356 mg sodium, 27 g carbo., 4 g fiber, 23 g pro.

BROCCOLI-CARROT LASAGNA

Serve this veggie-packed lasagna as a meal
in itself or make it a superlative side to accompany
roasted chicken or pork.

Prep: 30 minutes **Bake:** 35 minutes **Stand:** 15 minutes **Oven:** 350°F

- 9 dried lasagna noodles
- 3½ cups milk
- ½ cup all-purpose flour
- 1 teaspoon salt
- ½ teaspoon dry mustard
- ¼ teaspoon black pepper
- ¼ teaspoon bottled hot pepper sauce
- ¼ cup grated Parmesan cheese
- 1 16-ounce package frozen cut broccoli, thawed and drained
- 1 cup shredded carrots (2 medium)
- 2 cups shredded cheddar cheese (8 ounces)

1 Preheat oven to 350°F. Lightly grease a 9×13-inch baking dish; set aside. Cook lasagna noodles according to package directions; drain. Rinse with cold water; drain again. Place noodles in a single layer on a sheet of foil; set aside.

2 Meanwhile, for sauce: In a medium saucepan whisk together about 1 cup of the milk and the flour until smooth. Stir in the remaining milk, the salt, dry mustard, black pepper, and hot pepper sauce. Cook and stir on medium heat until thickened and bubbly. Remove from heat; stir in Parmesan cheese.

3 Arrange 3 of the cooked lasagna noodles in prepared baking dish. Top with half of the broccoli, half of the carrots, ¾ cup of the cheddar cheese, and 1 cup of the sauce. Repeat layers. Top with the remaining 3 cooked noodles, the remaining sauce, and the remaining ½ cup cheddar cheese.

4 Bake, uncovered, for 35 to 40 minutes or until heated through. Let stand for 15 minutes before serving.

Makes 8 servings.

Per Serving: 325 cal., 13 g total fat (8 g sat. fat), 41 mg chol., 574 mg sodium, 35 g carbo., 3 g fiber, 17 g pro.

VEGETABLE-POLENTA LASAGNA

When polenta chills, it becomes a thick
and sturdy layer that supports the vegetables
and cheese perfectly.

Prep: 25 minutes **Chill:** 30 minutes **Bake:** 40 minutes **Oven:** 350°F

- 2½   cups water
- 1½   cups yellow cornmeal
- 1½   cups water
- 1   teaspoon salt
- 1   small onion, thinly sliced
- 1   tablespoon olive oil
- 4   cups fresh mushrooms, halved
- ¼   teaspoon salt
- ¼   teaspoon black pepper
- 2   12-ounce jars roasted sweet red peppers, drained and cut into thin strips
- 1¼   cups marinara pasta sauce
- 1   cup shredded mozzarella cheese (4 ounces)
-    Snipped fresh Italian (flat-leaf) parsley (optional)

1 For polenta: In a medium saucepan bring the 2½ cups water to boiling. Meanwhile, in a small bowl combine cornmeal, the 1½ cups water, and the 1 teaspoon salt. Slowly add cornmeal mixture to the boiling water, stirring constantly. Cook and stir until mixture returns to boiling. Reduce heat to low. Cook, uncovered, for 10 to 15 minutes or until very thick, stirring frequently. Spread evenly in a 9×13-inch baking dish; cool. Cover and chill about 30 minutes or until firm.

2 Preheat oven to 350°F. In a large nonstick skillet cook onion in hot oil on medium for 3 to 4 minutes or until tender. Add mushrooms, the ¼ teaspoon salt, and the black pepper. Cook and stir about 5 minutes or until mushrooms are tender. Remove from heat. Stir in roasted sweet red peppers.

3 Spread marinara pasta sauce over chilled polenta. Top with vegetable mixture; sprinkle with cheese.

4 Cover with foil. Bake for 30 minutes. Uncover. Bake for 10 to 15 minutes more or until edges are bubbly. If desired, sprinkle with parsley.

Makes 8 servings.

Per Serving: 188 cal., 7 g total fat (2 g sat. fat), 8 mg chol., 649 mg sodium, 27 g carbo., 4 g fiber, 8 g pro.

BLACK BEAN LASAGNA

Cheesy and rich tasting, this Mexican-style vegetarian casserole is just as satisfying as a meat-filled version.

Prep: 45 minutes **Bake:** 35 minutes **Stand:** 10 minutes **Oven:** 350°F

9	dried lasagna noodles (8 ounces)
2	15-ounce cans black beans, rinsed and drained
1	egg, lightly beaten
1	12-ounce container (1½ cups) cottage cheese
1	8-ounce package cream cheese, cut into cubes and softened
1½	cups shredded Monterey Jack cheese (6 ounces)
1	cup chopped onion (1 large)
¾	cup chopped sweet green pepper (1 medium)
2	cloves garlic, minced
1	tablespoon vegetable oil
1	15-ounce can Italian-style tomato sauce
4	teaspoons dried cilantro, crushed
1	teaspoon ground cumin
	Coarsely chopped tomato

1 Preheat oven to 350°F. Lightly grease a 9×13-inch baking dish; set aside. Cook lasagna noodles according to package directions; drain. Rinse with cold water; drain again. Place noodles in a single layer on a sheet of foil; set aside.

2 In a small bowl mash 1 can of the beans with a potato masher; set aside. In a medium bowl combine egg, cottage cheese, cream cheese, and 1 cup of the Monterey Jack cheese; set aside.

3 In a large skillet cook onion, sweet pepper, and garlic in hot oil on medium-high heat until tender. Stir in mashed beans, the remaining 1 can of whole beans, the tomato sauce, cilantro, and cumin; heat through.

4 Arrange 3 of the cooked noodles in the prepared baking dish. Top with one-third of the bean mixture. Spoon half of the cheese mixture over bean mixture. Repeat layers. Top with the remaining 3 cooked noodles and the remaning bean mixture.

5 Cover with foil. Bake for 35 to 40 minutes or until heated through. Sprinkle with the remaining ½ cup Monterey Jack cheese. Let stand for 10 minutes before serving. Sprinkle with chopped tomato.

Makes 8 servings.

Per Serving: 456 cal., 22 g total fat (12 g sat. fat), 83 mg chol., 857 mg sodium, 46 g carbo., 8 g fiber, 25 g pro.

153

MOLE ENCHILADAS

**If you like, use half beans and half tofu.
Both are excellent flavor carriers
and each has its own nutritional benefits.**

Prep: 35 minutes   **Bake:** 30 minutes   **Oven:** 350°F

12	6- to 7-inch flour tortillas
½	cup chopped onion (1 medium)
1	medium fresh jalapeño or serrano chile, seeded and finely chopped*
2	cloves garlic, minced
1	tablespoon vegetable oil
⅓	cup sour cream
¼	cup purchased mole sauce
2	tablespoons water
2	15-ounce cans black beans or pinto beans, rinsed and drained, or one 16-ounce package firm or extra-firm tub-style tofu (fresh bean curd), drained and cut into ½-inch cubes
2	cups shredded asadero cheese, Monterey Jack cheese, or sharp cheddar cheese (8 ounces)
1	cup sour cream
2	tablespoons all-purpose flour
1	teaspoon ground cumin
¼	teaspoon salt
¾	cup milk
1	recipe Mango Salsa or 1½ cups desired salsa
	Lime wedges (optional)
	Snipped fresh cilantro

1 Preheat oven to 350°F. Stack tortillas and wrap tightly in foil. Bake about 10 minutes or until warm.

2 Meanwhile, grease a 9×13-inch baking dish; set aside. For filling: In a large skillet cook onion, jalapeño, and garlic in hot oil on medium heat until onion is tender. Remove from heat.

3 In a small bowl stir together the ⅓ cup sour cream, the mole sauce, and the water; stir into onion mixture. Gently stir in beans and 1 cup of the cheese. Spoon about ⅓ cup of the filling onto an edge of each tortilla. Starting at the edge with the filling, roll up tortilla. Arrange tortillas, seam sides down, in prepared baking dish.

4 For sauce: In a small bowl combine the 1 cup sour cream, the flour, cumin, and salt; whisk in milk. Pour sauce evenly over tortillas.

5 Cover with foil. Bake about 25 minutes or until heated through. Sprinkle with the remaining 1 cup cheese. Bake, uncovered, about 5 minutes more or until cheese melts. Serve with Mango Salsa and, if desired, lime wedges. Sprinkle with cilantro.

Makes 6 servings.

Per Serving: 851 cal., 31 g total fat (13 g sat. fat), 58 mg chol., 1,572 mg sodium, 116 g carbo., 13 g fiber, 34 g pro.

Mango Salsa: *In a small bowl combine 1 large mango, seeded, peeled, and chopped; 2 fresh jalapeños or serrano chiles, seeded and finely chopped;* 2 tablespoons snipped fresh cilantro; and 1 tablespoon lemon juice or lime juice.*

*Note: *Because chiles contain volatile oils that can burn your skin and eyes, avoid direct contact with them as much as possible. When working with chiles, wear plastic or rubber gloves. If your bare hands do touch the chiles, wash your hands and nails well with soap and warm water.*

CASSEROLE-STYLE CHILES RELLENOS

Authentic chiles rellenos is a marvelous
Mexican dish that is a lot of work to make. This creamy
casserole delivers great flavor without extra effort.

Prep: 35 minutes **Bake:** 15 minutes **Oven:** 450°F

- 4 large fresh poblano chiles* or sweet green peppers
- 6 eggs, lightly beaten
- ½ cup milk
- ½ teaspoon salt
- ½ cup chopped sweet red pepper (1 small)
- ½ cup chopped green onions (4)
- 1 tablespoon seeded and finely chopped fresh jalapeño*
- 2 cloves garlic, minced
- 1 tablespoon vegetable oil
- 1 cup shredded cheddar cheese (4 ounces)
- 1 cup picante sauce
- ½ cup sour cream

1 Preheat oven to 450°F. Generously grease a 9×13-inch baking dish; set aside. Halve poblano chiles or sweet green peppers lengthwise; remove seeds and membranes. Precook poblanos or green peppers in boiling water for 3 minutes. Invert onto paper towels to drain. Place poblanos or green peppers, cut sides up, in prepared baking dish.

2 In a medium bowl whisk together eggs, milk, and salt; set aside. In a large skillet cook sweet red pepper, green onions, jalapeño, and garlic in hot oil on medium heat just until sweet red pepper is tender. Remove vegetables from skillet; set aside.

3 Pour egg mixture into the same skillet. Cook on medium heat, without stirring, until mixture starts to set on the bottom and around the edges. Using a spatula or large spoon, lift and fold the partially cooked egg mixture so that the uncooked portion flows underneath. Continue cooking on medium heat for 2 to 3 minutes or until egg mixture is cooked through but is still glossy and moist.

4 Remove from heat. Fold in sweet red pepper mixture and ½ cup of the cheese. Fill poblano or green pepper halves with egg mixture. Sprinkle with the remaining ½ cup cheese.

5 Bake, uncovered, about 15 minutes or until heated through. Serve with picante sauce and sour cream.

Makes 8 servings.

Per Serving: 197 cal., 13 g total fat (6 g sat. fat), 181 mg chol., 516 mg sodium, 9 g carbo., 1 g fiber, 10 g pro.

*Note: *Because chiles contain volatile oils that can burn your skin and eyes, avoid direct contact with them as much as possible. When working with chiles, wear plastic or rubber gloves. If your bare hands do touch the chiles, wash your hands and nails well with soap and warm water.*

SPINACH CANNELLONI WITH FONTINA

Fontina—one of Italy's great cheeses—
is mild, nutty, buttery, and absolutely
outstanding with spinach.

Prep: 35 minutes **Bake:** 25 minutes **Stand:** 10 minutes **Oven:** 375°F

- 1 medium fennel bulb, cored and chopped (1 cup)
- 3 cloves garlic, minced
- 1 tablespoon olive oil
- 1 6-ounce package (about 5 cups) baby spinach
- 1 egg, lightly beaten
- 1 15-ounce carton ricotta cheese
- ²/₃ cup finely shredded Parmesan cheese
- ½ teaspoon dried Italian seasoning, crushed
- ½ teaspoon finely shredded lemon peel
- 1 17-ounce jar marinara pasta sauce
- 1 4.5- to 5-ounce package ready-to-use crepes
- 1 10-ounce container refrigerated Alfredo pasta sauce
- 1 cup shredded fontina cheese (4 ounces)

1 Preheat oven to 375°F. For filling: In an extra-large skillet cook fennel and garlic in hot oil on medium heat for 3 to 4 minutes or until tender. Add spinach; cook, covered, about 2 minutes more or until wilted. Transfer spinach mixture to a sieve. Using the back of a spoon, press out excess liquid; discard liquid.

2 In a large bowl combine egg, ricotta cheese, Parmesan cheese, Italian seasoning, and lemon peel. Stir in spinach mixture.

3 Spread half of the marinara pasta sauce in a 9×13-inch baking dish. Spoon about ⅓ cup of the filling along the center of each crepe; roll up crepe. Arrange crepes, seam sides down, on top of marinara sauce in baking dish. Spoon the remaining marinara sauce down center of crepes in baking dish. Pour Alfredo sauce over crepes, spreading evenly. Sprinkle with fontina cheese.

4 Bake, uncovered, for 25 to 30 minutes or until bubbly around the edges. Let stand for 10 minutes before serving.

Makes 5 servings.

Per Serving: 672 cal., 47 g total fat (15 g sat. fat), 159 mg chol., 1,297 mg sodium, 36 g carbo., 4 g fiber, 28 g pro.

CAJUN MAC AND CHEESE

Zesty Cajun spices give this macaroni
and cheese a load of spunk, while American
cheese makes it extra creamy.

Prep: 30 minutes   **Bake:** 35 minutes   **Stand:** 5 minutes   **Oven:** 350°F

- 3 cups dried tricolor or plain elbow macaroni (12 ounces)
- 2 cups shredded cheddar cheese (8 ounces)
- 4 ounces American cheese, cubed
- 2 tablespoons butter or margarine
- ¾ cup chopped sweet onion (such as Vidalia, Walla Walla, or Maui)
- 12 cloves garlic, minced (2 tablespoons)
- ½ cup sliced green onions (4)
- 1 cup chopped sweet red and/or green pepper (1 large)
- 2 eggs, lightly beaten
- 1 12-ounce can evaporated milk
- 2 tablespoons all-purpose flour
- 2 teaspoons yellow mustard
- 2 teaspoons bottled hot pepper sauce
- ½ teaspoon paprika
- ½ teaspoon salt

1 Preheat oven to 350°F. Grease a 9×13-inch baking dish; set aside.

2 In a large saucepan cook macaroni according to package directions; drain. Return to hot pan. Stir in cheeses; set aside.

3 Meanwhile, in a medium skillet melt butter on medium heat. Add sweet onion and garlic; cook until tender. Stir in green onions and sweet pepper. Cook and stir for 1 minute more; stir into cooked pasta mixture. Spoon into prepared baking dish; set aside.

4 In a medium bowl whisk together eggs, evaporated milk, flour, mustard, hot pepper sauce, paprika, and salt until smooth; pour evenly over pasta mixture.

5 Cover with foil. Bake for 20 minutes. Uncover. Bake for 15 to 20 minutes more or until bubbly and heated through. Let stand for 5 minutes before serving.

Makes 6 servings.

Per Serving: 600 cal., 29 g total fat (17 g sat. fat), 154 mg chol., 846 mg sodium, 56 g carbo., 3 g fiber, 28 g pro.

159

DEEP-DISH GARDEN VEGETABLE PIZZA

Looking for a way to sneak some vegetables
into your kids' diets? This pizza
makes it easy—and kids will clamor for it.

Prep: 30 minutes   **Bake:** 20 minutes   **Oven:** 400°F

- 1   egg, lightly beaten
- 1   8.5-ounce package corn muffin mix
- 1/3   cup all-purpose flour
- 3   tablespoons milk
- 1   tablespoon dried Italian seasoning, crushed
- 1   cup shredded carrots (2 medium)
- 1   cup fresh or frozen whole kernel corn, thawed
- 1   cup chopped sweet red or green pepper (1 large)
- 2   roma tomatoes, seeded and chopped
- 1   fresh jalapeño, seeded and finely chopped*
- 1   tablespoon snipped fresh oregano
- 1/4   cup bottled Italian salad dressing
- 1½   cups finely shredded Italian-style cheese blend (6 ounces)
- 1   tablespoon snipped fresh Italian (flat-leaf) parsley

1 Preheat oven to 400°F. Generously grease a 9×13-inch baking pan; set aside. In a medium bowl combine egg, corn muffin mix, flour, milk, and Italian seasoning. Mix until combined. On a well-floured surface knead dough 10 to 12 times or until easy to handle (dough will be soft). Using floured hands, pat dough into prepared baking pan.

2 Sprinkle carrots, corn, sweet pepper, tomatoes, jalapeño, and oregano over dough; drizzle with Italian dressing. Sprinkle with cheese.

3 Bake, uncovered, about 20 minutes or until a toothpick inserted near the center comes out clean. Sprinkle with parsley.

Makes 6 servings.

Per Serving: 368 cal., 15 g total fat (5 g sat. fat), 56 mg chol., 675 mg sodium, 47 g carbo., 2 g fiber, 13 g pro.

160

*__Note:__ *Because chiles contain volatile oils that can burn your skin and eyes, avoid direct contact with them as much as possible. When working with chiles, wear plastic or rubber gloves. If your bare hands do touch the chiles, wash your hands and nails well with soap and warm water.*

APPETIZERS & SIDES

People tend to think of appetizers and sides as second-fiddle supplements to the main attraction, but often they are the most memorable items on the table. There are plenty of those savory standouts in these pages—and each unforgettable option is on its way to your list of family favorites.

TANDOORI CHICKEN WINGS

Indian cuisine is the next
big food fashion. Be a trendsetter
with these India-inspired wings.

Prep: 45 minutes   Marinate: 4 to 24 hours   Bake: 25 minutes   Broil: 6 minutes   Oven: 400°F

- 50 chicken drumettes*
     (about 5 pounds)
- 1 medium onion, cut into
     wedges
- 1 8-ounce can tomato sauce
- 1 6-ounce carton plain fat-
     free yogurt
- 1 tablespoon ground
     coriander
- 4 cloves garlic, minced
- 2 teaspoons grated fresh
     ginger
- 1½ teaspoons salt
- 1 teaspoon cumin seeds
- 1 teaspoon garam masala
- ½ to 1 teaspoon cayenne
     pepper (optional)
- ¼ to ½ teaspoon red food
     coloring
- 2 whole cloves
     Lemon wedges (optional)
     Thin wedges red onion
     (optional)

1. Place the chicken drumettes in a 9×13-inch baking dish; set aside.

2. In a blender or food processor combine onion, tomato sauce, yogurt, coriander, garlic, ginger, salt, cumin seeds, garam masala, cayenne pepper (if desired), red food coloring, and whole cloves. Cover and blend or process to a very smooth paste. (The color should be deep red.)

3. Pour onion paste over chicken drumettes; turn drumettes to coat. Cover and marinate in the refrigerator for at least 4 or up to 24 hours. Drain chicken, discarding marinade.

4. Preheat oven to 400°F. Arrange as many of the chicken drumettes on the unheated rack of a broiler pan as will fit in a single layer. Bake, uncovered, for 25 minutes. Turn oven to broil.

5. Broil drumettes 4 to 5 inches from heat for 6 to 8 minutes or until chicken is no longer pink and pieces just start to blacken, turning once halfway through broiling.

6. Transfer chicken drumettes to a serving platter. Repeat baking and broiling with the remaining drumettes. If desired, serve with lemon wedges and red onion wedges.

Makes 16 appetizer servings.

Per Serving: 119 cal., 4 g total fat (1 g sat. fat), 62 mg chol., 363 mg sodium, 3 g carbo., 0 g fiber, 16 g pro.

163

*Note: *If you cannot find chicken drumettes, use 25 chicken wings. Cut off and discard tips of chicken wings. Cut wings at joints to form 50 pieces.*

BUFFALO-STYLE CHICKEN FINGERS

Since the first spicy wings flew from Buffalo, New York, to parties across the country, countless variations have appeared. This lean breast version may be the best.

Prep: 25 minutes   **Bake:** 12 minutes   **Oven:** 425°F

- ³/₄ cup crushed cornflakes
- 2 teaspoons finely snipped fresh parsley
- ¹/₈ teaspoon salt
- 12 ounces skinless, boneless chicken breast halves
- ¹/₄ cup bottled blue cheese salad dressing
- 1¹/₂ teaspoons water
- 1 teaspoon bottled hot pepper sauce
  Celery sticks
  Bottled blue cheese salad dressing

1 Preheat oven to 425°F. Lightly grease a 9×13-inch baking pan; set aside. In a shallow bowl or pie plate combine crushed cornflakes, parsley, and salt. Cut chicken breast halves into strips about ³⁄₄ inch wide and 3 inches long. In a large bowl combine the ¹⁄₄ cup dressing, the water, and hot pepper sauce. Add chicken; stir gently to coat. Roll chicken pieces, 1 at a time, in crumb mixture to coat. Place in a single layer in prepared baking pan.

2 Bake, uncovered, for 12 to 15 minutes or until chicken is no longer pink and crumbs are golden brown. Serve warm with celery sticks and additional blue cheese dressing for dipping.

Makes 8 appetizer servings.

Per Serving: 188 cal., 12 g total fat (2 g sat. fat), 32 mg chol., 356 mg sodium, 9 g carbo., 1 g fiber, 11 g pro.

SPICY CAJUN PECANS

When you need large quantities of nuts for recipes
like this one, head to your nearest wholesale warehouse—
you'll save a lot of money.

Prep: 10 minutes   Bake: 15 minutes   Oven: 350°F

- 4   cups pecan halves
- 2   tablespoons vegetable oil
- 1   tablespoon Worcestershire sauce
- 2   teaspoons lemon juice
- 2   teaspoons garlic salt
- 2   teaspoons paprika
- ½   teaspoon onion salt
- ½   teaspoon cayenne pepper
- ½   teaspoon dried thyme, crushed
- ¼   teaspoon black pepper

1 Preheat oven to 350°F. Spread pecans in a 9×13-inch baking pan. In a small bowl combine oil, Worcestershire sauce, lemon juice, garlic salt, paprika, onion salt, cayenne, thyme, and black pepper; drizzle over nuts. Toss to coat.

2 Bake, uncovered, about 15 minutes or until nuts are toasted, stirring occasionally. Spread on a piece of foil to cool. Store in an airtight container for up to 1 week.

Makes 16 (¼-cup) servings.

Per Serving: 205 cal., 21 g total fat (2 g sat. fat), 0 mg chol., 183 mg sodium, 4 g carbo., 3 g fiber, 3 g pro.

Sweet and Spicy Cajun Pecan Mix: *Prepare as above, except omit lemon juice, reduce oil to 1 tablespoon, and add 2 tablespoons dark corn syrup.*

NO-NUTS CEREAL SNACK

This quick nibble is perfect for anyone who is either allergic to nuts or just doesn't like them. It's especially good for small children.

Prep: 10 minutes **Bake:** 10 minutes **Cool:** 15 minutes **Oven:** 350°F

- 2 cups puffed corn cereal
- 2 cups round toasted oat cereal
- 1 cup small fish-shape cheese crackers
- 1 cup chow mein noodles
- 3 tablespoons vegetable oil
- 1 0.4-ounce envelope (1 tablespoon) dry buttermilk salad dressing mix

1 Preheat oven to 350°F. In a 9×13-inch baking pan stir together cereals, crackers, and chow mein noodles. Drizzle oil over cereal mixture; toss to coat. Sprinkle with dry dressing mix; toss to coat.

2 Bake, uncovered, for 10 minutes, stirring once. Cool in pan for 15 minutes. Store in an airtight container at room temperature for up to 1 week.

Makes 6 (1-cup) servings.

Per Serving: 236 cal., 12 g total fat (2 g sat. fat), 1 mg chol., 449 mg sodium, 28 g carbo., 2 g fiber, 4 g pro.

BACON-AND-CHEESE-STUFFED DATES

**Medjools are considered the
diamonds of dates. No other variety is as
big, plump, and sweet.**

Prep: 15 minutes   Bake: 5 minutes   Oven: 350°F

- ¼ **cup cooked bacon pieces or chopped prosciutto**
- ¼ **cup thinly sliced green onions (2)**
- 2 **cloves garlic, minced**
- 1 **3-ounce package cream cheese, softened**
- ½ **cup crumbled blue cheese (2 ounces)**
- 2 **teaspoons Dijon mustard**
- ⅛ **teaspoon black pepper**
- 24 **Medjool dates**

1 Preheat oven to 350°F. In a medium bowl stir together bacon, green onions, and garlic. Stir in cream cheese, blue cheese, mustard, and pepper.

2 Cut a slit in each date. Spread open slightly; remove pits. Fill each date with 1 rounded teaspoon of the bacon mixture.

3 Place dates, filling sides up, in a 9×13-inch baking pan. Bake, uncovered, for 5 to 8 minutes or until heated through. Serve warm.

Makes 24 appetizer servings.

Per Serving: 92 cal., 2 g total fat (1 g sat. fat), 6 mg chol., 70 mg sodium, 18 g carbo., 2 g fiber, 1 g pro.

BACON-AND-CHEESE-STUFFED MUSHROOMS

Dried bread crumbs are easy to find, but it's difficult to purchase fresh ones. To make your own, just tear up a few bread slices and give them a whirl in the food processor.

Prep: 30 minutes   **Bake:** 12 minutes   **Oven:** 400°F

- 1½ **cups soft bread crumbs (about 2 slices)**
- 1 **tablespoon olive oil**
- 6 **3- to 4-inch-diameter fresh portobello mushrooms (about 1¼ pounds)**
- 1 **cup finely shredded Colby and Monterey Jack cheese (4 ounces)**
- 4 **slices bacon, crisp-cooked, drained, and crumbled**
- ¼ **cup bottled creamy Italian salad dressing**
- ¼ **cup sliced green onions (2)**
- 1 **clove garlic, minced**
- 6 **cherry tomatoes, thinly sliced**

1 Preheat oven to 400°F. Place bread crumbs in a 9×13-inch baking pan; toss with oil. Bake, uncovered, for 5 to 7 minutes or until lightly toasted, stirring once. Cool on a wire rack.

2 Meanwhile, clean mushrooms; remove and discard stems and gills. Pat dry with paper towels. Place mushrooms, rounded sides down, on a baking sheet.

3 In a medium bowl combine ½ cup of the toasted bread crumbs, the cheese, bacon, salad dressing, green onions, and garlic. Spoon mixture into mushroom caps. Top with tomato slices. Sprinkle with the remaining crumbs.

4 Bake, uncovered, for 12 to 15 minutes or until mushrooms are tender. Cut mushrooms in half to serve.

Makes 12 appetizer servings.

Per Serving: 109 cal., 8 g total fat (3 g sat. fat), 11 mg chol., 253 mg sodium, 6 g carbo., 1 g fiber, 5 g pro.

ROASTED MUSHROOM MEDLEY

A special-event side like this is wonderful with roasted beef or chicken. Serve leftovers over buttered toast for lunch.

Prep: 25 minutes   **Roast:** 20 minutes   **Oven:** 400°F

- 1 pound assorted fresh mushrooms (such as cremini, stemmed shiitake, button, and/or porcini), quartered
- 6 cloves garlic, peeled and thinly sliced
- 2 tablespoons olive oil
- 2 teaspoons Worcestershire sauce
- 2 teaspoons balsamic vinegar
- 1 teaspoon dried oregano, crushed
- ¼ teaspoon salt
- ¼ teaspoon black pepper
- 2 tablespoons snipped fresh Italian (flat-leaf) parsley

1 Preheat oven to 400°F. Place mushrooms in a 9×13-inch baking pan. Stir garlic slices into mushrooms.

2 Drizzle mushroom mixture with oil, Worcestershire sauce, and balsamic vinegar. Sprinkle with oregano, salt, and pepper. Toss gently to coat.

3 Roast, uncovered, for 20 to 25 minutes or until mushrooms are tender, stirring twice. Stir in parsley just before serving.

Makes 6 servings.

Per Serving: 65 cal., 5 g total fat (1 g sat. fat), 0 mg chol., 124 mg sodium, 4 g carbo., 1 g fiber, 3 g pro.

ASPARAGUS WITH PARMESAN CHEESE

Asparagus, one of nature's most
elegant vegetables, has the most delectable
flavor when it's quick-roasted at high heat.

Prep: 10 minutes **Roast:** 15 minutes **Oven:** 450°F

1½ **pounds fresh asparagus**
⅛ **teaspoon black pepper**
4 **teaspoons olive oil**
¼ **cup finely shredded or grated Parmesan cheese**

1 Preheat oven to 450°F. Wash asparagus; break off woody bases where spears snap easily. If desired, scrape off scales. Place asparagus in a 9×13-inch baking pan or baking dish. Sprinkle with pepper. Drizzle with oil.

2 Roast, uncovered, about 15 minutes or until crisp-tender, using tongs to lightly toss twice during roasting. Transfer asparagus to a warm serving platter. Sprinkle with Parmesan cheese.

Makes 6 servings.

Per Serving: 56 cal., 4 g total fat (1 g sat. fat), 3 mg chol., 52 mg sodium, 2 g carbo., 1 g fiber, 3 g pro.

THYME-ROASTED BEETS

French chefs often roast beets to bring out
their mellow-sweet flavors. Here they get
extra punch with a fresh herb drizzle.

Prep: 20 minutes **Roast:** 40 minutes **Cool:** 15 minutes **Oven:** 400°F

3½ **to 4 pounds baby beets (assorted colors) or small beets**

6 **cloves garlic, peeled**

3 **sprigs fresh thyme**

5 **tablespoons olive oil**

½ **teaspoon kosher salt**

¼ **teaspoon freshly ground black pepper**

2 **tablespoons lemon juice**

1 **tablespoon snipped fresh thyme**

Snipped fresh thyme (optional)

1 Preheat oven to 400°F. Cut tops off the beets and trim the root ends. Wash beets thoroughly. If using small beets, cut into 1- to 1½-inch wedges. Place beets in a 9×13-inch baking dish. Add garlic and the thyme sprigs. In a small bowl stir together 3 tablespoons of the oil, the salt, and pepper. Drizzle over vegetables in baking dish; toss lightly to coat.

2 Cover with foil. Roast for 40 to 45 minutes or until tender. (A knife should easily slide into the beets when they are tender.) Uncover. Let beets cool in pan on a wire rack about 15 minutes. If using small beets, remove skins by wrapping the wedges, 1 at a time, in a paper towel and gently rubbing the skins off (use new paper towels as needed). (Baby beets do not need to be peeled.)

3 Remove garlic from dish and finely chop. Discard thyme sprigs. In a small bowl combine finely chopped garlic, the remaining 2 tablespoons oil, the lemon juice, and the 1 tablespoon snipped thyme. Drizzle mixture over beets; toss lightly to coat.

4 Serve warm or at room temperature. If desired, garnish with additional snipped thyme.

Makes 8 servings.

Per Serving: 165 cal., 9 g total fat (1 g sat. fat), 0 mg chol., 268 mg sodium, 20 g carbo., 6 g fiber, 3 g pro.

CHEESE AND VEGETABLE RICE CASSEROLE

Although this cheesy delight is meant to be a side dish, it makes a great entrée for meat-free meals as well.

Prep: 20 minutes   Bake: 35 minutes   Stand: 10 minutes   Oven: 350°F

- 1   16-ounce package frozen broccoli, cauliflower, and carrots, thawed
- 4   cups cooked rice
- 1   15-ounce can black beans, rinsed and drained
- 1   12-ounce jar roasted sweet red peppers, drained and coarsely chopped
- 1   cup frozen whole kernel corn, thawed
- 2   4-ounce cans diced green chiles, drained
- 2   cups shredded cheddar cheese (8 ounces)
- 1¼ cups chicken broth
- ½   cup seasoned fine dry bread crumbs
- 2   tablespoons butter, melted

1 Preheat oven to 350°F. Lightly grease a 9×13-inch baking dish; set aside.

2 In a large bowl stir together mixed vegetables, cooked rice, beans, roasted peppers, corn, and chiles. Stir in 1 cup of the cheese and the broth. Spoon into prepared baking dish. Sprinkle with the remaining 1 cup cheese.

3 In a small bowl combine bread crumbs and melted butter. Sprinkle over vegetable mixture.

4 Bake, uncovered, for 35 to 40 minutes or until mixture is heated through and crumbs are golden brown. Let stand for 10 minutes before serving.

Makes 6 servings.

Per Serving: 471 cal., 18 g total fat (10 g sat. fat), 50 mg chol., 1,423 mg sodium, 60 g carbo., 8 g fiber, 21 g pro.

175

POTATOES AU GRATIN

The best potatoes to use for baked dishes such as this gratin are all-purpose, medium-starch potatoes. Yukon gold or yellow Finn are good choices.

Prep: 40 minutes **Bake:** 70 minutes **Stand:** 10 minutes **Oven:** 350°F

- 6 **medium potatoes (2 pounds), peeled if desired and thinly sliced (about 6 cups)**
- ½ **cup chopped onion (1 medium)**
- 2 **large cloves garlic, minced**
- 2 **tablespoons olive oil or vegetable oil**
- ¼ **cup all-purpose flour**
- 1 **teaspoon salt**
- ¼ **teaspoon black pepper**
- 3 **cups milk**
- 1 **cup shredded Parmesan cheese (4 ounces)**

1 Preheat oven to 350°F. Grease a 9×13-inch baking dish; set aside. In a large covered saucepan cook potatoes in enough boiling salted water to cover for 5 minutes; drain. Set aside.

2 For sauce: In a medium saucepan cook the onion and garlic in hot oil on medium heat until tender. Stir in flour, salt, and pepper. Add milk all at once. Cook and stir until thickened and bubbly. Remove from heat.

3 Layer half of the potatoes in prepared baking dish. Pour half of the sauce over potatoes. Sprinkle with half of the cheese. Repeat with the remaining potatoes and the remaining sauce. Cover and refrigerate the remaining cheese.

4 Cover with foil. Bake for 35 minutes. Sprinkle with the remaining cheese. Bake, uncovered, about 35 minutes more or until potatoes are tender and top is golden brown. Let stand for 10 minutes before serving.

Makes 8 servings.

Per Serving: 220 cal., 8 g total fat (3 g sat. fat), 15 mg chol., 511 mg sodium, 27 g carbo., 2 g fiber, 10 g pro.

Granny Smith and Smoked Cheddar Gratin: *Prepare as directed for Potatoes au Gratin, except cut 2 large cored Granny Smith apples into thin wedges. Add 2 teaspoons snipped fresh thyme to sauce. Place half of the apples over each layer of potatoes, then pour the sauce over. Substitute smoked cheddar or Gouda for the Parmesan cheese.*

Per Serving: 253 cal., 10 g total fat (4 g sat. fat), 22 mg chol., 430 mg sodium, 32 g carbo., 3 g fiber, 10 g pro.

HERBED YUKON GOLD AND SWEET POTATO GRATIN

This beautiful layered dish depends on thinly sliced potatoes. If your knife skills need work, try slicing on a mandoline—it's a wonderful tool to have.

Prep: 25 minutes   **Bake:** 1¼ hours   **Stand:** 10 minutes   **Oven:** 350°F

½ cup chopped green onions (4)

1 tablespoon snipped fresh sage

1 tablespoon snipped fresh thyme

3 cloves garlic, minced

1 teaspoon salt

½ teaspoon black pepper

1½ pounds sweet potatoes, peeled and thinly sliced

1½ pounds Yukon gold potatoes, peeled and thinly sliced

½ cup shredded Gruyère cheese or Swiss cheese (2 ounces)

¼ cup finely shredded Parmesan cheese (1 ounce)

½ cup chicken broth

½ cup whipping cream

Fresh sage leaves (optional)

1 Preheat oven to 350°F. Grease a 9×13-inch baking dish; set aside. In a small bowl combine green onions, snipped sage, thyme, garlic, salt, and pepper; set aside.

2 Layer half of the sweet potatoes and half of the Yukon gold potatoes in the prepared baking dish, alternating rows if desired. Top with half of the herb mixture; sprinkle with half of the Gruyère cheese and half of the Parmesan cheese. Repeat layers. Pour broth and cream over layers in baking dish.

3 Cover with foil. Bake for 1 hour. Bake, uncovered, for 15 to 20 minutes more or until potatoes are tender and top is lightly browned. Let stand for 10 to 15 minutes before serving. If desired, garnish with sage leaves.

Makes 8 to 10 servings.

Per Serving: 240 cal., 9 g total fat (5 g sat. fat), 32 mg chol., 480 mg sodium, 34 g carbo., 5 g fiber, 7 g pro.

SWEET POTATO CASSEROLE

If you're looking for a classic side
to serve with Thanksgiving dinner,
this is one of the best.

Prep: 40 minutes   **Bake:** 30 minutes   **Oven:** 350°F

- **4** pounds sweet potatoes, peeled and quartered
- **4** eggs, lightly beaten
- **1** cup packed brown sugar
- **½** cup butter, cut up
- **¼** cup milk
- **3** to 4 tablespoons lemon juice
- **1** cup fresh or canned pineapple chunks, drained
- **½** cup crumbled blue cheese or feta cheese (2 ounces)

1 In a covered Dutch oven cook sweet potatoes in enough boiling salted water to cover for 25 to 30 minutes or until tender; drain. Return to hot pan.

2 Meanwhile, preheat oven to 350°F. Grease a 9×13-inch baking dish; set aside. Slightly mash potatoes with a potato masher. Stir in eggs, brown sugar, butter, milk, and lemon juice. Spoon into prepared baking dish. Top with pineapple and cheese.

3 Bake, uncovered, about 30 minutes or until heated through.

Makes 8 to 12 servings.

Per Serving: 482 cal., 17 g total fat (10 g sat. fat), 143 mg chol., 370 mg sodium, 76 g carbo., 7 g fiber, 9 g pro.

CARAMELIZED ACORN SQUASH

**This recipe for brown sugar-glazed squash
can be easily doubled for a large gathering.
Be sure to use two baking dishes.**

Prep: 30 minutes   **Bake:** 50 minutes   **Oven:** 350°F

- 2 1- to 1½-pound acorn squash
- ¼ cup butter
- ¼ cup packed brown sugar
- ¼ cup apple cider
- ½ teaspoon ground cinnamon
- ¼ teaspoon salt
- ¼ teaspoon freshly ground nutmeg

1 Preheat oven to 350°F. Line a shallow baking pan with parchment paper or aluminum foil. Cut each squash in half; discard and remove seeds and fibrous material. Place halves, cut sides down, in the prepared baking pan. Bake, uncovered, for 40 to 45 minutes or until the squash is tender. Let stand until cool enough to handle; cut squash into 1-inch slices.

2 Arrange squash slices in a 9×13-inch baking dish, overlapping if necessary.

3 For glaze: In a large skillet heat butter, brown sugar, cider, cinnamon, salt, and nutmeg to boiling, stirring to dissolve sugar. Reduce heat and boil gently, uncovered, about 5 minutes or until syrupy. Drizzle glaze over squash.

4 Bake, uncovered, about 10 minutes or until heated through. Spoon glaze over squash before serving.

Makes 6 servings.

Per Serving: 154 cal., 8 g total fat (5 g sat. fat), 20 mg chol., 160 mg sodium, 22 g carbo., 2 g fiber, 1 g pro.

POLENTA AND ROASTED ROOT
VEGETABLE CASSEROLE

Don't let the long ingredient list deter you. This dish goes together quickly and tastes heavenly.

Prep: 55 minutes   Bake: 25 minutes   Stand: 10 minutes   Oven: 375°F

- **3** large sweet red and/or yellow peppers, cut into 1-inch strips
- **5** medium carrots, cut into $3/4$-inch pieces
- **2** medium parsnips, peeled and cut into 1-inch pieces
- **1** medium fennel bulb, cored and cut into $1/2$-inch wedges
- **1** medium red onion, cut into $1/2$-inch wedges
- **2** tablespoons olive oil
- $1/2$ teaspoon salt
- $1/4$ teaspoon black pepper
- **4** cups milk
- **1** cup hot water
- **1** teaspoon salt
- **1** teaspoon garlic powder
- $1/4$ teaspoon black pepper
- $1 1/2$ cups yellow cornmeal
- $1/2$ cup grated Parmesan cheese
- $1/3$ cup shredded fresh basil
- $1/4$ cup whipping cream
- $1/2$ cup shredded fontina cheese (2 ounces)
- **1** teaspoon snipped fresh thyme

1 Preheat oven to 375°F. Grease a 9×13-inch baking dish; set aside.

2 In a large roasting pan toss together sweet peppers, carrots, parsnips, fennel, onion, olive oil, the $1/2$ teaspoon salt, and $1/4$ teaspoon pepper. Bake, uncovered, about 45 minutes or until tender, stirring twice.

3 Meanwhile, for polenta: In a large saucepan combine milk, the hot water, the 1 teaspoon salt, the garlic powder, and $1/4$ teaspoon pepper. Bring just to simmering over medium-high heat. Slowly add cornmeal, stirring constantly. Cook and stir until mixture returns to boiling. Reduce heat to low. Cook about 3 minutes or until thick, stirring frequently. Remove from heat. Stir in Parmesan cheese and basil.

4 Spread polenta evenly in the prepared baking dish. Top with vegetables. Drizzle with cream; sprinkle with fontina cheese and thyme.

5 Bake, uncovered, about 25 minutes or until heated through. Let stand for 10 minutes before serving.

Makes 8 servings.

Per Serving: 314 cal., 13 g total fat (6 g sat. fat), 33 mg chol., 677 mg sodium, 39 g carbo., 6 g fiber, 11 g pro.

SPICED BUTTERNUT SQUASH

To remove seeds and strings from
the butternut squash, use a
melon baller or ice cream scoop.

Prep: 30 minutes   **Roast:** 20 minutes   **Oven:** 450°F

- **1   2-pound butternut squash**
- **3   tablespoons butter, melted**
- **1   teaspoon curry powder, ginger powder, or five-spice powder**
- **Salt**

1 Preheat oven to 450°F. Cut squash in half lengthwise and remove seeds. Peel squash. Cut squash halves into 1- to 1½-inch pieces. Place squash pieces in a 9×13-inch baking dish. In a small bowl combine butter and curry powder. Drizzle over squash, tossing to coat.

2 Roast, uncovered, for 20 to 25 minutes or until tender and lightly browned, stirring once or twice. Serve warm or at room temperature. Season to taste with salt.

Makes 8 servings.

Per Serving: 69 cal., 5 g total fat (2 g sat. fat), 12 mg chol., 36 mg sodium, 7 g carbo., 1 g fiber, 1 g pro.

BUTTERNUT SQUASH GRATIN

Before peeling butternut squash, prick it in several places with a fork and microwave on high for 2 minutes— the skin will come off much more easily.

Prep: 45 minutes Bake: 20 minutes Oven: 375°F

- 3 ounces pancetta or bacon, chopped
- 3½ pounds butternut squash, peeled, seeded, and chopped (8 cups)
- 1 cup chopped onion (1 large)
- ½ teaspoon salt
- ¼ teaspoon black pepper
- 1 5- to 6-ounce package fresh baby spinach
- 2 tablespoons butter
- 2 tablespoons all-purpose flour
- 1⅓ cups half-and-half, light cream, or milk
- 8 ounces Gruyère cheese, shredded (2 cups)
  Nonstick cooking spray

1 Preheat oven to 375°F. In an extra-large skillet cook pancetta on medium heat until crisp. Using a slotted spoon, remove pancetta from skillet and drain on paper towels. If using bacon, drain all but 2 tablespoons drippings from the skillet.

2 Add squash, onion, salt, and pepper to the skillet. Cook, covered, for 12 to 15 minutes or until tender, stirring occasionally. Remove from skillet.

3 Add spinach to the skillet; cook and stir until spinach is wilted. Drain spinach in a colander, squeezing out as much of the excess liquid as possible.

4 For cheese sauce: In a small saucepan melt butter on medium heat. Stir in flour until combined. Add half-and-half all at once. Cook and stir until thickened and bubbly. Add 1½ cups of the Gruyère cheese, stirring until melted.

5 Lightly coat a 9×13-inch baking dish with cooking spray. In a large bowl combine squash, spinach, and pancetta. Add cheese sauce; toss to coat. Spoon into prepared baking dish. Sprinkle with the remaining ½ cup Gruyère cheese. Bake, uncovered, about 20 minutes or until heated through.

Makes 12 servings.

Per Serving: 217 cal., 14 g total fat (7 g sat. fat), 41 mg chol., 329 mg sodium, 17 g carbo., 3 g fiber, 9 g pro.

HERBED ROOT VEGETABLE COBBLER

Rutabagas are often dipped in wax to preserve their freshness. The wax is harmless and will come off easily with a vegetable peeler.

Prep: 45 minutes   Bake: 72 minutes   Stand: 20 minutes   Oven: 400°F

- 1 pound Yukon gold potatoes, cut into 1-inch pieces
- 1 pound rutabaga, peeled and cut into 1-inch pieces
- 4 medium carrots, cut into 1-inch pieces
- 2 medium parsnips, peeled and cut into 1-inch pieces
- 1 small red onion, cut into thin wedges
- 2 cloves garlic, minced
- 1 cup chicken broth
- 1½ teaspoons dried fines herbes, herbes de Provence, or Italian seasoning, crushed
- ½ teaspoon salt
- ¼ teaspoon black pepper
- 1 4- to 5.2-ounce container semisoft cheese with garlic and herbs
- 1 recipe Herbed Parmesan Dumplings

1 Preheat oven to 400°F. In a 9×13-inch baking dish combine potatoes, rutabaga, carrots, parsnips, onion, and garlic.

2 In a small bowl combine broth, fines herbes, salt, and pepper. Pour over vegetables, stirring to coat. Cover with foil. Bake about 1 hour or until vegetables are nearly tender. Carefully uncover vegetables;* stir in semisoft cheese.

3 Drop Herbed Parmesan Dumplings into 12 mounds on top of hot vegetables. Bake, uncovered, for 12 to 15 minutes more or until a toothpick inserted in centers of dumplings comes out clean. Let stand for 20 minutes before serving.

Makes 12 servings.

Per Serving: 235 cal., 11 g total fat [6 g sat. fat], 61 mg chol., 424 mg sodium, 29 g carbo., 4 g fiber, 6 g pro.

Herbed Parmesan Dumplings: *In a medium bowl stir together 1½ cups all-purpose flour; 2 teaspoons baking powder; 1½ teaspoons dried fines herbes, herbes de Provence, or Italian seasoning, crushed; and ½ teaspoon salt. Using a pastry blender, cut in 6 tablespoons butter until mixture resembles coarse crumbs. Stir in ¼ cup finely shredded Parmesan cheese [1 ounce]. In a small bowl use a fork to lightly beat together 2 eggs and ⅓ cup milk. Add all at once to flour mixture, stirring just until moistened.*

---

*Note: *Be sure to uncover the vegetables so the steam escapes away from you.*

ZUCCHINI AND EGGPLANT BAKE

This cheese-and-veggie-packed casserole delivers Italian flavors in style.

Prep: 35 minutes **Bake:** 20 minutes **Stand:** 10 minutes **Oven:** 350°F

4	cups thinly sliced zucchini (3 medium)
2	cups coarsely chopped sweet red peppers (2 large)
1	cup coarsely chopped onion (1 large)
5	cups coarsely chopped, peeled eggplant (1 medium)
2	cloves garlic, minced
½	teaspoon salt
¼	teaspoon black pepper
3	tablespoons olive oil
4	eggs
½	cup light mayonnaise
4	ounces Pecorino-Romano cheese, grated (1 cup)
1	8-ounce package shredded mozzarella cheese (2 cups)
12	rich round crackers, crushed (about ⅔ cup)

1 Preheat oven to 350°F. Grease 9×13-inch baking dish; set aside. In a large skillet cook zucchini, sweet peppers, onion, eggplant, garlic, salt, and black pepper in hot oil on medium-high heat for 10 to 15 minutes or until vegetables are tender, stirring occasionally.

2 Meanwhile, in an extra-large bowl whisk together eggs and mayonnaise until combined. Stir in Pecorino-Romano cheese and half of the mozzarella cheese. Add cooked vegetables; toss to combine. Spread vegetable mixture evenly in prepared baking dish. Top with the remaining mozzarella cheese and the cracker crumbs.

3 Bake, uncovered, for 20 to 25 minutes or until top is lightly browned and knife inserted near center comes out clean. Let stand for 10 minutes before serving.

Makes 6 to 8 servings.

Per Serving: 440 cal., 32 g total fat (11 g sat. fat), 188 mg chol., 942 mg sodium, 21 g carbo., 5 g fiber, 23 g pro.

187

LEEK AND ROOT VEGETABLE GRATIN

When choosing leeks, go for
the small ones—they tend to be
sweeter than the large ones.

Prep: 35 minutes   **Bake:** 55 minutes   **Stand:** 10 minutes   **Oven:** 350°F/400°F

- 8 ounces mild cheddar cheese or Muenster cheese, shredded (2 cups)
- 1 tablespoon finely snipped fresh herbs (such as parsley, thyme, chives, sage, and/or chervil)
- 1 tablespoon olive oil
- 3 large turnips or rutabagas, peeled and thinly sliced (about 1 pound)
- 1 pound russet potatoes, thinly sliced
- 6 medium thinly sliced leeks (2 cups)
- 1 pound parsnips, peeled and thinly sliced
- 1½ pounds sweet potatoes, peeled and thinly sliced
- Salt
- Freshly ground black pepper
- Assorted fresh herbs (optional)

1 Preheat oven to 350°F. In a small bowl toss together cheese and the 1 tablespoon snipped herbs; set aside. Coat a 9×13-inch baking dish with the olive oil.

2 In the prepared baking dish layer half of each sliced vegetable in the following order, sprinkling salt, pepper, and 3 to 4 tablespoons of the cheese mixture between layers: turnips, russet potatoes, leeks, parsnips, and sweet potatoes. Repeat layers, reserving the remaining cheese mixture.

3 Cover with foil. Bake for 40 to 50 minutes or until vegetables are nearly tender. Sprinkle with the remaining cheese mixture. Increase oven temperature to 400°F. Bake, uncovered, about 15 minutes more or until cheese melts and is starting to brown.

4 Let stand for 10 minutes before serving. If desired, sprinkle with additional fresh herbs.

Makes 8 to 10 servings.

Per Serving: 309 cal., 11 g total fat (6 g sat. fat), 27 mg chol., 422 mg sodium, 44 g carbo., 8 g fiber, 11 g pro.

CHORIZO CORN BREAD STUFFING

To kick this superlative stuffing up
another notch, combine the fennel and apple,
using equal amounts of each.

Prep: 40 minutes   **Bake:** 45 minutes   **Oven:** 350°F

15 to 16 ounces uncooked chorizo sausage, casings removed if present

½ cup butter

2 cups chopped onions (2 large)

2 medium fennel bulbs, trimmed, cored, and cut into thin wedges (reserve feathery tops for garnish), or 2 large apples, cored and chopped (2 cups)

¾ cup chopped celery

2 cloves garlic, minced

1 16-ounce package corn bread stuffing mix

1 cup dry-roasted salted pistachio nuts

¾ cup dried cranberries

2 eggs, lightly beaten

1 14-ounce can reduced-sodium chicken broth

1 Preheat oven to 350°F. Grease a 9×13-inch baking pan or baking dish; set aside. In a large skillet cook sausage until cooked through, stirring to break up sausage as it cooks. Drain off fat. Transfer sausage to an extra-large bowl. Set aside.

2 Carefully wipe out skillet. Melt butter in the skillet on medium heat. Add onions, fennel (if using), celery, and garlic. Cook for 10 to 15 minutes or until tender, stirring occasionally. Add apple (if using). Cook and stir for 2 minutes more.

3 Add onion mixture, stuffing mix, nuts, and cranberries to sausage in bowl; toss to combine. In a medium bowl combine eggs and broth. Drizzle broth mixture over onion-stuffing mixture to moisten, tossing lightly to combine. (For moister stuffing, add ½ cup water.) Spoon into prepared baking pan or dish.

4 Cover with foil. Bake for 35 minutes. Uncover. Bake for 10 to 15 minutes more or until heated through and top is light brown. (Stuffing is done when an instant-read thermometer inserted in center of stuffing mixture registers 165°F.) If desired, garnish with fennel tops.

Makes 12 servings.

Per Serving: 504 cal., 30 g total fat (11 g sat. fat), 356 mg chol., 1,054 mg sodium, 42 g carbo., 3 g fiber, 17 g pro.

CAROLINA LOW COUNTRY DRESSING

**Although safe to eat and available
year 'round, oystersare always best in the
winter months, when waters are cold.**

Prep: 45 minutes   **Bake:** 1 hour   **Oven:** 350°F

- 1 **pint shucked oysters**
- ½ **cup butter**
- 1 **stalk celery, chopped (½ cup)**
- 1 **medium onion, chopped (½ cup)**
- 1 **teaspoon dried sage, crushed**
- ½ **teaspoon salt**
- ½ **teaspoon black pepper**
- 8 **cups crumbled corn bread***
- 6 **2¼-inch baked flaky biscuits, torn into bite-size pieces (about 3 cups)**
- 1 **cup cooked white or brown rice**
- 2 **eggs, lightly beaten**
- ½ **to 1 cup chicken broth**

1 | Preheat oven to 350°F. Drain oysters; reserving liquid. Coarsely chop oysters; set aside.

2 | In a large skillet melt butter on medium heat. Add celery, onion, sage, salt, and pepper; cook about 5 minutes or until tender. Add chopped oysters; cook and stir for 2 minutes more.

3 | In an extra-large bowl combine corn bread, biscuits, rice, oyster mixture, and eggs. Toss just until combined. Drizzle with reserved oyster liquid and enough broth to moisten, tossing lightly to combine. Spoon into a 9×13-inch baking dish.

4 | Cover with foil. Bake for 45 minutes. Uncover. Bake about 15 minutes more or until heated through and light brown. (Stuffing is done when an instant-read thermometer inserted in center of stuffing mixture registers 170°F.)

Makes 16 servings.

Per Serving: 319 cal., 14 g total fat (6 g sat. fat), 90 mg chol., 808 mg sodium, 39 g carbo., 2 g fiber, 9 g pro.

---

*Note: *To make 8 cups of crumbled corn bread, prepare and bake two 8.5-ounce packages corn bread according to package directions.*

SMOKED ALMOND AND ONION BAKE

This bacon- and cheese-enhanced
onion custard reaches silken perfection
while it bakes in a crispy almond crust.

Prep: 45 minutes   **Bake:** 30 minutes   **Cool:** 15 minutes   **Oven:** 350°F

- 1 cup smoke-flavor whole almonds
- 1 cup all-purpose flour
- ½ cup butter
- 1 teaspoon water
- 6 slices bacon, chopped
- 3 large onions, halved and sliced (5 cups)
- ½ cup sliced green onions (4)
- 4 eggs, beaten
- 2 cups milk
- 1 8-ounce package shredded Swiss cheese (2 cups)
- ½ teaspoon salt
- ¼ teaspoon black pepper
- ¼ teaspoon ground nutmeg
- 2 cups shredded romaine or fresh spinach
- 2 tablespoons bottled balsamic vinaigrette

1 Preheat oven to 350°F. For crust: Place almonds in a food processor. Cover and process until finely ground. Add flour; process until combined. Add butter. Cover and process with several on/off turns until mixture resembles coarse crumbs. Add the water; cover and process with on/off turns until mixture holds together.

2 Press almond mixture evenly into a 9×13-inch baking dish. Bake, uncovered, for 12 minutes. Transfer to a wire rack.

3 Meanwhile, in a large skillet cook bacon until crisp. Using a slotted spoon, transfer cooked bacon to paper towels, reserving 2 tablespoons drippings in skillet. Add sliced onions to skillet. Cook, covered, on medium-low heat for 20 minutes, stirring occasionally. Uncover. Cook for 5 minutes more. Remove from heat; stir in green onions.

4 Spoon onion mixture evenly over crust. Sprinkle with cooked bacon. In a large bowl combine eggs, milk, cheese, salt, pepper, and nutmeg; pour evenly over onion-bacon layers.

5 Bake, uncovered, about 30 minutes or until top is light brown and egg mixture is just set. Let cool on a wire rack for 15 minutes. Cut into rectangles to serve. In a medium bowl toss romaine with vinaigrette; spoon some on top of each serving.

Makes 8 servings.

Per Serving: 486 cal., 34 g total fat (15 g sat. fat), 172 mg chol., 599 mg sodium, 27 g carbo., 3 g fiber, 20 g pro.

ROASTED VEGETABLE SALAD

Grilling enthusiasts enjoy firing up the coals well after the summer season wanes. This recipe is perfect for fall grilling, served alongside your favorite meat.

Prep: 20 minutes **Roast:** 40 minutes **Oven:** 425°F

- 1 pound tiny new potatoes
- 1 recipe Fresh Herb Vinaigrette
- 8 ounces fresh asparagus spears
- ¾ cup grape tomatoes
- 6 cups mixed salad greens (such as small romaine, radicchio, arugula, or leaf lettuce)
- 2 ounces thinly sliced prosciutto, cut into strips
- 1 ounce Asiago cheese, shaved

1 Preheat oven to 425°F. Scrub potatoes thoroughly; cut in half. In a 9×13-inch baking pan toss potatoes with 2 tablespoons of the Fresh Herb Vinaigrette.

2 Roast, uncovered, for 30 minutes, stirring once halfway through roasting.

3 Meanwhile, wash asparagus. Break off woody bases where spears snap easily. Add the asparagus, tomatoes, and another 2 tablespoons of the Fresh Herb Vinaigrette to the pan with the potatoes. Roast, uncovered, for 10 minutes more, stirring once.

4 To serve, arrange salad greens on a large platter. Arrange potatoes, asparagus, and tomatoes on top. Top with strips of prosciutto and shaved Asiago cheese. Serve with the remaining Fresh Herb Vinaigrette.

Makes 6 servings.

Per Serving: 199 cal., 12 g total fat (3 g sat. fat), 12 mg chol., 404 mg sodium, 17 g carbo., 3 g fiber, 7 g pro.

194

Fresh Herb Vinaigrette: *In a screw-top jar combine ¼ cup olive oil; ¼ cup white wine vinegar; 1 tablespoon finely chopped red onion; 1 tablespoon snipped fresh herbs (such as thyme, basil, and/or oregano); 1 clove garlic, minced; ¼ teaspoon Dijon mustard; ¼ teaspoon kosher salt; and ⅛ teaspoon black pepper. Cover and shake well.*

ROASTED ASPARAGUS-CANNELLINI BEAN SALAD

This light and lovely salad would make a wonderful main dish too. Add toasted garlic bread and you're good to go.

Prep: 20 minutes   Roast: 12 minutes   Chill: 2 hours   Oven: 400°F

12 ounces fresh asparagus spears, trimmed and cut into 1½-inch pieces

3 tablespoons olive oil

1 clove garlic, minced

1 19-ounce can cannellini beans (white kidney beans), rinsed and drained

¾ cup chopped sweet red pepper (1 medium)

¼ cup chopped red onion

2 tablespoons snipped fresh basil

3 tablespoons balsamic vinegar

4 teaspoons toasted sesame oil

1 tablespoon Dijon mustard

¼ teaspoon salt

¼ teaspoon black pepper

4 cups mixed baby greens or mesclun

1 tablespoon sesame seeds, toasted

1 Preheat oven to 400°F. Spread asparagus in a 9×13-inch baking pan. Drizzle with 1 tablespoon of the olive oil and the garlic; toss to coat. Roast, uncovered, for 12 minutes, stirring once halfway through roasting time.

2 In a large bowl combine asparagus, cannellini beans, sweet pepper, onion, and basil.

3 In a screw-top jar combine the remaining 2 tablespoons olive oil, the balsamic vinegar, sesame oil, mustard, salt, and black pepper. Cover and shake well to combine. Add to asparagus mixture; toss to coat. Cover and chill about 2 hours or until well chilled.

4 To serve, spread greens on a serving platter. Top with asparagus mixture. Sprinkle with toasted sesame seeds.

Makes 4 to 6 servings.

Per Serving: 271 cal., 16 g total fat (2 g sat. fat), 0 mg chol., 452 mg sodium, 29 g carbo., 9 g fiber, 11 g pro.

DINNER ROLLS

Brushing the rolls with melted butter after
you remove them from the oven gives
them a soft, shiny crust.

Prep: 45 minutes **Rise:** 1½ hours **Rest:** 10 minutes **Bake:** 20 minutes **Oven:** 375°F

4½ to 5 cups all-purpose flour
1 package active dry yeast
1 cup milk
⅓ cup sugar
⅓ cup butter, margarine, or shortening
1 teaspoon salt
2 eggs

1 In a large bowl stir together 2 cups of the flour and the yeast. In a small saucepan heat and stir milk, sugar, butter, and salt just until warm (120°F to 130°F) and butter almost melts; add to flour mixture along with eggs. Beat with an electric mixer on low to medium for 30 seconds, scraping sides of bowl constantly. Beat on high for 3 minutes. Using a wooden spoon, stir in as much of the remaining flour as you can.

2 Turn out dough onto a lightly floured surface. Knead in enough of the remaining flour to make a moderately stiff dough that is smooth and elastic (6 to 8 minutes total). Shape dough into a ball. Place in a greased bowl; turn once to grease surface. Cover; let rise in a warm place until double in size (about 1 hour).

3 Punch down dough. Turn out dough onto a lightly floured surface. Divide dough in half. Cover; let rest for 10 minutes. Meanwhile, lightly grease a 9×13-inch baking pan.

4 Shape dough into 24 balls. Place dough balls in prepared baking pan. Cover and let rise in a warm place until nearly double in size (about 30 minutes).

5 Meanwhile, preheat oven to 375°F. Bake, uncovered, about 20 minutes or until golden brown. Immediately invert pan onto a wire rack. Lift off pan. Cool rolls on the wire rack.

Makes 24 rolls.

Per Roll: 132 cal., 4 g total fat (2 g sat. fat), 26 mg chol., 127 mg sodium, 21 g carbo., 1 g fiber, 3 g pro.

197

CHEDDAR-CORN BREAD ROLLS

These yummy rolls—spiked with nuggets of cheddar and crunchy cornmeal— start with a hot roll mix.

Prep: 10 minutes   Rest: 5 minutes   Rise: 20 minutes   Bake: 20 minutes   Oven: 375°F

- 1 **16-ounce package hot roll mix**
- 1 **cup shredded cheddar cheese, Monterey Jack cheese, or Monterey Jack cheese with jalapeños (4 ounces)**
- ⅓ **cup cornmeal**
- 1¼ **cups hot water (120°F to 130°F)**
- 2 **tablespoons olive oil**
- 1 **egg, lightly beaten**
  Milk
  Cornmeal

1 In a large bowl stir together the flour from the hot roll mix, the contents of the yeast packet, the cheese, and the ⅓ cup cornmeal. Add the hot water, oil, and egg; stir until combined.

2 Turn out dough onto a well-floured surface. Knead dough about 5 minutes or until smooth and elastic. Cover and let rest for 5 minutes. Lightly grease a 9×13-inch baking pan; set aside.

3 Shape dough into 15 balls. Place dough balls in prepared baking pan. Cover and let rise in a warm place for 20 minutes.

4 Meanwhile, preheat oven to 375°F. Brush rolls with milk and sprinkle with additional cornmeal. Bake, uncovered, for 20 to 22 minutes or until golden brown.

Makes 15 rolls.

Per Roll: 176 cal., 5 g total fat (2 g sat. fat), 22 mg chol., 228 mg sodium, 26 g carbo., 0 g fiber, 7 g pro.

TWO-TONE BALSAMIC-ONION
SPIRAL ROLLS

These amazingly easy beauties look like they rolled off the rolling pin of an expert baker. Without much work, that expert baker can be you.

Prep: 35 minutes **Rise:** 45 minutes **Bake:** 25 minutes **Cool:** 15 minutes **Oven:** 375°F

- 2 slices bacon
- 2 cups chopped onions (2 large)
- ¼ cup balsamic vinegar
- ½ cup grated Parmesan cheese
- ¼ teaspoon black pepper
- 1 1-pound loaf frozen white bread dough, thawed
- 1 1-pound loaf frozen whole wheat bread dough, thawed
- 1 egg yolk, lightly beaten
- 1 tablespoon milk

1 Grease a 9×13-inch baking pan; set aside. In a large skillet cook bacon until crisp. Using a slotted spoon, transfer bacon to paper towels, reserving drippings in skillet. Crumble bacon and set aside. Add onions to skillet; cook on medium heat about 5 minutes or until tender. Carefully stir in balsamic vinegar. Simmer, uncovered, on medium-low heat for 1 to 2 minutes or until most of the liquid has evaporated. Remove from heat. Stir in Parmesan cheese and pepper. Cool completely.

2 Meanwhile, on a lightly floured surface roll each loaf of bread dough into a 10×16-inch rectangle. Spread onion mixture over white dough rectangle; sprinkle with bacon. Top with wheat dough rectangle. Starting from a long side, roll up rectangles together. Seal seam. Slice roll crosswise into 16 pieces. Place pieces, cut sides down, in prepared baking pan.

3 Cover loosely and let rise in a warm place until nearly double in size (about 45 minutes). Meanwhile, preheat oven to 375°F. In a small bowl beat together egg yolk and milk; brush over rolls.

4 Bake, uncovered, about 25 minutes or until roll tops are light brown. Invert rolls onto a wire rack. Lift off pan. Cool for 15 minutes. Invert again onto a serving platter. Serve warm.

Makes 16 rolls.

Per Roll: 189 cal., 4 g total fat (1 g sat. fat), 18 mg chol., 237 mg sodium, 29 g carbo., 1 g fiber, 7 g pro.

HOME RUN GARLIC ROLLS

Brush the butter mixture over the unbaked rolls gently so they don't deflate.

Prep: 20 minutes   Rise: 1½ hours   Bake: 15 minutes   Oven: 350°F

- 1   **16-ounce package frozen white or whole wheat bread dough, thawed**
- 1   **tablespoon butter, melted**
- 2   **cloves garlic, minced**
- 2   **tablespoons grated Parmesan cheese**

1 Lightly grease a 9×13-inch baking pan; set aside. Shape dough into 24 balls. Place dough balls in prepared baking pan. Cover and let rise in a warm place until nearly double in size (1½ to 2 hours).

2 Preheat oven to 350°F. In a small bowl stir together melted butter and garlic. Brush butter mixture over rolls. Sprinkle with Parmesan cheese. Bake, uncovered, for 15 to 20 minutes or until golden brown. Immediately invert pan onto a wire rack. Lift off pan. Cool rolls slightly on the wire rack. Serve warm.

Makes 24 rolls.

Per Roll: 55 cal., 1 g total fat (0 g sat. fat), 2 mg chol., 99 mg sodium, 9 g carbo., 0 g fiber, 1 g pro.

CORN BREAD WITH TOMATO-BACON RIBBON

Corn muffin mix comes to
the rescue, allowing you to easily make
this impressive bread.

Prep: 25 minutes   Bake: 35 minutes   Cool: 15 minutes   Oven: 375°F

Nonstick cooking spray

1 8-ounce package cream cheese, softened

2 tablespoons butter, softened

2 tablespoons cornstarch

1/2 teaspoon black pepper

2 eggs

1/4 cup milk

4 slices bacon, crisp-cooked, drained, and crumbled

1/4 cup oil-pack dried tomatoes, drained and chopped

2 8.5-ounce packages corn muffin mix

1 Preheat oven to 375°F. Lightly coat a 9×13-inch baking pan with cooking spray; set aside.

2 In a medium bowl beat cream cheese, butter, cornstarch, and pepper with an electric mixer on medium until smooth. Beat in eggs and milk until combined. Stir in bacon and tomatoes; set aside.

3 In a large bowl prepare corn muffin mixes according to package directions. Spread about two-thirds of the batter into prepared baking pan. Pour cream cheese mixture evenly over batter in pan. Drop the remaining batter in small mounds over cream cheese mixture.

4 Bake, uncovered, about 35 minutes or until top springs back when lightly touched. Cool in pan on a wire rack for 15 to 20 minutes before serving. Serve warm.

Makes 12 to 15 servings.

Per Serving: 290 cal., 16 g total fat (7 g sat. fat), 65 mg chol., 597 mg sodium, 31 g carbo., 3 g fiber, 7 g pro.

BROWNIES & BARS

Baked from batter and scored into squares, brownies and bars bundle family-favored fare, one-pan simplicity, and blissfully easy preparation into one sweet little package. You'll find the perfect treat for any occasion here, and whatever variety you decide to bake—chock-full of chocolate, studded with nuts, or filled with fruit—you'll be on your way to packing a whole lot of pleasure into one pan.

ORANGE-KISSED CHOCOLATE BROWNIES

The combination of chocolate and orange is popular in Italian cuisine. Be sure to shred the orange peel before you squeeze the juice for this recipe.

Prep: 30 minutes **Bake:** 25 minutes **Chill:** 30 minutes **Oven:** 350°F

- 4   eggs
- 2   cups sugar
- 1¼ cups all-purpose flour
- 1   cup unsweetened Dutch-process cocoa powder
- 1   cup butter, melted
- 1   recipe Orange Butter Frosting
- 4   ounces semisweet chocolate, chopped
- ½   cup butter
- 2   tablespoons light-color corn syrup

1 Preheat oven to 350°F. Line a 9×13-inch baking pan with foil, extending foil over edges of pan. Lightly grease foil; set pan aside. In a large bowl combine eggs and sugar. Beat with an electric mixer on medium for 3 to 5 minutes or until mixture is pale yellow and thickened. In a small bowl stir together flour and cocoa powder. Add flour mixture to egg mixture, beating just until smooth. Stir in 1 cup melted butter until combined. Spread batter evenly in prepared baking pan.

2 Bake, uncovered, for 25 to 30 minutes or until a toothpick inserted near the center comes out clean. Cool in pan on a wire rack.

3 Spread brownies with Orange Butter Frosting. Cover and chill for 30 minutes.

4 Meanwhile, in a medium saucepan combine semisweet chocolate and ½ cup butter. Cook and stir over low heat until melted. Remove from heat. Stir in corn syrup. Cool for 15 minutes.

5 Slowly pour chocolate mixture over frosted brownies. Tilt pan gently to spread chocolate over the entire top. Chill until chocolate is set. Using edges of foil, lift brownies out of pan. Cut into bars.

Makes 32 brownies.

Per Brownie: 244 cal., 12 g total fat (7 g sat. fat), 53 mg chol., 82 mg sodium, 34 g carbo., 1 g fiber, 2 g pro.

Orange Butter Frosting: *In a large bowl combine ¼ cup softened butter and 1 teaspoon finely shredded orange peel. Beat with an electric mixer on medium until smooth. Add 1 cup powdered sugar and 1 tablespoon orange juice, beating well. Beat in 2½ cups additional powdered sugar and 1 to 2 tablespoons additional orange juice to make a frosting of spreading consistency.*

PEANUT BUTTER BROWNIE BITES

These bodacious, mix-based
bites are bound to be
bake sale best sellers.

Prep: 20 minutes **Bake:** 30 minutes **Cool:** 1 hour **Oven:** 350°F

1 **18- to 21-ounce package fudge brownie mix**

½ **cup chopped peanuts (optional)**

1 **cup creamy peanut butter**

1 **3-ounce package cream cheese, softened**

1 **egg yolk**

2 **tablespoons milk**

1 **16-ounce can chocolate frosting**

Chopped peanuts (optional)

206

1 Preheat oven to 350°F. Lightly grease a 9×13-inch baking pan; set aside. Prepare brownie mix according to package directions. If desired, stir in ½ cup chopped peanuts. Spread batter evenly in prepared baking pan.

2 In a medium bowl combine ½ cup of the peanut butter, the cream cheese, egg yolk, and milk. Beat with an electric mixer on medium until smooth. Spoon mixture into a decorating bag fitted with a small round tip (or spoon it into a resealable plastic bag and snip off one corner of the bag). Pipe mixture over batter.

3 Bake, uncovered, for 30 minutes. Cool in pan on a wire rack for 1 hour.

4 In a medium bowl combine frosting and the remaining ½ cup peanut butter. Spread over brownies. If desired, sprinkle with additional peanuts. Cut into small bars.

Makes 64 brownies.

Per Brownie: 101 cal., 6 g total fat (1 g sat. fat), 10 mg chol., 73 mg sodium, 11 g carbo., 0 g fiber, 2 g pro.

CHOCOLATE-CHIPOTLE BROWNIES

Chipotle chile powder—ground from smoke-dried
jalapeño chiles—adds depth of flavor
with just a touch of heat to these brownies.

Prep: 25 minutes   **Bake:** 35 minutes   **Oven:** 325°F

8   ounces semisweet chocolate, chopped

1   cup butter

2   cups all-purpose flour

¼   cup unsweetened Dutch-process cocoa powder

2½   cups sugar

1   tablespoon instant espresso coffee powder or instant coffee crystals

1½   teaspoons ground cinnamon

1   to 2 teaspoons ground chipotle chile

2   teaspoons vanilla

6   eggs

Unsweetened Dutch-process cocoa powder

1 Preheat oven to 325°F. Line a 9×13-inch baking pan with foil, extending foil over edges of pan. Grease foil; set pan aside. In a small saucepan combine chocolate and butter. Cook and stir over low heat until melted. Cool slightly. In a small bowl combine flour and ¼ cup cocoa powder; set aside.

2 In a large bowl combine sugar, coffee powder, cinnamon, and ground chipotle chile. Add chocolate mixture and vanilla. Beat with an electric mixer on medium for 1 minute, scraping sides of bowl occasionally. Add eggs, 1 at a time, beating on low just until combined. Add flour mixture, ½ cup at a time, beating after each addition just until combined. Beat on medium for 1 minute more. Spread batter evenly in prepared baking pan.

3 Bake, uncovered, for 35 to 40 minutes or until edges start to pull away from sides of pan. Cool in pan on a wire rack. Using edges of foil, lift brownies out of pan. Cut into bars. Sift additional cocoa powder over tops of brownies.

Makes 32 brownies.

Per Brownie: 194 cal., 9 g total fat (5 g sat. fat), 55 mg chol., 55 mg sodium, 26 g carbo., 1 g fiber, 3 g pro.

CARAMEL-HAZELNUT BROWNIES

These dreamy delights feature three luscious
layers: fudgy brownie, hazelnut-flecked caramel,
and a topping of satiny dark chocolate.

Prep: 30 minutes **Bake:** 45 minutes **Oven:** 350°F

- 3 cups all-purpose flour
- 1½ cups unsweetened cocoa powder
- 2 teaspoons baking powder
- 1 teaspoon salt
- 2⅔ cups sugar
- 1½ cups butter, melted
- 4 eggs
- 2 teaspoons vanilla
- 1 14-ounce package vanilla caramels, unwrapped
- 2 tablespoons milk
- 1 cup hazelnuts (filberts), toasted and chopped
- 2 tablespoons hazelnut liqueur
- 2 cups dark or bittersweet chocolate pieces

1 Preheat oven to 350°F. Line a 9×13-inch baking pan with foil, extending foil over edges of pan. Generously grease foil; set pan aside. In a large bowl stir together flour, cocoa powder, baking power, and salt; set aside.

2 In an extra-large bowl combine sugar and melted butter. Beat with an electric mixer on low until well mixed. Beat in eggs and vanilla until combined. Add flour mixture, ½ cup at a time, beating well after each addition (batter will be thick). Spread batter evenly in prepared baking pan.

3 In a large microwave-safe bowl combine caramels and milk. Microwave, uncovered, on high for 1¼ to 2 minutes or until caramels are melted, stirring every 30 seconds. Stir in ½ cup of the hazelnuts and the liqueur. Drizzle caramel mixture over batter in pan.

4 Bake, uncovered, for 45 minutes. Remove from oven. Immediately sprinkle with chocolate pieces. Let stand about 2 minutes or until chocolate is softened. Spread chocolate evenly over brownies. Sprinkle with the remaining ½ cup hazelnuts.

5 Cool in pan on a wire rack. (If necessary, chill until chocolate is set.) Using edges of foil, lift brownies out of pan. Cut into bars.

Makes 36 brownies.

Per Brownie: 311 cal., 15 g total fat (7 g sat. fat), 45 mg chol., 183 mg sodium, 40 g carbo., 1 g fiber, 4 g pro.

SHORTBREAD BROWNIES

A buttery-rich base topped with a layer of dense chocolate blesses these brownies with striking architectural elements.

Prep: 25 minutes **Bake:** 45 minutes **Oven:** 350°F

2½   cups all-purpose flour
⅓   cup packed brown sugar
¾   cup butter
1¼   cups miniature semisweet chocolate pieces
2   cups granulated sugar
¾   cup unsweetened cocoa powder
2¼   teaspoons baking powder
1   teaspoon salt
5   eggs
½   cup butter, melted
1   tablespoon vanilla

1 Preheat oven to 350°F. Line a 9×13-inch baking pan with foil, extending foil over edges of pan; set aside. For crust: In a medium bowl stir together 1½ cups of the flour and the brown sugar. Cut in ¾ cup butter until mixture resembles coarse crumbs. Stir in ½ cup of the chocolate pieces. Press dough evenly into prepared pan. Bake, uncovered, for 10 minutes.

2 Meanwhile, in a large bowl stir together granulated sugar, the remaining 1 cup flour, the cocoa powder, baking powder, and salt. Add eggs, the ½ cup melted butter, and vanilla; beat by hand until smooth. Stir in the remaining ¾ cup chocolate pieces. Carefully spoon over crust in pan, spreading evenly.

3 Bake, uncovered, for 35 minutes more. Cool in pan on a wire rack. Using edges of foil, lift brownies out of pan. Cut into bars.

Makes 36 brownies.

Per Brownie: 180 cal., 9 g total fat (4 g sat. fat), 44 mg chol., 121 mg sodium, 23 g carbo., 1 g fiber, 3 g pro.

HAZELNUT SACHER BROWNIES

These fruit-and nut-embellished brownies are adapted from the Sachertorte, a classic Viennese pastry created in the 19th century.

Prep: 30 minutes **Bake:** 32 minutes **Chill:** 20 minutes **Oven:** 350°F

- ¾ cup powdered sugar
- ½ cup butter, softened
- ¾ cup all-purpose flour
- ½ cup hazelnuts (fliberts), toasted and finely ground
- ¾ cup apricot preserves
- ½ cup butter
- 3 ounces unsweetened chocolate, cut up
- 1 egg
- 1 egg yolk
- 1 cup granulated sugar
- ¼ teaspoon salt
- 1 teaspoon vanilla
- ½ cup all-purpose flour
- 3 ounces semisweet chocolate, melted
- 1 ounce white baking chocolate, melted

1 Preheat oven to 350°F. Line a 9×13-inch baking pan with foil, extending foil over edges of pan. Grease foil; set pan aside.

2 For crust: In a small bowl beat powdered sugar and ½ cup softened butter with an electric mixer on medium to high until combined. Beat in the ¾ cup flour and the ground nuts. Press crust evenly into prepared baking pan. Bake, uncovered, for 12 minutes. Cool in pan on a wire rack.

3 Place preserves in a blender or food processor. Cover and blend or process until smooth. Spread preserves over baked crust. Chill for 20 minutes.

4 Meanwhile, in a small saucepan combine ½ cup butter and the unsweetened chocolate. Cook and stir on low heat until melted. Cool slightly. In a medium bowl combine egg, egg yolk, granulated sugar, and salt. Beat with an electric mixer on medium for 5 minutes. Beat in melted unsweetened chocolate and vanilla. Stir in the ½ cup flour. Carefully spread batter over chilled preserves layer.

5 Bake, uncovered, for 20 minutes more. Cool in pan on a wire rack. Using edges of foil, lift brownies out of pan. Spread brownies with melted semisweet chocolate. Let stand until chocolate is set. Drizzle brownies with melted white chocolate. Let stand until white chocolate is set. Cut into bars.

Makes 48 brownies.

Per Brownie: 116 cal., 7 g total fat (4 g sat. fat), 19 mg chol., 44 mg sodium, 14 g carbo., 1 g fiber, 1 g pro.

CHOCOLATE-BUTTERMILK BROWNIES

This chocolaty dessert—known also as Texas sheet cake or chocolate-buttermilk sheet cake—is so rich and moist, it's a cross between a brownie and a cake.

Prep: 30 minutes **Bake:** 35 minutes **Oven:** 350°F

- 2 cups all-purpose flour
- 2 cups granulated sugar
- 1 teaspoon baking soda
- ¼ teaspoon salt
- 1 cup butter
- 1 cup water
- ⅓ cup unsweetened cocoa powder
- 2 eggs
- ½ cup buttermilk or sour milk
- 1½ teaspoons vanilla
- 1 recipe Chocolate-Buttermilk Frosting

1. Preheat oven to 350°F. Grease a 9×13-inch baking pan; set aside. In a medium bowl stir together flour, granulated sugar, baking soda, and salt; set aside.

2. In a medium saucepan combine butter, the water, and cocoa powder. Bring to boiling, stirring constantly. Add to flour mixture. Beat with an electric mixer on medium until combined. Add eggs, buttermilk, and vanilla. Beat for 1 minute (batter will be thin). Pour batter into prepared baking pan.

3. Bake, uncovered, about 35 minutes or until a toothpick inserted in the center comes out clean.

4. Pour warm Chocolate-Buttermilk Frosting over brownies, spreading evenly. Cool in pan on a wire rack. Cut into bars.

Makes 24 brownies.

Per Brownie: 244 cal., 11 g total fat (6 g sat. fat), 45 mg chol., 193 mg sodium, 35 g carbo., 0 g fiber, 2 g pro.

213

Chocolate-Buttermilk Frosting: *In a medium saucepan combine ¼ cup butter, 3 tablespoons unsweetened cocoa powder, and 3 tablespoons buttermilk or sour milk. Bring to boiling. Remove from heat. Beat in 2 ¼ cups powdered sugar and ½ teaspoon vanilla until smooth. If desired, stir in ¾ cup coarsely chopped toasted pecans.*

COFFEE AND COOKIE BROWNIES

These quick-to-make java-spiked brownies are a perfect choice when you need sweet treats in a hurry.

Prep: 15 minutes **Bake:** 40 minutes **Oven:** 350°F

- 1 **16.5-ounce roll refrigerated sugar cookie dough**
- 2 **eggs, lightly beaten**
- 1 **19.5-ounce package milk chocolate brownie mix**
- ½ **cup vegetable oil**
- ⅓ **cup coffee liqueur or cooled strong coffee**
- 1 **cup semisweet or bittersweet chocolate pieces**

1 Preheat oven to 350°F. Press sugar cookie dough evenly into a 9×13-inch baking pan; set aside.

2 In a large bowl stir together eggs, brownie mix, oil, and liqueur just until combined. Spread over sugar cookie dough. Sprinkle with chocolate pieces.

3 Bake, uncovered, about 40 minutes or until edges are set. Cool in pan on a wire rack. Cut into bars.

Makes 24 brownies.

Per Brownie: 279 cal., 15 g total fat (3 g sat. fat), 23 mg chol., 159 mg sodium, 36 g carbo., 1 g fiber, 3 g pro.

BLONDIES

This recipe calls for lots of brown sugar, which is sold in both light and dark versions. Dark brown sugar will create more richly flavored bars.

Prep: 20 minutes **Bake:** 25 minutes **Oven:** 350°F

- 2 **cups packed brown sugar**
- ²/₃ **cup butter**
- 2 **eggs**
- 2 **teaspoons vanilla**
- 2 **cups all-purpose flour**
- 1 **teaspoon baking powder**
- ¼ **teaspoon baking soda**
- 1½ **cups sliced almonds or broken pecans**

1 | Preheat oven to 350°F. Grease a 9×13-inch baking pan; set aside.

2 | In a medium saucepan combine brown sugar and butter. Cook and stir on medium heat until smooth. Cool slightly. Add eggs, 1 at a time, stirring after each addition just until combined. Stir in vanilla. Stir in flour, baking powder, and baking soda.

3 | Spread batter in prepared baking pan. Sprinkle with nuts. Bake, uncovered, for 25 to 30 minutes or until a toothpick inserted near the center comes out clean. Cool slightly in pan on a wire rack. While warm, cut into bars.

Makes 36 bars.

Per Bar: 129 cal., 6 g total fat (2 g sat. fat), 21 mg chol., 48 mg sodium, 18 g carbo., 1 g fiber, 2 g pro.

Chocolate-Chunk Blondies: *Prepare as directed, except reduce nuts to ¾ cup and stir ¾ cup chopped semisweet or white baking chocolate into batter.*

CARROT SPICE BARS

These inviting bars taste exactly
like carrot cake but offer
whole grain goodness too.

Prep: 25 minutes **Bake:** 25 minutes **Oven:** 350°F

Nonstick cooking spray

- ¾ cup whole wheat flour
- ¾ cup rolled oats
- ½ cup unbleached all-purpose flour
- 1 teaspoon baking powder
- ½ teaspoon ground ginger
- ½ teaspoon ground cinnamon
- ¼ teaspoon baking soda
- ¼ teaspoon salt
- 3 egg whites, lightly beaten
- 2 cups finely shredded carrots
- ¾ cup packed brown sugar
- ½ cup canola or vegetable oil
- ¼ cup honey
- 1 teaspoon vanilla
- ½ cup pecans, toasted and chopped

Sifted powdered sugar

1 Preheat oven to 350°F. Line a 9×13-inch baking pan with foil, extending foil over edges of pan. Lightly coat foil with cooking spray; set pan aside.

2 In a large bowl stir together whole wheat flour, oats, unbleached flour, baking powder, ginger, cinnamon, baking soda, and salt. In a medium bowl stir together egg whites, carrots, brown sugar, oil, honey, vanilla, and pecans. Add carrot mixture to flour mixture, stirring just until combined. Spread batter evenly into prepared baking pan.

3 Bake, uncovered, about 25 minutes or until a toothpick inserted near the center comes out clean. Cool in pan on a wire rack. Using edges of foil, lift uncut bars out of pan. Sprinkle with powdered sugar. Cut into bars.

Makes 28 bars.

Per Bar: 113 cal., 6 g total fat (0 g sat. fat), 0 mg chol., 54 mg sodium, 15 g carbo., 1 g fiber, 2 g pro.

WHOLE WHEAT GINGERBREAD BARS

Prep: 25 minutes **Bake:** 25 minutes **Oven:** 375°F

½ cup shortening

1 cup all-purpose flour

½ cup whole wheat flour

½ cup mild-flavor molasses

½ cup hot water

¼ cup packed brown sugar

1 egg

¾ teaspoon baking powder

¾ teaspoon ground cinnamon

½ teaspoon ground ginger

¼ teaspoon baking soda

¼ teaspoon salt

½ cup chopped walnuts

1 recipe Maple Frosting

1 Preheat the oven to 375°F. Grease a 9×13-inch baking pan; set aside. In a medium bowl beat shortening with an electric mixer on medium to high for 30 seconds. Add all-purpose flour, whole wheat flour, molasses, hot water, brown sugar, egg, baking powder, cinnamon, ginger, baking soda, and salt. Beat until combined, scraping side of bowl occasionally. Stir in walnuts.

2 Spread batter evenly in prepared baking pan. Bake, uncovered, about 25 minutes or until a toothpick inserted in the center comes out clean. Cool in pan on a wire rack. Spread with Maple Frosting. Cut into bars.

Makes 36 bars.

Per Bar: 149 cal., 6 g total fat (2 g sat. fat), 10 mg chol., 47 mg sodium, 24 g carbo., 0 g fiber, 1 g pro.

Maple Frosting: *In a large bowl beat ⅓ cup softened butter with an electric mixer on medium until fluffy. Gradually beat in 2 cups powdered sugar. Beat in ¼ cup milk and ½ teaspoon maple flavoring. Gradually beat in 2½ cups additional powdered sugar. If necessary, beat in additional milk, 1 teaspoon at a time, to make a frosting of spreading consistency.*

FRESH STRAWBERRY BARS

The rich peanut butter base for
these super-stunning berry-topped bars
can be made ahead and frozen.

Prep: 25 minutes   **Bake:** 25 minutes   **Oven:** 350°F

- ³/₄ cup butter, softened
- ³/₄ cup peanut butter
- 1 cup packed brown sugar
- ½ cup granulated sugar
- 2 teaspoons baking powder
- ¼ teaspoon salt
- 2 eggs
- 1 teaspoon vanilla
- 2¼ cups all-purpose flour
- ½ cup strawberry jam
- 4 cups small whole fresh strawberries, halved or quartered
- Snipped fresh mint (optional)

1 Heat oven to 350°F. Line a 9×13-inch baking pan with foil, extending foil over edges of pan; set aside.

2 In large bowl combine butter and peanut butter; beat on medium to high for 30 seconds. Beat in brown sugar, granulated sugar, baking powder, and salt until combined. Add eggs and vanilla; beat until combined. Beat in as much of the flour as you can with mixer. Using a wooden spoon, stir in any remaining flour.

3 Spread dough in prepared baking pan. Bake, uncovered, about 25 minutes or until top is lightly browned and a toothpick inserted near center comes out clean.

4 Cool in pan on a wire rack. Using edges of foil, lift uncut bars out of pan. Spread jam over uncut bars; top with berries. Cut into bars. Serve immediately or chill for up to 6 hours. Before serving, if desired, sprinkle with a little snipped fresh mint.

Makes 24 bars.

Per Bar: 225 cal., 10 g total fat (5 g sat. fat), 33 mg chol., 143 mg sodium, 30 g carbo., 1 g fiber, 4 g pro.

220

CHERRY REVEL BARS

If fresh cherries are not available,
you may substitute 10 ounces frozen
sweet cherries, thawed and drained.

Prep: 35 minutes   **Bake:** 25 minutes   **Chill:** 2 hours   **Oven:** 350°F

1	cup butter, softened
2½	cups packed brown sugar
½	teaspoon baking soda
¼	teaspoon salt
4	eggs
1½	teaspoons vanilla
2½	cups all-purpose flour
1½	cups quick-cooking rolled oats
6	ounces bittersweet chocolate, chopped
2	cups sweet cherries (such as Bing or Royal Ann), pitted
½	cup slivered almonds, toasted and coarsely chopped

1 Preheat oven to 350°F. Line a 9×13-inch baking pan with foil, extending foil over edges of pan; set aside. In a large bowl beat ½ cup of the butter with an electric mixer on medium to high for 30 seconds. Add 1 cup of the brown sugar, the baking soda, and salt. Beat until combined, scraping sides of bowl occasionally. Beat in 1 of the eggs and ½ teaspoon of the vanilla until combined. Beat or stir in 1¼ cups of the flour. Stir in oats.

2 For filling: In a medium saucepan combine the remaining butter and the remaining brown sugar. Cook and stir on medium heat until smooth; cool slightly. Stir in the remaining eggs and the remaining vanilla. Stir in the remaining flour and the chocolate.

3 Reserve ¾ cup of the oat mixture for topping. Press the remaining mixture evenly into prepared baking pan. Spread with filling; top with cherries. Crumble the reserved ¾ cup oat mixture evenly over layers in pan; sprinkle with almonds.

4 Bake, uncovered, about 25 minutes or until top is lightly browned (filling will still look moist). Cool in pan on a wire rack. Cover and chill for at least 2 hours. Using edges of foil, lift uncut bars out of pan. Cut into bars.

Makes 25 bars.

Per Bar: 280 cal., 13 g total fat (6 g sat. fat), 54 mg chol., 124 mg sodium, 40 g carbo., 2 g fiber, 4 g pro.

223

TOFFEE BARS

Don't forget the salt! Even though the amount is small, it plays a big role in bringing out the toffee flavor in these bars.

Prep: 15 minutes   **Bake:** 15 minutes   **Oven:** 350°F

½   **cup butter, softened**

1   **egg**

¾   **cup packed brown sugar**

½   **teaspoon vanilla**

1   **cup all-purpose flour**

⅛   **teaspoon salt**

¾   **cup semisweet chocolate pieces**

½   **cup broken pecans or walnuts**

½   **cup chopped chocolate-covered English toffee**

1 Preheat oven to 350°F. For crust: In a large bowl beat butter with an electric mixer on medium to high for 30 seconds. Add egg, brown sugar, and vanilla. Beat until combined, scraping side of bowl occasionally. Beat in flour and salt until combined.

2 Spread dough evenly into a 9×13-inch baking pan. Bake, uncovered, about 15 minutes or until top is dry and edges are starting to brown. Remove from oven.

3 Sprinkle chocolate pieces over hot crust. Let stand about 2 minutes or until softened. Spread chocolate over uncut bars. Sprinkle with nuts and toffee. Cool in pan on a wire rack. Cut into bars.

Makes 36 bars.

Per Bar: 88 cal., 5 g total fat (2 g sat. fat), 14 mg chol., 46 mg sodium, 9 g carbo., 1 g fiber, 1 g pro.

ULTIMATE BAR COOKIES

To enhance the flavor of the nuts
in these bars, lightly toast them in a 350°F oven
for about 8 minutes before you chop them.

Prep: 15 minutes **Bake:** 30 minutes **Oven:** 350°F

- 2 cups all-purpose flour
- ½ cup packed brown sugar
- ½ cup butter, softened
- 1 cup coarsely chopped walnuts
- 1 3.5-ounce jar macadamia nuts, coarsely chopped
- 1 6-ounce package white baking chocolate with cocoa butter, coarsely chopped
- 1 cup milk chocolate pieces
- ¾ cup butter
- ½ cup packed brown sugar

1 Preheat oven to 350°F. For crust: In a medium bowl combine flour, ½ cup brown sugar, and the ½ cup butter. Beat with an electric mixer on medium until mixture resembles fine crumbs. Press evenly into a 9×13-inch baking pan.

2 Bake, uncovered, about 15 minutes or until lightly browned. Remove from oven. Sprinkle walnuts, macadamia nuts, white chocolate, and milk chocolate over hot crust.

3 In a small saucepan combine the ¾ cup butter and ½ cup brown sugar. Cook and stir on medium heat until bubbly. Cook and stir for 1 minute more. Pour evenly over layers in baking pan.

4 Bake, uncovered, about 15 minutes more or just until bubbly around edges. Cool in pan on a wire rack. Cut into bars.

Makes 36 bars.

Per Bar: 204 cal., 14 g total fat (7 g sat. fat), 19 mg chol., 62 mg sodium, 19 g carbo., 1 g fiber, 2 g pro.

CHOCO-CRAN CUT-UPS

Children will enjoy measuring, mixing,
and munching the ingredients
in this simple, kid-friendly recipe.

Prep: 25 minutes **Chill:** 1 hour

- 1   16-ounce box toasted honey-flavored corn and wheat cereal flakes with oats (8 cups)
- ³/₄ cup chopped peanuts
- ²/₃ cup dried cranberries
- 1   cup semisweet chocolate pieces
- ¹/₄ cup honey
- 3   tablespoons butter
- 5   cups tiny marshmallows
- 2   teaspoons shortening

228

1. Line a 9×13-inch baking pan with foil, extending foil over edges of pan. Grease foil; set pan aside.

2. In a very large bowl combine cereal, peanuts, cranberries, and ½ cup of the chocolate pieces; set aside.

3. In a large microwave-safe bowl combine honey and butter. Microwave, uncovered, on high for minute. Stir until butter melts. Add marshmallows; toss to coat. Microwave on high for 1½ minutes. Stir until melted and combined. Add marshmallow mixture to cereal mixture; toss to coat. Press cereal-marshmallow mixture firmly into prepared baking pan.

4. In a small bowl combine remaining chocolate pieces and shortening. Microwave on medium about 1 minute or until melted, stirring once. Drizzle over bars.

5. Chill about 1 hour or until set. Using edges of foil, lift uncut bars out of pan. Cut into bars. Store, covered, at room temperature for up to 3 days.

Makes 32 bars.

Per Bar: 144 cal., 5 g total fat (2 g sat. fat), 3 mg chol., 94 mg sodium, 24 g carbo., 1 g fiber, 2 g pro.

LEMON-LIME BARS

> If the lemon-lime mixture appears
> curdled before it is baked, don't panic—it's
> supposed to look that way.

Prep: 20 minutes **Bake:** 40 minutes **Chill:** 2 hours **Oven:** 350°F

- ⅔ cup butter, softened
- ½ cup packed brown sugar
- 2 cups all-purpose flour
- 4 teaspoons finely shredded lemon peel
- 6 eggs
- 2¼ cups granulated sugar
- ½ cup all-purpose flour
- ½ cup lemon juice
- ¾ teaspoon baking powder
- ⅛ teaspoon ground nutmeg
- 1 teaspoon finely shredded lime peel
- 2 tablespoons powdered sugar
- 1 recipe Candied Citrus Slices and/or Candied Citrus Strips

1 Preheat oven to 350°F. Line a 9×13-inch baking pan with parchment paper or foil, extending paper or foil over edges of pan; set pan aside.

2 For crust: In a large bowl beat butter with an electric mixer on medium to high for 30 seconds. Add brown sugar. Beat until combined, scraping sides of bowl occasionally. Beat in the 2 cups flour until mixture is crumbly. Stir in 2 teaspoons of the lemon peel. Press evenly into prepared baking pan. Bake, uncovered, for 20 minutes.

3 Meanwhile, for filling: In a medium bowl combine eggs, granulated sugar, the ½ cup flour, the lemon juice, baking powder, and nutmeg. Beat on medium for 2 minutes. Stir in the remaining 2 teaspoons lemon peel and the lime peel. Pour over hot crust.

4 Bake, uncovered, about 20 minutes more or until edges are browned and center appears set. Cool in pan on a wire rack. Cover and chill for 2 hours.

5 Sprinkle with powdered sugar. Using edges of paper or foil, lift uncut bars out of pan. Cut into bars. Top with Candied Citrus Slices and/or Candied Citrus Strips.

Makes 16 to 20 bars.

Per Bar: 307 cal., 10 g total fat (5 g sat. fat), 100 mg chol., 96 mg sodium, 52 g carbo., 0 g fiber, 4 g pro.

Candied Citrus Slices: *Thinly slice 2 lemons or 10 Key limes. In a large skillet combine ¾ cup granulated sugar and ¼ cup water. Bring to boiling; reduce heat. Add citrus slices. Simmer gently, uncovered, for 1 to 2 minutes or just until softened. Transfer to a wire rack; cool.*

Candied Citrus Strips: *Remove peel from 2 lemons or 2 limes; scrape away the white pith. Cut peel into thin strips. Cook as directed for Candied Citrus Slices.*

LEMON BARS

The lusciously thick filling in these all-time favorite bars gets its signature citrusy flavor from the combination of lemon juice and peel.

Prep: 25 minutes **Bake:** 33 minutes **Oven:** 350°F

2 cups all-purpose flour
½ cup powdered sugar
2 tablespoons cornstarch
¼ teaspoon salt
¾ cup butter
4 eggs, lightly beaten
1½ cups granulated sugar
1 teaspoon finely shredded lemon peel
¾ cup lemon juice
¼ cup half-and-half, light cream, or milk
3 tablespoons all-purpose flour
Powdered sugar

1 Preheat oven to 350°F. Line a 9×13-inch baking pan with foil, extending foil over edges of pan. Grease foil; set pan aside. For crust: In a large bowl combine the 2 cups flour, the ½ cup powdered sugar, the cornstarch, and salt. Using a pastry blender, cut in butter until mixture resembles coarse crumbs. Press mixture evenly into prepared baking pan. Bake, uncovered, for 18 to 20 minutes or until edges are golden brown.

2 Meanwhile, for filling: In a medium bowl stir together eggs, granulated sugar, lemon peel, lemon juice, half-and-half, and the 3 tablespoons flour. Pour filling over hot crust. Bake, uncovered, for 15 to 20 minutes more or until center is set. Cool in pan on a wire rack.

3 Using edges of foil, lift uncut bars out of pan. Cut into bars. Before serving, sprinkle bars with powdered sugar.

Makes 36 bars.

Per Bar: 115 cal., 5 g total fat (3 g sat. fat), 34 mg chol., 52 mg sodium, 17 g carbo., 0 g fiber, 2 g pro.

SOUR CREAM AND RAISIN BARS

Raisin pie fans will love these Southern-style bars with their buttery oatmeal crust and crumb topper.

Prep: 30 minutes **Bake:** 30 minutes **Chill:** 2 hours **Oven:** 350°F

1³/₄ cups quick-cooking rolled oats

1³/₄ cups all-purpose flour

1 cup packed brown sugar

1 teaspoon baking soda

1 cup butter, melted

4 egg yolks

2 cups sour cream

2 cups raisins

1¹/₂ cups granulated sugar

3 tablespoons cornstarch

1 Preheat oven to 350°F. Line a 9×13-inch baking pan with foil, extending foil over edges of pan; set aside. For crust: In a large bowl combine oats, flour, brown sugar, and baking soda. Stir in melted butter until combined.

2 Press 3 cups of the mixture evenly into prepared baking pan. Bake, uncovered, for 15 to 20 minutes or until set and lightly browned. Cool in pan on a wire rack.

3 Meanwhile, in a medium saucepan combine egg yolks, sour cream, raisins, granulated sugar, and cornstarch. Cook and stir on medium heat until thickened and bubbly. Pour raisin mixture over crust. Crumble the remaining oat mixture evenly over top.

4 Bake, uncovered, for 15 to 20 minutes more or until filling is set and top is lightly browned. Cool in pan on a wire rack. Cover and chill for at least 2 hours. Using edges of foil, lift uncut bars out of pan. Cut into bars.

Makes 24 bars.

Per Bar: 286 cal., 12 g total fat (7 g sat. fat), 64 mg chol., 125 mg sodium, 44 g carbo., 1 g fiber, 3 g pro.

DOUBLE PEANUT BUTTER-
CHOCOLATE BARS

Warm the ice cream topping according to package directions, if needed, to make drizzling consistency.

Prep: 20 minutes **Bake:** 24 minutes **Oven:** 375°F

- **2** **16.5-ounce rolls refrigerated peanut butter cookie dough**
- **1** **9.5-ounce package (18 cookies) fudge-covered round cookies with peanut butter filling, chopped**
- **⅓** **cup chocolate-flavor ice cream topping**
- **½** **cup peanut butter-flavor pieces**
- **½** **cup semisweet chocolate pieces**
- **⅓** **cup chopped honey-roasted peanuts**

1 Preheat oven to 375°F. For crust: Press two-thirds (about 3 cups) of the cookie dough into a 9×13-inch baking pan. Bake, uncovered, for 12 minutes. Remove from oven.

2 Sprinkle hot crust with chopped cookies; drizzle with ice cream topping. Sprinkle evenly with peanut butter pieces, chocolate pieces, and peanuts. Dot top with small pieces of the remaining cookie dough.

3 Bake, uncovered, about 12 minutes more or until top is lightly browned. Cool in pan on a wire rack. Cut into bars.

Makes 24 bars.

Per Bar: 308 cal., 17 g total fat (6 g sat. fat), 10 mg chol., 217 mg sodium, 35 g carbo., 1 g fiber, 5 g pro.

BANANA-CHOCOLATE CHIP BARS

Even dyed-in-the-wool, only-from-scratch bakers agree that the new refrigerated cookie dough products are pretty darn good.

Prep: 20 minutes   **Bake:** 25 minutes   **Oven:** 350°F

- 1 **16.5-ounce roll refrigerated peanut butter cookie dough**
- 1 **cup regular rolled oats**
- ½ **cup mashed banana (1 large)**
- ½ **cup miniature semisweet chocolate pieces**
- ½ **cup chopped peanuts**
- 1 **16-ounce can chocolate or vanilla frosting**

1 Preheat oven to 350°F. Lightly grease a 9×13-inch baking pan; set aside. In a large bowl stir together cookie dough, oats, mashed banana, chocolate pieces, and peanuts until combined. Press dough evenly into prepared baking pan.

2 Bake, uncovered, about 25 minutes or until golden brown. Cool in pan on a wire rack.

3 Frost with desired frosting. (For a decorative touch, use half a can chocolate frosting and half a can vanilla frosting and swirl frostings together.) Cut into bars.

Makes 36 bars.

Per Bar: 158 cal., 8 g total fat (2 g sat. fat), 4 mg chol., 75 mg sodium, 21 g carbo., 1 g fiber, 3 g pro.

CHEWY CHERRY-ALMOND BARS

Of all the great flavor combinations, the marriage of cherries and almonds is one of the happiest.

Prep: 20 minutes **Bake:** 35 minutes **Oven:** 350°F

- 1 cup butter, softened
- 2 cups packed brown sugar
- 2 teaspoons baking powder
- 1 egg
- 1 teaspoon almond extract
- 2 cups all-purpose flour
- 2 cups regular rolled oats
- ½ cup sliced almonds
- 1 12-ounce jar (1 cup) cherry preserves

1 Preheat oven to 350°F. Line a 9×13-inch baking pan with foil, extending foil over edges of pan. Grease foil; set pan aside.

2 In a large bowl beat butter with an electric mixer on medium to high for 30 seconds. Add brown sugar and baking powder. Beat until combined, scraping sides of bowl occasionally. Beat in egg and almond extract until combined. Beat in as much of the flour as you can with the mixer. Using a wooden spoon, stir in any remaining flour, the oats, and almonds.

3 Remove ½ cup of the dough and set aside. Press the remaining dough evenly into prepared baking pan. Spread with preserves. Crumble the reserved ½ cup dough evenly over preserves layer.

4 Bake, uncovered, about 35 minutes or until lightly browned. Cool in pan on a wire rack. Using edges of foil, lift uncut bars out of pan. Cut into bars.

Makes 36 bars.

Per Bar: 170 cal., 6 g total fat (3 g sat. fat), 9 mg chol., 58 mg sodium, 27 g carbo., 1 g fiber, 2 g pro.

CARAMEL-NUT CHOCOLATE CHIP BARS

If chewy-rich, ooey and gooey
sweets are on your list of loves, you'll
adore these candylike bars.

Prep: 15 minutes **Bake:** 35 minutes **Oven:** 350°F

- 1 **18-ounce roll refrigerated chocolate chip cookie dough**
- 2 **cups quick-cooking rolled oats**
- 1½ **cups chopped honey-roasted peanuts or cashews**
- 1 **14-ounce can sweetened condensed milk**
- ¼ **cup caramel ice cream topping**
- ½ **cup flaked coconut**

1. Preheat oven to 350°F. Line a 9×13-inch baking pan with foil, extending the foil over the edges of the pan. Grease foil; set pan aside.

2. In a large bowl stir together cookie dough, oats, and ½ cup of the nuts until combined. Press dough evenly into the prepared pan. Bake, uncovered, for 15 minutes.

3. Meanwhile, in a small bowl stir together sweetened condensed milk and caramel topping. Drizzle over partially baked cookies. Sprinkle evenly with the remaining 1 cup nuts and the coconut.

4. Bake, uncovered, for 20 to 25 minutes more or until top is golden brown. Cool in pan on a wire rack. Using edges of foil, lift uncut bars out of pan. Cut into bars.

Makes 36 bars.

Per Bar: 157 cal., 7 g total fat (2 g sat. fat), 7 mg chol., 74 mg sodium, 21 g carbo., 1 g fiber, 3 g pro.

CHOCOLATE-MINT BARS

If desired, substitute semisweet chocolate pieces
for the mint-flavor chocolate pieces and add ¼ teaspoon
mint extract along with the vanilla.

Prep: 30 minutes **Bake:** 30 minutes **Oven:** 350°F

- ½ cup butter, softened
- ½ cup shortening
- 1 cup sugar
- 1 teaspoon baking powder
- ¼ teaspoon salt
- 1 egg
- 1 teaspoon vanilla
- 2¼ cups all-purpose flour
- 1½ cups mint-flavor semisweet chocolate pieces
- 1 14-ounce can sweetened condensed milk
- ½ cup chopped walnuts
- 1 teaspoon vanilla

1 Preheat oven to 350°F. In a large bowl combine butter and shortening. Beat with an electric mixer on medium to high for 30 seconds. Add sugar, baking powder, and salt. Beat until combined, scraping sides of bowl occasionally. Beat in egg and vanilla until combined. Beat in as much of the flour as you can with the mixer. Using a wooden spoon, stir in any remaining flour. Set aside.

2 For filling: In a medium saucepan combine chocolate pieces and sweetened condensed milk. Cook on low heat until chocolate is melted, stirring occasionally. Remove from heat. Stir in walnuts and vanilla.

3 Press about two-thirds of the dough evenly into a 9×13-inch baking pan. Spread with filling. Drop spoonfuls of the remaining dough onto filling. Bake, uncovered, for 30 to 35 minutes or until golden brown. Cool in pan on a wire rack. Cut into bars.

Makes 36 bars.

Per Bar: 193 cal., 11 g total fat (5 g sat. fat), 16 mg chol., 60 mg sodium, 24 g carbo., 0 g fiber, 2 g pro.

SALTED PEANUT BARS

This treat contains all the salty-sweet
goodness of a salted-peanut candy bar. A smooth
caramel topping is like icing on the cake.

Prep: 25 minutes **Bake:** 12 minutes **Oven:** 350°F

- 1 cup all-purpose flour
- ½ cup crushed pretzels
- ½ teaspoon baking powder
- ¼ teaspoon baking soda
- ½ cup butter, softened
- 2 egg yolks
- ⅔ cup packed brown sugar
- 2 teaspoons vanilla
- 1 7-ounce jar marshmallow creme
- ½ cup creamy peanut butter
- ¼ cup powdered sugar
- 1 cup salted cocktail peanuts
- 1 14-ounce package vanilla caramels, unwrapped
- 3 tablespoons milk

1 Preheat oven to 350°F. Line a 9×13-inch baking pan with foil, extending foil over edges of pan; set aside. In a small bowl combine flour, pretzels, baking powder, and baking soda; set aside.

2 For crust: In a large bowl beat butter with an electric mixer on medium to high for 30 seconds. Add egg yolks, brown sugar, and vanilla. Beat until combined, scraping sides of bowl occasionally. Beat in as much of the flour mixture as you can with the mixer. Using a wooden spoon, stir in any remaining flour mixture. Press mixture evenly into prepared baking pan.

3 Bake, uncovered, for 12 to 14 minutes or until lightly browned. Meanwhile, in a microwave-safe medium bowl combine marshmallow creme and peanut butter. Microwave on high about 1 minute or until softened and slightly melted, stirring after 30 seconds. Stir in powdered sugar. Spread mixture over hot crust. Sprinkle with peanuts.

4 In a heavy large saucepan combine caramels and milk. Cook and stir on medium-low heat until melted. Pour caramel mixture evenly over peanut layer. Cool in pan on a wire rack. Using edges of foil, lift uncut bars out of pan. Cut into bars.

Makes 48 bars.

Per Bar: 127 cal., 6 g total fat (2 g sat. fat), 15 mg chol., 81 mg sodium, 17 g carbo., 1 g fiber, 2 g pro.

PECAN-CRUSTED MOJITO BARS

The refreshing taste of the mojito {moe-HEE-toe}, a traditional Cuban cocktail, makes these bars a superlative summer treat.

Prep: 15 minutes **Bake:** 40 minutes **Oven:** 350°F

1³/₄ cups all-purpose flour

1 cup chopped pecans

³/₄ cup granulated sugar

1 cup butter, cut into slices

4 eggs, lightly beaten

1¹/₂ cups granulated sugar

2 tablespoons finely shredded lime peel

¹/₂ cup lime juice

¹/₄ cup all-purpose flour

2 tablespoons milk

1 tablespoon snipped fresh mint

¹/₂ teaspoon baking powder

¹/₄ teaspoon salt

Powdered sugar

Finely shredded lime peel (optional)

Small fresh mint leaves (optional)

244

1 Preheat oven to 350°F. Line a 9×13-inch baking pan with foil, extending foil over edges of pan; set aside. For crust: In a food processor combine the 1³/₄ cups flour, the chopped pecans, and the ³/₄ cup granulated sugar. Add butter slices. Cover and pulse with several on/off turns until the mixture resembles coarse crumbs. Press crumb mixture into prepared baking pan. Bake, uncovered, for 20 to 22 minutes or until crust is light brown.

2 Meanwhile, for filling: In a medium bowl whisk together eggs, the 1¹/₂ cups sugar, the 2 tablespoons lime peel, the lime juice, the ¹/₄ cup flour, the milk, snipped fresh mint, baking powder, and salt until well mixed. Pour filling over hot crust.

3 Bake, uncovered, for 20 to 25 minutes more or until filling is set and edges just begin to brown. Cool in pan on a wire rack. Using edges of foil, lift uncut bars out of pan. Cut into bars. Sift powdered sugar over bars. If desired, sprinkle with additional lime peel and garnish with small fresh mint leaves before serving.

Makes 36 bars.

Per Bar: 150 cal., 8 g total fat (4 g sat. fat), 37 mg chol., 64 mg sodium, 19 g carbo., 1 g fiber, 1 g pro.

PIÑA COLADA SQUARES

Literally translated, the term "piña colada"
means "strained pineapple." Here pineapple preserves
give these tasty bars their tropical flair.

Prep: 25 minutes **Bake:** 30 minutes **Oven:** 350°F

- **2** cups all-purpose flour
- **2** cups quick-cooking rolled oats
- **1⅓** cups packed brown sugar
- **¼** teaspoon baking soda
- **1** cup butter
- **1** cup pineapple ice cream topping
- **1** teaspoon rum extract
- **1** cup flaked coconut
  Semisweet chocolate, melted

1 Preheat oven to 350°F. For crust: In a large bowl combine flour, oats, brown sugar, and baking soda. Using a pastry blender, cut in butter until mixture resembles coarse crumbs. Set aside 1 cup of the oats mixture for topping. Press the remaining oats mixture evenly into a 9×13-inch baking pan. Set aside.

2 For filling: In a small bowl stir together pineapple topping and rum extract. Spread pineapple mixture evenly over crust.

3 For topping: Stir coconut into the reserved 1 cup oats mixture. Sprinkle evenly over filling. Bake, uncovered, about 30 minutes or until top is golden brown. Cool in pan on a wire rack. Cut into bars. Drizzle with melted chocolate.

Makes 48 bars.

Per Bar: 117 cal., 5 g total fat (3 g sat. fat), 11 mg chol., 55 mg sodium, 18 g carbo., 1 g fiber, 1 g pro.

245

GOOEY MIXED-NUT BARS

Stirring in a batch of mixed nuts right
out of the can puts a supercrunchy
spin on these sweet bars.

Prep: 25 minutes **Bake:** 45 minutes **Oven:** 350°F

1 package 2-layer-size yellow cake mix

½ cup butter

4 eggs

1 cup packed brown sugar

½ cup light-color corn syrup

⅓ cup butter, melted

1 teaspoon vanilla

½ teaspoon ground cinnamon

2 cups mixed nuts, coarsely chopped

1 Preheat oven to 350°F. Line a 9×13-inch baking pan with foil, extending foil over edges of pan. Grease foil; set pan aside.

2 For crust: Place cake mix in a large bowl. Using a pastry blender, cut in the ½ cup butter until mixture resembles coarse crumbs. Press evenly into prepared baking pan. Bake, uncovered, for 15 to 20 minutes or until lightly browned and set.

3 Meanwhile, in a large bowl whisk together eggs, brown sugar, corn syrup, the ⅓ cup melted butter, the vanilla, and cinnamon. Stir in mixed nuts. Pour nut mixture over hot crust. Bake, uncovered, about 30 minutes more or until golden brown and bubbly around edges.

4 Cool in pan on a wire rack. Using edges of foil, lift uncut bars out of pan. Cut into bars.

Makes 32 bars.

Per Bar: 207 cal., 11 g total fat (4 g sat. fat), 39 mg chol., 155 mg sodium, 26 g carbo., 1 g fiber, 3 g pro.

PEAR-CINNAMON STREUSEL SQUARES

When picking pears for these fall
favorites, choose pears that are
slightly firm to the touch.

Prep: 30 minutes **Bake:** 45 minutes **Oven:** 350°F

2	cups all-purpose flour
1¼	cups quick-cooking rolled oats
¾	cup packed brown sugar
2	teaspoons ground cinnamon
1	cup butter
2	eggs
1	cup granulated sugar
2	tablespoons all-purpose flour
¼	teaspoon baking powder
¼	teaspoon salt
2	cups peeled and chopped pears or apples
¾	cup cinnamon-flavor pieces
1	recipe Powdered Sugar Icing

1 Preheat oven to 350°F. Lightly grease a 9×13-inch baking pan; set aside. In a large bowl stir together the 2 cups flour, the oats, brown sugar, and cinnamon. Using a pastry blender, cut in butter until mixture resembles coarse crumbs. Set aside 1½ cups of the oats mixture for topping. Press the remaining oats mixture evenly into the prepared baking pan. Bake, uncovered, for 15 minutes.

2 Meanwhile, for filling: In a medium bowl combine eggs and granulated sugar. Stir in the 2 tablespoons flour, the baking powder, and salt. Stir in pears and cinnamon pieces. Spread filling evenly over hot crust. Sprinkle with the reserved 1½ cups oats mixture.

3 Bake, uncovered, for 30 to 35 minutes more or until top is golden brown. Cool in pan on a wire rack. Cut into bars. Drizzle with Powdered Sugar Icing.

Makes 32 bars.

Per Bar: 193 cal., 8 g total fat (5 g sat. fat), 29 mg chol., 81 mg sodium, 29 g carbo., 1 g fiber, 2 g pro.

Powdered Sugar Icing: *In a small bowl stir together 1 cup powdered sugar, 1 tablespoon milk, and ¼ teaspoon vanilla. Stir in enough additional milk, 1 teaspoon at a time, to make an icing of drizzling consistency.*

DESSERTS

You'll always be a star when you serve a homemade dessert—especially with this selection of simple-to-make cakes, cobblers, custards, fruits, and frozen fantasies, all of which fit beautifully in your trusty 9×13 pan. Choose any one of these happy endings. This array of grand finales is sure to delight you and your guests on any occasion or at any time of year.

CHOCOLATE-ORANGE HAZELNUT BAKLAVA

A delicious variation of the classic Middle Eastern
dessert, this chocolate baklava is soaked in an
enchanting orange-hazelnut syrup.

Prep: 45 minutes   **Bake:** 35 minutes   **Oven:** 325°F

- **3** cups hazelnuts (filberts), toasted and finely chopped
- **1⅓** cups sugar
- **¼** cup unsweetened Dutch-process cocoa powder
- **¾** cup butter, melted
- **½** of a 16-ounce package (9×14-inch rectangles) frozen phyllo dough, thawed
- **¼** cup water
- **¼** cup hazelnut syrup
- **1** teaspoon finely shredded orange peel
- **¼** cup orange juice
  Unsweetened Dutch-process cocoa powder

1 Preheat oven to 325°F. For filling: In a large bowl stir together hazelnuts, ⅓ cup of the sugar, and the ¼ cup cocoa powder; set aside.

2 Brush the bottom of a 9×13-inch baking pan with some of the melted butter. Unfold phyllo dough; remove 1 sheet of the phyllo dough and brush with butter. (As you work, cover the remaining phyllo dough with plastic wrap to prevent it from drying out.) Layer 5 or 6 of the phyllo sheets in the prepared baking pan, brushing each sheet with butter. Sprinkle with about 1¼ cups of the filling. Repeat layering phyllo sheets and filling 2 more times, brushing each sheet with butter. Layer the remaining phyllo sheets on top of the filling, brushing each sheet with butter. Drizzle with any remaining butter. Using a sharp knife, cut into 24 to 48 diamond-, rectangle-, or square-shape pieces.

3 Bake, uncovered, for 35 to 45 minutes or until golden brown. Cool slightly in pan on a wire rack.

4 Meanwhile, for syrup: In a medium saucepan stir together the remaining 1 cup sugar, the water, syrup, orange peel, and orange juice. Bring to boiling; reduce heat. Simmer, uncovered, about 15 minutes or until reduced to 1 cup. Pour syrup evenly over baklava in pan. Cool completely. Before serving, sprinkle with additional cocoa powder.

Makes 24 to 48 pieces.

Per Piece: 240 cal., 17 g total fat (5 g sat. fat), 15 mg chol., 87 mg sodium, 22 g carbo., 2 g fiber, 4 g pro.

TROPICAL FRUIT-TOPPED SPICE CAKE

Nutmeg and mace—the secrets to this cake's sweet success—come from the same tree. Mace is the lacelike red membrane that covers the nutmeg seed.

Prep: 30 minutes   **Bake:** 30 minutes   **Oven:** 350°F

2 cups all-purpose flour

1¼ teaspoons ground nutmeg

1 teaspoon baking powder

1 teaspoon baking soda

¼ teaspoon salt

¼ teaspoon ground allspice

½ cup butter, softened

1½ cups sugar

½ teaspoon vanilla

3 eggs

1 cup buttermilk or sour milk*

½ cup orange marmalade

3 cups coarsely chopped tropical fruits, such as papayas, peeled and seeded; kiwifruits, peeled; pineapple, peeled and cored; mango, peeled and pitted; and/or carambola (star fruit)

1 Preheat oven to 350°F. Grease and lightly flour a 9×13-inch baking pan; set aside. In a medium bowl stir together flour, 1 teaspoon of the nutmeg, the baking powder, baking soda, salt, and allspice. In a large bowl beat butter with an electric mixer on medium about 30 seconds. Add sugar and vanilla; beat until combined. Add eggs, 1 at a time, beating on medium for 1 minute after each addition.

2 Alternately add flour mixture and buttermilk to beaten mixture, beating on low after each addition. Pour batter into prepared baking pan. Bake, uncovered, about 30 minutes or until a toothpick inserted in center comes out clean and top springs back when lightly touched. Cool in pan on a wire rack.

3 Meanwhile, in a medium saucepan cook orange marmalade on low heat just until melted. Remove from heat; stir in the remaining ¼ teaspoon nutmeg and the fruit. Spoon warm fruit mixture over cake squares. (Or cover fruit mixture and chill for up to 4 hours before serving.)

Makes 16 servings.

Per Serving: 233 cal., 7 g total fat (4 g sat. fat), 56 mg chol., 208 mg sodium, 40 g carbo., 1 g fiber, 3 g pro.

***Note:** To make sour milk, place 1 tablespoon lemon juice or vinegar in a measuring cup; add enough milk to make 1 cup liquid. Let stand for 5 minutes.*

DOUBLE BERRY STREUSEL-TOPPED CAKE

**Thanks to frozen berries,
you can make this tender
spring-inspired cake year 'round.**

Prep: 25 minutes   Bake: 25 minutes   Cool: 30 minutes   Oven: 400°F

2	cups all-purpose flour
¼	cup sugar
1	tablespoon baking powder
½	teaspoon salt
6	tablespoons butter
¾	cup milk
1	egg, lightly beaten
1	teaspoon vanilla
1	cup frozen blueberries, thawed and drained
1	16-ounce container frozen sweetened sliced strawberries, thawed
⅓	cup all-purpose flour
3	tablespoons sugar
3	tablespoons butter
	Sweetened whipped cream (optional)

1 Preheat oven to 400°F. Grease bottom of a 9×13-inch baking pan or lightly coat with cooking spray; set aside.

2 In a medium bowl stir together the 2 cups flour, the ¼ cup sugar, the baking powder, and salt. Cut in the 6 tablespoons butter until mixture resembles coarse meal; set aside.

3 In a small bowl stir together milk, egg, and vanilla; add to flour mixture, stirring until moistened. Fold in blueberries. Spread evenly in prepared baking pan (batter will be thin in pan). Spoon undrained strawberries over batter in pan.

4 In another small bowl stir together the ⅓ cup flour and the 3 tablespoons sugar. Cut in the 3 tablespoons butter until mixture resembles fine crumbs. Sprinkle over berries.

5 Bake, uncovered, for 25 to 30 minutes or until set and top is evenly browned. Cool about 30 minutes before serving. If desired, serve with whipped cream.

Makes 12 servings.

Per Serving: 256 cal., 10 g total fat (6 g sat. fat), 42 mg chol., 231 mg sodium, 38 g carbo., 2 g fiber, 4 g pro.

GOOEY CHOCOLATE-CARAMEL CAKE

The amount of sweetened condensed milk and caramel sauce may seem generous, but go ahead and pour it all on.

Prep: 15 minutes **Bake:** according to package directions

- 1 **package 2-layer-size German chocolate cake mix**
- 1 **14-ounce can sweetened condensed milk**
- 1 **12- to 12.5-ounce jar caramel ice cream topping**
- 1 **8-ounce carton frozen whipped dessert topping, thawed**
- 3 **1.4-ounces bars chocolate-covered English toffee, chopped**

1 Prepare and bake cake mix according to package directions for a 9×13-inch baking pan. Cool in pan on a wire rack.

2 Using the handle of a wooden spoon, poke holes about 1 inch apart over surface of cake. Pour the sweetened condensed milk over the cake. Pour caramel topping over cake. Spread dessert topping evenly over top. Sprinkle with the chopped toffee bars. Store leftovers, covered, in the refrigerator for up to 24 hours.

Makes 30 servings.

Per Serving: 220 cal., 7 g total fat (4 g sat. fat), 6 mg chol., 174 mg sodium, 33 g carbo., 0 g fiber, 2 g pro.

PUMPKIN PEAR CAKE

Before you bake, check to make sure that you are using solid pumpkin—not pumpkin pie fillling.

Prep: 25 minutes **Bake:** 35 minutes **Cool:** 35 minutes **Oven:** 350°F

1 cup packed brown sugar

⅓ cup butter, melted

1½ teaspoons cornstarch

2 15-ounce cans pear halves in light syrup

½ cup coarsely chopped pecans

1 package 2-layer-size spice cake mix

1 cup canned pumpkin

1 Preheat oven to 350°F. In a small bowl combine brown sugar, butter, and cornstarch. Drain pears, reserving 3 tablespoons of the syrup. Stir reserved syrup into brown sugar mixture. Pour mixture into a 9×13-inch baking pan. If desired, cut pear halves into fans by making 3 or 4 lengthwise cuts, starting ¼ inch from the stem end of each pear half and cutting to the bottom of the pear half. Arrange whole or fanned pear halves, cored sides down, on top of the syrup in the pan. Sprinkle pecans evenly into the pan.

2 Prepare cake mix according to package directions, except decrease oil to 2 tablespoons and add the pumpkin. Slowly pour cake batter into baking pan, spreading evenly.

3 Bake, uncovered, for 35 to 40 minutes or until a toothpick inserted near center comes out clean. Cool in pan on a wire rack for 5 minutes. Run a thin metal spatula around edges of cake. Carefully invert cake into a 10×15-inch baking pan or onto a very large serving platter with slightly raised sides. Cool about 30 minutes before serving. Serve warm.

Makes 16 servings.

Per Serving: 337 cal., 15 g total fat (4 g sat. fat), 51 mg chol., 254 mg sodium, 51 g carbo., 2 g fiber, 3 g pro.

CARAMEL APPLE TRIFLE PARFAITS

Make the cake the day before serving; the rest of this fun fall dessert goes together in a snap.

Prep: 45 minutes **Bake:** according to package directions

- 1 package 2-layer-size spice cake mix
- 1 8-ounce package cream cheese, softened
- 1 12.25-ounce jar caramel ice cream topping
- 1½ cups whipping cream
- 1 21-ounce can apple pie filling
- ⅔ cup chopped walnuts, toasted
- ½ cup golden raisins (optional)
- Chopped toasted walnuts and/or golden raisins (optional)

1 Prepare and bake cake mix according to package directions for a 9×13-inch baking pan. Cool in pan on a wire rack. Cut half of the cake into 1-inch cubes (you should have 8 cups). Set aside. Reserve remaining cake for another use.

2 In a large bowl beat cream cheese with an electric mixer on medium until light and fluffy. Slowly add ice cream topping, beating on low just until combined. In a medium bowl beat whipping cream until stiff peaks form (tips stand straight). Fold whipped cream into cream cheese mixture.

3 Using eight 14-ounce stemmed glasses or tumblers, spoon 2 rounded tablespoons of the whipped cream mixture into each glass or tumbler. Top each with ½ cup of the cake cubes. Top each with 2 rounded tablespoons of the whipped cream mixture. Top each with ¼ cup of the apple pie filling. Sprinkle walnuts and raisins (if using) over pie filling. Top each with another ½ cup of the cake cubes. Spoon the remaining whipped cream mixture over.

4 If desired, sprinkle with additional chopped walnuts and raisins. Serve immediately. Or cover and chill for up to 4 hours before serving.)

Makes 8 servings.

Per Serving: 803 cal., 38 g total fat (19 g sat. fat), 93 mg chol., 670 mg sodium, 108 g carbo., 2 g fiber, 6 g pro.

CHUTNEY-STYLE SPICED APPLE COBBLER

There is no need to tediously peel the apples for use in this this scrumptious spicy cobbler.

Prep: 35 minutes   Bake: 25 minutes   Oven: 400°F

- 3 pounds cooking apples, cored and thinly sliced (about 10 cups)
- 2 tablespoons lemon juice
- 1¼ cups packed dark brown sugar
- 3 tablespoons cornstarch
- ⅔ cup water
- ½ cup coarsely chopped dried apricots
- ¼ cup dried cranberries
- 1 small fresh jalapeño, seeded and finely chopped*
- 1 teaspoon pumpkin pie spice
- 2 cups all-purpose flour
- ¼ cup granulated sugar
- 1 tablespoon baking powder
- 1 teaspoon salt
- 1 teaspoon finely shredded lemon peel
- ½ cup butter
- 1¼ cups buttermilk or sour milk**

  Vanilla yogurt

  Snipped dried apricots and/or chopped jalapeños (optional)

  Pumpkin pie spice (optional)

1 Preheat oven to 400°F. In a very large bowl combine apples and lemon juice; toss to coat.

2 In a 4- to 6-quart Dutch oven stir together brown sugar and cornstarch. Stir in the water, apricots, cranberries, the 1 jalapeño, and the 1 teaspoon pumpkin pie spice. Cook and stir on medium heat until boiling. Cook and stir for 1 minute more. Remove from heat. Stir in apple mixture. Spoon into a 9×13-inch baking dish.

3 In a large bowl combine flour, granulated sugar, baking powder, salt, and lemon peel. Using a pastry blender, cut in butter until pieces are pea size. Add buttermilk, stirring just until combined. Drop topping into 12 mounds on top of filling. If desired, sprinkle with additional pumpkin pie spice.

4 Bake, uncovered, for 25 to 30 minutes or until topping is golden brown and filling is bubbly. Cool in pan on a wire rack. Top cobbler with vanilla yogurt and additional apricots and/or jalapeños and, if desired, additional pumpkin pie spice.

Makes 12 servings.

Per Serving with Yogurt: 393 cal., 9 g total fat (6 g sat. fat), 24 mg chol., 415 mg sodium, 75 g carbo., 4 g fiber, 7 g pro.

259

*Note: *Because hot chile peppers contain volatile oils that can burn your skin and eyes, avoid direct contact with chiles as much as possible. When working with chile peppers, wear plastic or rubber gloves. If your bare hands do touch the chile peppers, wash your hands and fingernails well with soap and warm water.*

**Note: *To make sour milk, place 4 teaspoons lemon juice or vinegar in a 2-cup glass measure. Add enough milk to equal 1¼ cups total. Let stand 5 minutes before using.*

ROASTED PLUMS WITH FROZEN VANILLA CREAM

An egg-rich custard combined
with whipped cream creates a sweet
accompaniment to wine-roasted plums.

Prep: 35 minutes   **Roast:** 40 minutes   **Freeze:** 6 hours   **Oven:** 350°F

1	vanilla bean,* split lengthwise
3	eggs
2	egg yolks
²/₃	cup sugar
1	teaspoon vanilla extract*
1³/₄	cups whipping cream
12	ripe plums, halved lengthwise
1½	cups late-harvest Riesling or other dessert wine
2	tablespoons sugar

1 For vanilla cream: Use the tip of a small sharp knife to scrape seeds from vanilla bean. Discard pod or reserve for another use. In a medium heatproof bowl whisk together vanilla seeds, eggs, egg yolks, the ²/₃ cup sugar, and the 1 teaspoon vanilla extract.

2 Place heatproof bowl on the edges of a saucepan of simmering water (bowl should not touch water).** Cook and whisk constantly for 5 to 10 minutes or until egg mixture reaches 165°F or mixture reaches and remains at 140°F for 3 minutes. Carefully remove bowl from saucepan. Beat mixture with an electric mixer on medium to high for 3 to 5 minutes or until thick and light colored.

3 In a large bowl beat whipping cream with an electric mixer on medium until soft peaks form (tips curl). Fold egg mixture into whipped cream. Transfer to a freezer container. Cover and freeze for at least 6 or up to 24 hours.

4 Preheat oven to 350°F. Place plums, cut sides up, in a 9×13-inch baking dish. Pour wine over plums; sprinkle with the 2 tablespoons sugar.

5 Roast, uncovered, for 40 to 50 minutes or until plums are soft and edges start to brown. Serve warm plums with scoops of frozen vanilla cream.

Makes 6 to 8 servings.

Per Serving: 555 cal., 30 g total fat (17 g sat. fat), 270 mg chol., 70 mg sodium, 51 g carbo., 2 g fiber, 7 g pro.

260

*Note: If you prefer, substitute 2 teaspoons vanilla extract for the vanilla bean and 1 teaspoon vanilla extract.

**Note: If you don't have a heatproof bowl that can easily rest on the edges of a saucepan, use a double broiler and transfer mixture to a mixing bowl before beating.

POT-OF-GOLD BAKED APPLES

If you would like to make this delightful dessert a bit less caloric, substitute Neufchâtel cheese for the cream cheese.

Prep: 25 minutes **Bake:** 35 minutes **Oven:** 350°F

6 large Golden Delicious apples

1 3-ounce package cream cheese, softened

¼ cup peach preserves

½ teaspoon ground cinnamon

¼ teaspoon ground ginger

¼ teaspoon ground nutmeg

¼ teaspoon almond extract

⅛ teaspoon salt

¾ cup crushed gingersnap cookies (12)

¼ cup butter, melted

1 Preheat oven to 350°F. Using an apple corer or sharp knife, remove cores from apples. Peel a 1-inch strip from the top of each apple. Place apples in a 9×13-inch baking dish. Set aside.

2 In a medium bowl beat cream cheese with an electric mixer on medium to high for 30 seconds. Stir in preserves, cinnamon, ginger, nutmeg, almond extract, and salt. Spoon mixture into centers of apples.

3 In a small bowl combine gingersnap crumbs and butter. Spoon crumb mixture on top of apples.

4 Cover with foil. Bake for 20 minutes. Bake, uncovered, for 15 to 20 minutes more or until apples are tender. Serve warm.

Makes 6 servings.

Per Serving: 309 cal., 14 g total fat (8 g sat. fat), 36 mg chol., 246 mg sodium, 46 g carbo., 5 g fiber, 2 g pro.

SAUCY APPLE DUMPLINGS

Frozen puff pastry—a miracle of the
modern kitchen—makes these dumplings look
like they were made by a pastry chef.

Prep: 30 minutes **Bake:** 30 minutes **Oven:** 375°F

- ½ of a 17.3-ounce package (1 sheet) frozen puff pastry, thawed
- 4 medium Granny Smith apples
- 1 tablespoon sugar
- ½ teaspoon ground cinnamon
- 1 egg
- 1 teaspoon water
- ½ cup caramel ice cream topping
- ⅓ cup chopped pecans, toasted

1 Unfold puff pastry on a lightly floured surface. Roll pastry into a 14-inch square. Using a knife, cut pastry into four 7-inch squares. Set aside.

2 Preheat oven to 375°F. Peel and core apples. If necessary, trim bottoms of apples so they stand upright. Place an apple in the center of each pastry square. In a small bowl combine sugar and cinnamon; spoon into centers of apples.

3 In another small bowl beat egg and the water with a fork. Moisten the edges of the pastry squares with egg mixture; fold corners to center over fruit. Pinch to seal, pleating and folding pastry along seams as necessary. Place dumplings in a 9×13-inch baking pan.

4 If desired, cut leaf shapes from pastry trimmings with a small cookie cutter or knife; score veins in leaves. For curved leaves, drape over crumpled foil on another baking sheet.

5 Brush wrapped apples and leaf cutouts with egg mixture. Sprinkle leaves with sugar. Bake, uncovered, for 30 to 35 minutes or until fruit is tender and pastry is golden brown.

6 Meanwhile, for sauce: In a microwave-safe 2-cup glass measure combine caramel ice cream topping and chopped pecans. Microwave, uncovered, on high for 30 to 60 seconds or until topping is heated through.

7 To serve, moisten the bottoms of pastry leaves with caramel sauce; place on top of the baked dumplings, gently pressing in place. Serve dumplings warm with caramel-pecan sauce.

Makes 4 servings.

Per Serving: 567 cal., 28 g total fat (1 g sat. fat), 53 mg chol., 362 mg sodium, 77 g carbo., 5 g fiber, 5 g pro.

PUFFED EGYPTIAN BREAD PUDDING

Desserts of sunny Middle Eastern countries are defined by their delicious use of nuts and dried fruits.

Prep: 30 minutes   **Bake:** 35 minutes   **Oven:** 400°F/350°F

- **1** **17.3-ounce package (2 sheets) frozen puff pastry sheets, thawed**
- **³/₄** **cup packed brown sugar**
- **1** **teaspoon ground cinnamon**
- **1½** **cups flaked coconut**
- **³/₄** **cup golden raisins**
- **½** **cup sliced almonds**
- **2** **eggs, lightly beaten**
- **2** **12-ounce cans evaporated milk**
- **1** **tablespoon cornstarch**
- **2** **tablespoons honey (optional)**

1 Preheat oven to 400°F. Cut puff pastry sheets along creases; cut each piece in half lengthwise. Cut pieces crosswise into about 1½-inch squares. Arrange squares about 1 inch apart on 2 ungreased large baking sheets. Bake on separate oven racks about 15 minutes or until pastry squares are golden, rearranging baking sheets once during baking. Reduce oven temperature to 350°F.

2 Place hot baked squares in a 9×13-inch baking dish. In a small bowl combine brown sugar and cinnamon; sprinkle about two-thirds of the sugar mixture over pastry. Top with coconut, raisins, and almonds. In a 4-cup glass measure whisk together eggs, evaporated milk, and cornstarch; pour evenly over mixture in baking dish. Sprinkle with the remaining brown sugar mixture.

3 Cover with foil. Bake for 20 minutes. Bake, uncovered, for 15 to 20 minutes more or until top is golden brown and mixture is set. Cool in pan on a wire rack for 20 minutes. Serve warm. If desired, drizzle with honey.

Makes 12 servings.

Per Serving: 450 cal., 25 g total fat (7 g sat. fat), 52 mg chol., 274 mg sodium, 49 g carbo., 2 g fiber, 9 g pro.

264

HARVEST PUDDING

This autumnal pudding possesses
a rustic, chunky texture—the kind that is especially
appealing on a chilly fall night.

Prep: 25 minutes   **Bake:** 45 minutes   **Cool:** 30 minutes   **Oven:** 350°F

⅓ cup quick-cooking rolled oats

¼ cup all-purpose flour

2 tablespoons packed brown sugar

⅛ teaspoon ground cinnamon

¼ cup butter

2 tablespoons chopped walnuts

1 package 2-layer-size sour cream white cake mix

3 eggs

Sour cream

Pear nectar

2 medium pears, cored and finely chopped (2 cups)

1 medium cooking apple, cored and finely chopped (⅔ cup)

1 Preheat oven to 350°F. Grease a 9×13-inch baking dish; set aside. For topping: In a small bowl combine the oats, flour, brown sugar, and cinnamon. Using a pastry blender, cut in butter until pieces are pea size. Stir in walnuts. Set aside.

2 Prepare cake mix according to package directions, except use 3 whole eggs instead of the egg whites, sour cream instead of the oil, use half of the water called for, and use pear nectar for the other half of the water called for. Stir in pears and apple. Pour into prepared baking dish, spreading evenly.

3 Bake, uncovered, for 20 minutes. Sprinkle with topping. Bake, uncovered, for 25 to 30 minutes more or until a toothpick inserted near the center comes out clean. Cool in pan on a wire rack for 30 minutes. Serve warm.

Makes 12 servings.

Per Serving: 333 cal., 12 g total fat (5 g sat. fat), 66 mg chol., 431 mg sodium, 53 g carbo., 1 g fiber, 5 g pro.

HONEYED BAKED PEARS WITH ZABAGLIONE

> **Zabaglione (zah-bahl-YOH-nay) is a rich-tasting, yet light and foamy custardlike sauce. It's one of the dessert classics of Italian cuisine.**

Prep: 25 minutes **Bake:** 45 minutes **Cool:** 1 hour **Cook:** 15 minutes **Oven:** 325°F

4	pears
	Lime juice
1/2	cup honey
3	tablespoons butter
8	egg yolks
1/2	cup sugar
	Dash salt
1/2	cup plus 2 tablespoons apple juice
2	tablespoons Calvados or apple brandy
1	cup whipping cream
	Chopped pecans, toasted

1. Preheat oven to 325°F. Cut unpeeled pears in half lengthwise, leaving the stem on one half. Using a spoon, remove core and seeds. Brush the cut sides of the pears with lime juice. Place pears, cut sides down, in a 9×13-inch baking dish; set aside. In a small saucepan combine honey and butter. Cook and stir on medium heat until butter is melted. Spoon honey mixture over pears.

2. Bake, uncovered, about 45 minutes or until pears are tender. Let cool in pan on a wire rack about 1 hour or until pears are just slightly warm.

3. Meanwhile, for zabaglione: In a large heatproof bowl or the top of a double boiler combine egg yolks, sugar, and salt. Place bowl over a large saucepan of simmering (not boiling) water. (Upper bowl should not touch water.) Gradually whisk in apple juice and Calvados. Cook over simmering water, beating constantly with a wire whisk until mixture thickens and mounds slightly (about 15 minutes). Remove from heat. Place bowl in a larger bowl with ice water and whisk constantly until mixture has cooled completely. Remove from ice water.

4. In a large bowl beat whipping cream with an electric mixer on medium until soft peaks form (tips curl). Fold whipped cream into cooled egg mixture. (If not serving immediately, cover and chill zabaglione for up to 2 hours before serving.)

5. Spoon zabaglione into dessert dishes. Top with pear halves. Drizzle with some of the juices from baking dish and sprinkle with pecans.

Makes 4 servings.

Per Serving: 792 cal., 45 g total fat (23 g sat. fat), 515 mg chol., 141 mg sodium, 93 g carbo., 6 g fiber, 8 g pro.

FLAN

It's elegant, simple, and sweet. No wonder
the Mexicans quickly adopted this caramel-coated
baked custard from the Spaniards.

Prep: 30 minutes **Bake:** 35 minutes **Chill:** 4 to 24 hours **Oven:** 325°F

⅓ cup sugar

3 eggs, lightly beaten

1 12-ounce can (1½ cups)
  evaporated milk

⅓ cup sugar

  Fresh fruit (optional)

  Edible flowers (optional)

1 To caramelize sugar: In a heavy skillet cook ⅓ cup sugar on medium-high heat until the sugar begins to melt, shaking the skillet occasionally to heat sugar evenly. Do not stir. Once the sugar starts to melt, reduce heat to low and cook about 5 minutes more or until all of the sugar is melted and golden brown, stirring as needed with a wooden spoon. Immediately divide the caramelized sugar among six 6-ounce custard cups or pour caramelized sugar into an 8-inch flan pan or an 8×1½-inch round baking pan. Working quickly, tilt cups or pan so sugar coats the bottom as evenly as possible. Let stand.

2 Preheat oven to 325°F. In a medium bowl combine eggs, evaporated milk, and ⅓ cup sugar. Place custard cups or round pan in a 9×13-inch baking pan on an oven rack. Pour egg mixture into cups or round pan. Pour the hottest tap water available into the 9×13-inch baking pan around the cups or round pan to a depth of about ½ inch.

3 Bake, uncovered, for 35 to 40 minutes for custard cups (30 to 35 minutes for round pan) or until a knife inserted near the centers comes out clean. Immediately remove cups or round pan from hot water. Cool on a wire rack. Cover and chill for at least 4 or up to 24 hours.

4 To unmold flan, loosen edges with a knife, slipping the point of the knife down the sides to let air in. Invert a dessert plate over each custard cup or a serving platter over round pan; turn dishes over together to release custard. Remove cup or pan. Spoon any caramelized sugar that remains in pan onto the top of flan. If desired, serve with fresh fruit and garnish with edible flowers.

Makes 6 servings.

Per Serving: 202 cal., 7 g total fat (3 g sat. fat), 123 mg chol., 92 mg sodium, 28 g carbo., 0 g fiber, 7 g pro.

LEMON-LAVENDER CUSTARDS

Lemon curd is really just a very thick
lemon sauce. You'll find it shelved along with jams
and jellies in most markets.

Prep: 25 minutes   **Bake:** 40 minutes   **Chill:** 2 to 24 hours   **Oven:** 325°F

- 2 cups milk
- 2 tablespoons sugar
- 1½ teaspoons dried lavender buds or 2 sprigs fresh lemon thyme or thyme
- 3 eggs, lightly beaten
- ⅓ cup lemon curd
- 1 teaspoon vanilla

1. Preheat oven to 325°F. In a medium saucepan combine milk, sugar, and lavender. Cook on medium-low heat just until mixture starts to simmer, stirring frequently. Remove from heat. Strain mixture through a fine-mesh sieve into a bowl; discard lavender.

2. In a medium bowl whisk eggs, lemon curd, and vanilla until combined. Gradually whisk the warm strained milk mixture into egg mixture.

3. Place six 6-ounce custard cups in a 9×13-inch baking dish. Divide milk mixture evenly among custard cups. Place baking dish on an oven rack. Pour enough boiling water into baking dish to reach halfway up the sides of the custard cups.

4. Bake, uncovered, about 40 minutes or until edges are set and centers appear nearly set when gently shaken. Remove custard cups from water; cool on a wire rack. Cover and chill for at least 2 or up to 24 hours.

5. Using a knife, loosen custards from sides of custard cups and invert onto dessert plates.

Makes 6 servings.

Per Serving: 117 cal., 1 g total fat (1 g sat. fat), 15 mg chol., 105 mg sodium, 22 g carbo., 2 g fiber, 6 g pro.

SYRUP-TOPPED MILK CUSTARD

> This Greek-inspired dessert features a
> creamy layer of custard between two layers of
> crisp and buttery phyllo pastry.

Prep: 25 minutes **Bake:** 45 minutes **Cool:** 30 minutes **Chill:** 4 to 8 hours **Oven:** 350°F

- ½ cup sugar
- ¼ cup all-purpose flour
- ¼ cup cornstarch
- 1 quart milk (4 cups)
- 2 tablespoons butter
- 6 eggs, lightly beaten
- 1 teaspoon vanilla
- ¾ cup butter, melted
- 10 sheets (9×14-inch rectangles) frozen phyllo dough, thawed and halved crosswise
- 1½ cups sugar
- 1 cup water
- 1 slice lemon

1 Preheat oven to 350°F. For custard: In a large saucepan stir together the ½ cup sugar, the flour, and cornstarch. Stir in milk and the 2 tablespoons butter. Cook and stir on medium heat until mixture is bubbly. Cook and stir for 2 minutes more. Gradually stir about 2 cups of the hot mixture into eggs. Return egg mixture to saucepan. Cook and stir on medium-low heat just until mixture starts to bubble. Remove from heat. Stir in vanilla.

2 Brush bottom of a 9×13-inch baking dish with some of the melted butter. Place 1 half-sheet of phyllo dough on a clean work surface. (As you work, cover the remaining phyllo dough with plastic wrap to prevent it from drying out.) Brush the half-sheet with some of the melted butter. Top with 9 more half-sheets of phyllo dough, brushing each with butter. Place phyllo stack in the baking dish.

3 Pour custard over phyllo stack in dish. Repeat with the remaining 10 half-sheets of phyllo dough, brushing each with butter. Place phyllo stack on top of custard. Bake, uncovered, for 45 minutes, covering loosely with foil if necessary to prevent overbrowning.

4 Meanwhile, for syrup: In a small saucepan combine the 1½ cups sugar, the water, and lemon. Bring to boiling, stirring until sugar is dissolved. Reduce heat. Simmer, uncovered, for 15 minutes. Remove from heat. Remove and discard lemon.

5 Cool in dish on a wire rack about 30 minutes or until custard is set. Pour syrup over dessert. Cover and chill for at least 4 hours or up to 8 hours. To serve, cut into squares.

Makes 24 servings.

Per Serving: 188 cal., 9 g total fat (5 g sat. fat), 74 mg chol., 100 mg sodium, 24 g carbo., 0 g fiber, 4 g pro.

TINY VANILLA CRÈME BRÛLÉE

Following an ample meal, just a bite of dessert is all you need. These petite pleasures are perfect.

Prep: 30 minutes **Stand:** 15 minutes **Bake:** 25 minutes **Chill:** 4 to 8 hours **Oven:** 300°F

- 1³⁄₄ **cups whipping cream**
- ¹⁄₂ **cup sugar**
- ¹⁄₄ **cup half-and-half or light cream**
- ¹⁄₂ **of a vanilla bean, split lengthwise**
- 6 **egg yolks**
- ¹⁄₄ **cup sugar**

1 Preheat oven to 300°F. In a heavy medium saucepan combine whipping cream, the ¹⁄₂ cup sugar, and the half-and-half. Using the tip of a small sharp knife, scrape seeds from vanilla bean. Add vanilla seeds and pod to cream mixture. Cook and stir on medium heat just until mixture comes to boiling. Remove from heat. Cover and let stand for 15 minutes to infuse cream mixture with vanilla flavor. Remove vanilla pod; discard or reserve for another use.

2 Meanwhile, in a medium bowl whisk egg yolks until combined. Gradually whisk warm cream mixture into egg yolks.

3 Place ten 2-ounce ramekins in a 9×13-inch baking pan. Divide cream mixture evenly among ramekins. Place baking pan on an oven rack. Pour hot water into baking pan around ramekins to reach a depth of ³⁄₄ inch.

4 Bake, uncovered, for 25 to 30 minutes or until centers appear set when gently shaken. Remove ramekins from water; cool on a wire rack. Cover and chill for at least 4 hours or up to 8 hours.

5 To serve, sprinkle the ¹⁄₄ cup sugar evenly over tops of custards. Using a culinary blow torch, heat sugar until a bubbly brown crust forms.*

Makes 10 servings.

Per Serving: 244 cal., 19 g total fat (11 g sat. fat), 186 mg chol., 23 mg sodium, 17 g carbo., 0 g fiber, 3 g pro.

273

*Note: *If your ramekins are broiler-safe, you can melt the sugar under the broiler. Preheat broiler. Return chilled custards to the baking pan and surround with ice cubes and a little cold water. Broil about 5 inches from the heat about 2 minutes or until a bubbly brown crust forms.*

MANGO YOGURT POPS

These healthful frozen treats are
sure to make you popular with the little
ones—and the not-so-little ones too.

Prep: 15 minutes   **Freeze:** 3 hours + overnight

- **2** **medium ripe mangoes, seeded and peeled**
- **½** **cup water**
- **¼** **cup sugar**
- **¼** **cup lemon juice**
- **3** **6-ounce cartons vanilla low-fat yogurt**
- **2- to 3-ounce pop molds or 4-ounce paper cups***
- **Wooden crafts sticks* (optional)**

1 In a blender combine mangoes, the water, sugar, and lemon juice; cover and blend until smooth. Add yogurt; cover and blend until combined. Pour into a 9×13-inch baking dish. Cover and freeze about 3 hours or until edges are firm but center is slightly soft, stirring 2 or 3 times.

2 Scrape mango mixture into a chilled large bowl. Beat with an electric mixer on medium until smooth. Pour mixture into pop molds; cover with lids. Cover and freeze overnight. Remove from molds to serve.

Makes 12 to 16 pops.

Per Pop: 75 cal., 1 g total fat (0 g sat. fat), 2 mg chol., 29 mg sodium, 16 g carbo., 1 g fiber, 2 g pro.

***Note:** If using paper cups, cover each filled cup with a square of foil. Use a table knife to make a small slit in center of each foil square. Slide a crafts stick through each hole and into the fruit mixture in the cup. Peel off paper to serve.*

ORANGE SHERBET CHEESECAKE SQUARES

Casual summertime suppers will be even
more special when you serve this cool and
refreshing make-ahead dessert.

Prep: 25 minutes   **Bake:** 12 minutes   **Freeze:** 1 hour + overnight   **Stand:** 10 minutes   **Oven:** 350°F

- ½ **cup butter, melted**
- 2 **cups crushed vanilla wafers**
- 2 **8-ounce packages cream cheese, softened**
- 1 **14-ounce can sweetened condensed milk**
- 1 **quart orange sherbet**
- 3 **medium oranges, peeled, sectioned, and chopped**
- 1 **cup flaked coconut, toasted**
- ⅓ **cup dried tart cherries, chopped**
- 1 **8-ounce container frozen whipped dessert topping, thawed**

1 Preheat oven to 350°F. For crust: In a medium bowl combine butter and crushed wafers; press into a 9×13-inch baking pan. Bake, uncovered, for 12 to 15 minutes or until brown and set. Cool in pan on a wire rack.

2 In a large bowl beat cream cheese with an electric mixer on low to medium until smooth; gradually beat in sweetened condensed milk. Stir sherbet to soften;* fold into cream cheese mixture. Cover and freeze for 1 to 2 hours or until almost firm.

3 In a small bowl combine oranges, half of the coconut, and the cherries; set aside. Fold into sherbet mixture. Spread over crust in pan. Top with whipped dessert topping and sprinkle with the remaining coconut.

4 Cover and freeze overnight. Before serving, let stand for 10 minutes at room temperature. Cut into squares.

Makes 12 to 15 servings.

Per Serving: 591 cal., 35 g total fat (22 g sat. fat), 73 mg chol., 321 mg sodium, 63 g carbo., 3 g fiber, 8 g pro.

276

*****Note:** *To soften sherbet, place sherbet in a chilled bowl; use a wooden spoon to press sherbet against sides of bowl until softened.*

INDEX

Note: Boldface page references
indicate recipe photographs.

281

MEAT ROASTING CHART

Place meat, fat side up, on a roasting rack in a 9×13-inch baking pan or baking dish. (Roasts with a bone do not need a rack.) Insert an oven-going meat thermometer into meat so the stem end is at least 2 inches into the center of the largest muscle or thickest portion of the meat. The thermometer should not touch fat, bone, or the baking pan or baking dish. Do not add water or liquid and do not cover. Roast in a 325°F oven (unless chart says otherwise) for the time given and until the thermometer registers the "final roasting temperature." (This will be 5°F to 10°F below the "final doneness temperature.") Remove the roast from the oven; cover with foil and let it stand for 15 minutes before carving. The temperature of the meat will rise 5°F to 10°F during the time it stands.

Cut	Weight	Approximate Roasting Time	Final Roasting Temperature (when to remove from oven)	Final Doneness Temperature (after standing 15 minutes)
BEEF				
Boneless tri-tip roast (bottom sirloin) Roast at 425°F	1½ to 2 pounds	30 to 35 minutes 40 to 45 minutes	135°F 150°F	145°F medium rare 160°F medium
Eye round roast Roasting past medium rare is not recommended.	2 to 3 pounds	1½ to 1¾ hours	135°F	145°F medium rare
Ribeye roast Roast at 350°F	3 to 4 pounds 4 to 6 pounds	1½ to 1¾ hours 1¾ hours to 2 hours 1¾ hours to 2 hours 2 to 2½ hours	135°F 150°F 135°F 150°F	145°F medium rare 160°F medium 145°F medium rare 160°F medium
Rib roast (chine bone removed) Roast at 350°F	4 to 6 pounds	1¾ to 2¼ hours 2¼ to 2¾ hours	135°F 150°F	145°F medium rare 160°F medium
Round tip roast	3 to 4 pounds 4 to 6 pounds 6 to 8 pounds	1¾ to 2 hours 2¼ to 2½ hours 2 to 2½ hours 2½ to 3 hours 2½ to 3 hours 3 to 3½ hours	135°F 150°F 135°F 150°F 135°F 150°F	145°F medium rare 160°F medium 145°F medium rare 160°F medium 145°F medium rare 160°F medium
Tenderloin roast Roast at 425°F	2 to 3 pounds 4 to 5 pounds	35 to 40 minutes 45 to 50 minutes 50 to 60 minutes 60 to 70 minutes	135°F 150°F 135°F 150°F	145°F medium rare 160°F medium 145°F medium rare 160°F medium
Top round roast Roasting past medium rare is not recommended.	4 to 6 pounds 6 to 8 pounds	1¾ to 2½ hours 2½ to 3 hours	135°F 135°F	145°F medium rare 145°F medium rare
PORK				
Boneless sirloin roast	1½ to 2 pounds	¾ to 1¼ hours	150°F	160°F medium
Boneless top loin roast (double loin)	3 to 4 pounds 4 to 5 pounds	1½ to 2¼ hours 2 to 2½ hours	150°F 150°F	160°F medium 160°F medium
Boneless top loin roast (single loin)	2 to 3 pounds	1¼ to 1¾ hours	150°F	160°F medium
Loin center rib roast (backbone loosened)	3 to 4 pounds 4 to 6 pounds	1¼ to 1¾ hours 1¾ to 2½ hours	150°F 150°F	160°F medium 160°F medium
Tenderloin Roast at 425°F	¾ to 1 pound	25 to 35 minutes	155°F	160°F medium
Ham, cooked (boneless)	1½ to 3 pounds 3 to 5 pounds 6 to 8 pounds 8 to 10 pounds*	¾ to 1¼ hours 1 to 1¾ hours 1¾ to 2½ hours 2¼ to 2¾ hours	140°F 140°F 140°F 140°F	No standing time No standing time No standing time No standing time
Ham, cook before eating (with bone)	3 to 5 pounds	1¾ to 3 hours	150°F	160°F medium
Smoked shoulder picnic, cooked (with bone)	4 to 6 pounds	1¼ to 2 hours	140°F	No standing time

All roasting times are based on meat removed directly from refrigerator.

POULTRY ROASTiNG CHART

To prepare a bird for roasting, follow the steps below. Because birds vary in size and shape, use the times as general guides.

1. If desired, thoroughly rinse a whole bird's body cavity and neck cavity. Pat dry with paper towels. If desired, sprinkle the body cavity with salt.

2. For an unstuffed bird, if desired, place quartered onions and celery in body cavity. To stuff a bird (do not stuff a duckling), just before roasting, loosely spoon some stuffing into the neck and body cavities. For both a stuffed and unstuffed bird, pull neck skin to the back and fasten with a short skewer. If a band of skin crosses tail, tuck drumsticks under band. If there is no band, tie drumsticks to tail with 100%-cotton kitchen string. Twist wing tips under back.

3. Place bird, breast side up, on a roasting rack in a 9×13-inch baking pan or baking dish; brush with cooking oil or melted butter and, if desired, sprinkle with a crushed dried herb, such as thyme or oregano. (When cooking a domestic duckling, use a fork to prick skin generously all over and omit cooking oil or butter.) For whole birds, insert an oven-going thermometer into center of one of the inside thigh muscles. The thermometer should not touch the bone.

4. Cover Cornish game hen, pheasant, and squab with foil, leaving air space between bird and foil. Lightly press the foil to the ends of drumsticks and neck to enclose bird. Leave all other types of poultry uncovered.

5. Two-thirds through roasting time, cut the band of skin or string between drumsticks. Uncover small birds the last 30 minutes of roasting. Continue roasting until the meat thermometer registers 180°F in thigh muscle (check temperature of thigh in several places) or until drumsticks move easily in their sockets and juices run clear. (For a turkey breast, the meat thermometer should register 170°F.) Center of stuffing should register 165°F. Remove bird from oven; cover. Allow whole birds and turkey portions to stand for 15 minutes before carving.

Type of Bird	Weight	Oven Temperature	Roasting Time
CHICKEN			
Capon	5 to 7 pounds	325°F	1¾ to 2½ hours
Meaty pieces (breast halves, drumsticks, and thighs with bone)	2½ to 3 pounds	375°F	45 to 55 minutes
Whole	2½ to 3 pounds 3½ to 4 pounds 4½ to 5 pounds	375°F 375°F 375°F	1 to 1¼ hours 1¼ to 1¾ hours 1½ to 2 hours
GAME			
Cornish game hen	1¼ to 1½ pounds	375°F	1 to 1¼ hours
Duckling, domestic	4 to 6 pounds	350°F	1½ to 2 hours
Pheasant	2 to 3 pounds	350°F	1¼ to 1½ hours
Squab, domestic	12 to 16 ounces	375°F	45 to 60 minutes
TURKEY			
Boneless whole	2½ to 3½ pounds	325°F	2 to 2½ hours
Breast, whole	4 to 6 pounds 6 to 8 pounds	325°F 325°F	1½ to 2¼ hours 2¼ to 3¼ hours
Drumstick	1 to 1½ pounds	325°F	1¼ to 1¾ hours
Thigh	1½ to 1¾ pounds	325°F	1½ to 1¾ hours

METRIC INFORMATION

The charts on this page provide a guide for converting measurements from the U.S. customary system, which is used throughout this book, to the metric system.

Product Differences

Most of the ingredients called for in the recipes in this book are available in most countries. However, some are known by different names. Here are some common American ingredients and their possible counterparts:

- Sugar (white) is granulated, fine granulated, or castor sugar.
- Powdered sugar is icing sugar.
- All-purpose flour is enriched, bleached or unbleached white household flour. When self-rising flour is used in place of all-purpose flour in a recipe that calls for leavening, omit the leavening agent (baking soda or baking powder) and salt.
- Light-color corn syrup is golden syrup.
- Cornstarch is cornflour.
- Baking soda is bicarbonate of soda.
- Vanilla or vanilla extract is vanilla essence.
- Green, red, or yellow sweet peppers are capsicums or bell peppers.
- Golden raisins are sultanas.

Volume and Weight

The United States traditionally uses cup measures for liquid and solid ingredients. The chart below shows the approximate imperial and metric equivalents. If you are accustomed to weighing solid ingredients, the following approximate equivalents will be helpful.

- 1 cup butter, castor sugar, or rice = 8 ounces = ½ pound = 250 grams
- 1 cup flour = 4 ounces = ¼ pound = 125 grams
- 1 cup icing sugar = 5 ounces = 150 grams
- Canadian and U.S. volume for a cup measure is 8 fluid ounces (237 ml), but the standard metric equivalent is 250 ml.
- 1 British imperial cup is 10 fluid ounces.
- In Australia, 1 tablespoon equals 20 ml, and there are 4 teaspoons in the Australian tablespoon.
- Spoon measures are used for smaller amounts of ingredients. Although the size of the tablespoon varies slightly in different countries, for practical purposes and for recipes in this book, a straight substitution is all that's necessary. Measurements made using cups or spoons always should be level unless stated otherwise.

Common Weight Range Replacements

Imperial / U.S.	Metric
½ ounce	15 g
1 ounce	25 g or 30 g
4 ounces (¼ pound)	115 g or 125 g
8 ounces (½ pound)	225 g or 250 g
16 ounces (1 pound)	450 g or 500 g
1¼ pounds	625 g
1½ pounds	750 g
2 pounds or 2¼ pounds	1,000 g or 1 Kg

Oven Temperature Equivalents

Fahrenheit Setting	Celsius Setting	Gas Setting
300°F	150°C	Gas Mark 2 (very low)
325°F	160°C	Gas Mark 3 (low)
350°F	180°C	Gas Mark 4 (moderate)
375°F	190°C	Gas Mark 5 (moderate)
400°F	200°C	Gas Mark 6 (hot)
425°F	220°C	Gas Mark 7 (hot)
450°F	230°C	Gas Mark 8 (very hot)
475°F	240°C	Gas Mark 9 (very hot)
500°F	260°C	Gas Mark 10 (extremely hot)
Broil	Broil	Grill

*Electric and gas ovens may be calibrated using celsius. However, for an electric oven, increase celsius setting 10 to 20 degrees when cooking above 160°C. For convection or forced air ovens (gas or electric), lower the temperature setting 25°F/10°C when cooking at all heat levels.

Baking Pan Sizes

Imperial / U.S.	Metric
9×1½-inch round cake pan	22- or 23×4-cm (1.5 L)
9×1½-inch pie plate	22- or 23×4-cm (1 L)
8×8×2-inch square cake pan	20×5-cm (2 L)
9×9×2-inch square cake pan	22- or 23×4.5-cm (2.5 L)
11×7×1½-inch baking pan	28×17×4-cm (2 L)
2-quart rectangular baking pan	30×19×4.5-cm (3 L)
13×9×2-inch baking pan	34×22×4.5-cm (3.5 L)
15×10×1-inch jelly roll pan	40×25×2-cm
9×5×3-inch loaf pan	23×13×8-cm (2 L)
2-quart casserole	2 L

U.S. / Standard Metric Equivalents

⅛ teaspoon = 0.5 ml	
¼ teaspoon = 1 ml	
½ teaspoon = 2 ml	
1 teaspoon = 5 ml	
1 tablespoon = 15 ml	
2 tablespoons = 25 ml	
¼ cup = 2 fluid ounces = 50 ml	
⅓ cup = 3 fluid ounces = 75 ml	
½ cup = 4 fluid ounces = 125 ml	
⅔ cup = 5 fluid ounces = 150 ml	
¾ cup = 6 fluid ounces = 175 ml	
1 cup = 8 fluid ounces = 250 ml	
2 cups = 1 pint = 500 ml	
1 quart = 1 litre	